Southeast Asian Modern

From Roots to Contemporary Turns

Southeast Asian Modern

From Roots to Contemporary Turns

Peter G. Rowe
and Yun Fu

Birkhäuser
Basel

This publication was supported in part by the Graduate School of Design, Harvard University

To my parents Youngming and Lina,
who lived the region's modern history

Te hunga nō Aotearoa

Graphic Design, Cover, and Layout:
Reinhard Steger
Mariana Uccello
Cristina Mosillo
proxi.me

Production: Heike Strempel, Berlin

Printing: optimal media GmbH, Röbel/Müritz
Paper: 135g/m² Condat matt Perigord

Editor for the Publisher: Michael Wachholz, Berlin

Library of Congress Control Number: 2022933620

Bibliographic information published
by the German National Library
The German National Library lists this
publication in the Deutsche Nationalbibliografie;
detailed bibliographic data are available on the
Internet at http://dnb.dnb.de.

This work is subject to copyright.
All rights are reserved, whether the whole or
part of the material is concerned, specifically the
rights of translation, reprinting, re-use of illustrations,
recitation, broadcasting, reproduction on microfilms
or in other ways, and storage in databases.
For any kind of use, permission of the copyright
owner must be obtained.

This publication is also available as an e-book
(ISBN PDF 978-3-0356-2459-5).

© 2022 Birkhäuser Verlag GmbH, Basel
P.O. Box 44, 4009 Basel, Switzerland
Part of Walter de Gruyter GmbH, Berlin/Boston

Printed on acid-free paper produced from
chlorine-free pulp. TCF ∞

Printed in Germany

ISBN 978-3-0356-2457-1

9 8 7 6 5 4 3 2 1

www.birkhauser.com

Southeast Asian Modern
From Roots to Contemporary Turns

Intro–duction

Chapter 1

This book is about the modernization of architecture within the geography of Southeast Asia and parts of Austronesia, including the twelve nation states of Brunei, Cambodia, East Timor, Indonesia, Laos, Malaysia, Myanmar, the Philippines, Singapore, Taiwan, Thailand and Vietnam, as well as portions of the ocean peoples of Polynesia, Melanesia and Micronesia. Today, the total population stands at around 681 million inhabitants and roughly 9 percent of the world's population (Latadmin, 2020). In addition to its national heterogeneity, this is a region of geomorphological complexity and ecological diversity with the coming together of several tectonic plates, volcanic and earthquake activity, as well as tropical cyclones and tsunamis in many places. Relatively rich in natural resources, this area has been swept by inter-island travelers along with major politico-religious groups from the north and west and principally from China and India. These include several Buddhist regimes and dynasties and Hindu as well as Muslim followers. Western colonization followed, roughly from the 16th century through mainly the 19th century with Portuguese, Spanish, Dutch, British, French and American traders, military personnel and administrators. From these mixed roots, the architecture of different places varied, echoing local vernacular traditions and those of colonial hegemonies from both East and West. In many cases a distinctiveness and quality emerged in the contemporary era of the past half-century to 30 years ago. Moreover, this book aims to tell the story of these largely separate roots culminating in today's contemporary architectural production.

Prehistoric Making of Territories

Geomorphologically, what is now regarded as Southeast Asia arose primarily from Sundaland, Sahul and Wallacea. Sundaland encompassed the Sunda Shelf, which was a tectonically stable extension of Southeast Asia's continental shelf from the Eurasian plate. Its western and southern boundaries are clearly marked by deep waters of the Sunda Trench and the Indian Ocean, with its eastern boundary defined by the Wallace Line, essentially the boundary of the Indo-Malayan and Australian or Sahul realms, as shown on the map opposite (Gupta, 2005). The islands east of the Wallace Line are known to be in Wallacea, and greater parts of Sundaland were exposed during the late glacial period some 10,000 to 12,000 years ago (Wallace, 1869). Now, all of what was once Sundaland is in the tropics with no predictable dry seasons. Eco-regions there are comprised of tropical and sub-tropical broadleaf forests, tropical and sub-tropical conifer forests, montane grasslands and shrublands, as well as mangroves (Ashton, 2014). Particularly in the Borneo segment of Sundaland, there is an evolutionary hotspot for biodiversity, though much of the broader region is likewise inclined (de Bruyn, Stelbrink, Morley et al., 2014). Today, the archipelago of

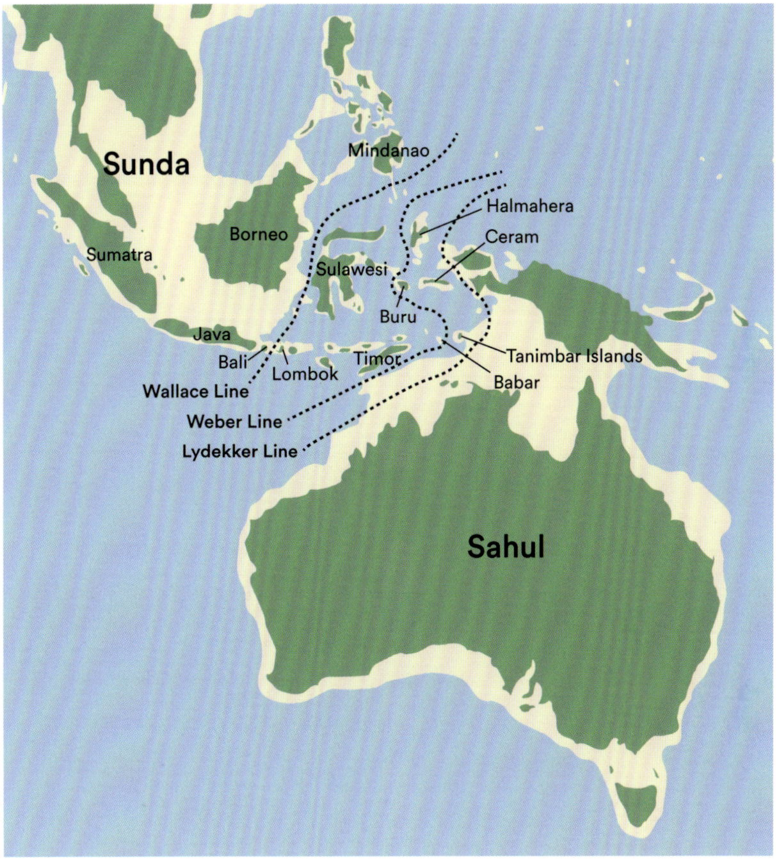

The Sunda and Sahul Shelves

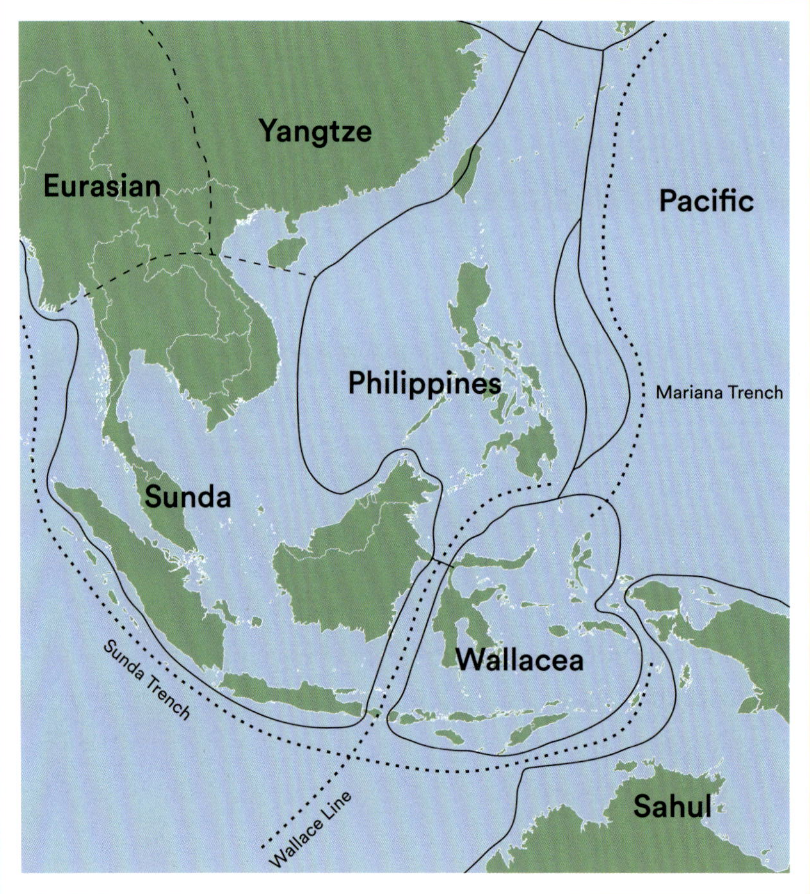

Map of Southeast Asia and Tectonic Plates

islands associated with Sundaland is comprised of the Greater Sunda Islands, including Sumatra, Borneo, Java, Sulawesi, mainly in Indonesia, whereas the Lesser Sunda Islands include Bali, Lombok, Sumbawa, Flores, Sumba, Timor, Alor Islands, Barat Daya Islands and the Tanimbar Islands, mainly in the biogeographical area of Wallacea and eastern Indonesia. The Sahul Shelf, sometimes referred to as Australinea or Meganesia, is made up of Australia, including Tasmania, as well as New Guinea. It is the smallest of the seven continents of the world and, though close by, outside of Southeast Asia *per se.* As shown on the map opposite, the Philippines is somewhat separate and a part of the Philippine Mobile Belt, a complex tectonic boundary between the Philippine Sea Plate and the Larger Eurasian Plate to the northwest. This is a very active area of tectonic activity even today.

Another contemporary geomorphological feature of Southeast Asia is its major river valleys, depicted diagrammatically on the map on p. 14. All are located downstream of rivers flowing into the Western Pacific and Indian Oceans, though many come from considerable distances upriver. The Mekong River, for instance, is some 4,350 kilometers in length, before reaching the sea in Laos and near the junction with Vietnam. In effect it flows from China in the north through Myanmar and Thailand to Laos in the southeast. The combined Salween and Irrawaddy Rivers are the second in length at 2,165 kilometers, flowing through Myanmar and entering the Indian Ocean at the city of Yangon, or formerly Rangoon (Middleton and Lamb, 2019). The Red River is next in length, emanating from southwestern China before reaching the ocean to the south of Hanoi in Vietnam and with a length of 1,149 kilometers. The Khwae Yai River, of western Thailand, has a similar riverine pattern and outflow, whereas the Chao Phraya River on the other side of the peninsula serves Bangkok, Thailand, and a basin of some 370 or so kilometers in length. The Perfume River, by contrast, is comparatively short, though serving the city of Hue, roughly halfway down the Vietnamese side of the former Indochina and the South China Sea. Finally, the Citarum River in West Java is the third-longest on the island after the Bengawan Solo and Brantas, but plays a crucially important role supporting agriculture, industry, fisheries and water supply for substantial populations. In addition, the Sepik River in New Guinea,

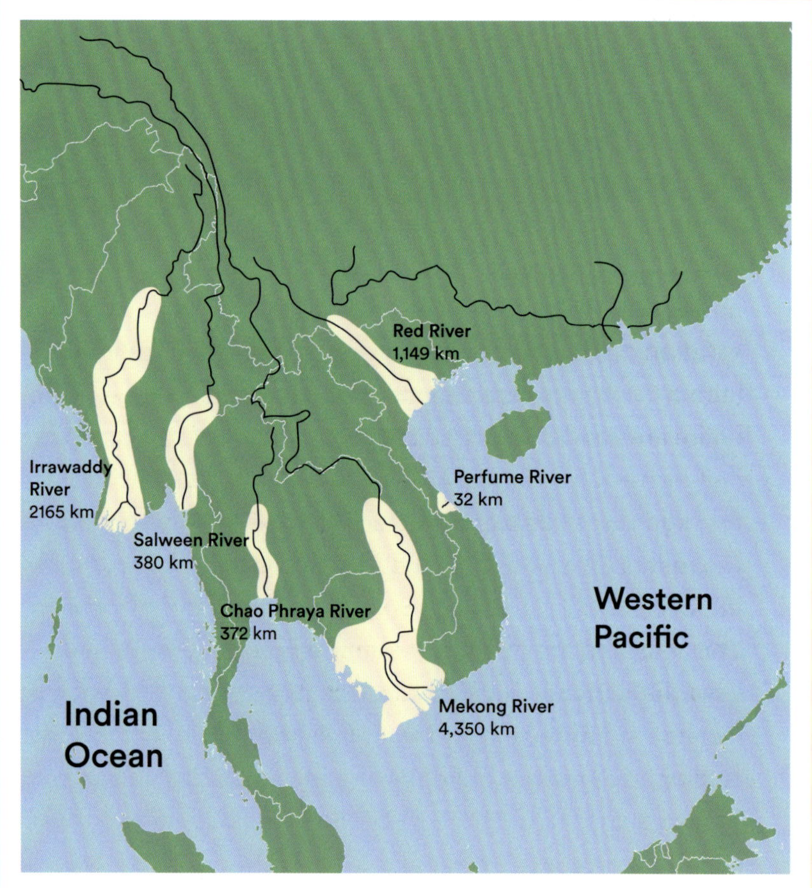

Major River Valleys of Southeast Asia

at 1,127 kilometers in length, is embraced by a large catchment area containing what is reputed to be the largest uncontaminated freshwater wetland system in the Asia-Pacific region (World Wildlife Fund, 1999). More important though, as in other parts of the world, these river valleys and coastally aligned basins host many of the region's major cities and productive developmental areas, especially when one thinks of Yangon, Bangkok, Ho Chi Minh City, Hue and Hanoi.

The tropical rainforests of Southeast Asia are a part of the earth's oldest existing tropical systems and the third-largest. They span across Brunei, Cambodia, Indonesia, Laos, Malaysia, Myanmar, the Philippines, Singapore and Vietnam, as shown on the map on p. 17. Historically, they have always been lush and green, teeming sites of biodiversity. Now, however, the rainforest has suffered the effects of incessant deforestation and logging. They have existed since the Pleistocene Period (about 70 million years ago). Later, about 8,000 years ago, almost the entire area of Southeast Asia was covered by forest, compared to about half of the initially forested area remaining today. One of the reasons for high levels of biodiversity is because millions of years ago when the rest of the world's climate underwent extreme cooling and warming cycles, the climate of Southeast Asia remained relatively stable. This was due to the ecosystem's proximity to the equator and water, with the consequence of significant rain. The rise of oceans creating isolated islands also contributed to speciation. This resulted in 'forest refugia', or unique wildlife reservoirs. Additionally, Borneo, Malaysia, Sumatra and Java (the Greater Sunda Islands) belonged to the same singular landmass – Sundaland. With the subsequent isolation of the islands, extensive diversification of species occurred due to the need to adapt to local conditions (Nee, 2014, p. 463).

Unfortunately, anthropogenic impacts are having detrimental impacts, through conversion to agriculture, logging and encroachment of oil palm plantations, not to mention greenhouse gas emissions from forest burning. This has driven many endemic tropical plants and animal species to the brink of endangerment and extinction, resulting also in a grave loss of biodiversity. Among the deforestation drivers, some 44 percent is due to intensive agriculture, a further 44 percent to subsistence agriculture and a further 6 percent each to logging and ranching (Stoly, 2011). Of 25 hotspots of diversity worldwide, four are in Southeast Asia. As elsewhere, the rates of species extinction are pegged to endism of hotspots. For Sundaland, recent studies have shown that endism was around 35 percent for mammals, 61 percent for reptiles, 18 percent for birds, 80 percent for amphibians and 60 percent for plants. The chart on p. 17, bottom, shows these data in more detail. Conservation challenges span social, scientific and logistical elements. Among social elements are population growth, poverty, shortages of conservation resources, and corruption. Scientific elements include neglect of research, low levels of research and publication as well as recognition of results; and logistical elements encompass the diversity of habitat types and numbers and scope of protected areas (Rowe and Hee, 2019, pp. 104–106).

Forests of Southeast Asia

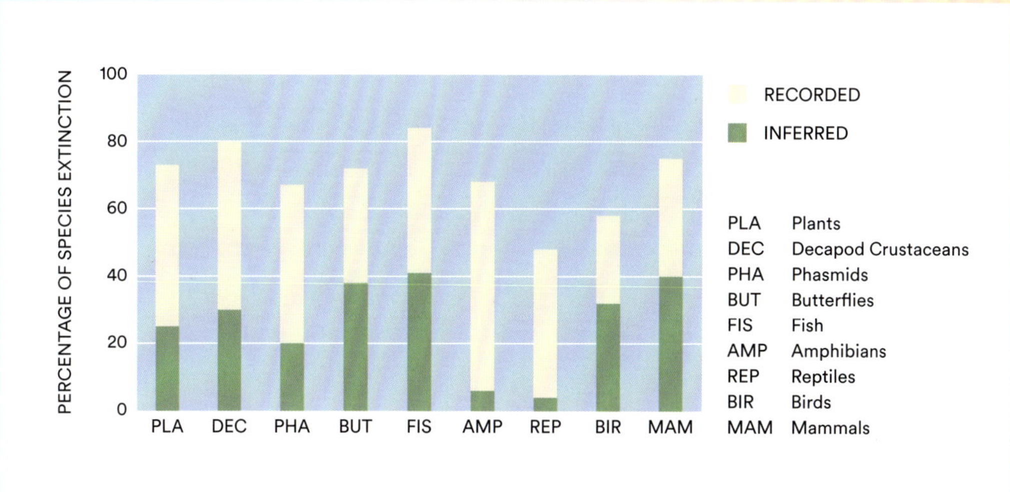

Species Extinction by Taxonomic Groups in Sundaland

Pre-Modern Cultures and Geographies

Austronesian peoples, sometimes referred to as Austronesian-speaking peoples, are named after a linguistic superfamily of languages in Taiwan, maritime Southeast Asia, Oceania and Madagascar. Based on current scientific consensus, they originate from prehistoric seaborne migrations from Taiwan around 5000 BCE, known as the 'Austronesian Expansion'. It reached southeast to the Philippines between 5000 and 4000 BCE, followed by remote Oceania around 1000 BCE, Melanesia about 1200 BCE and Polynesia between 900 and 800 BCE. Expansion as far as the Cook Islands and Tahiti occurred about 700 CE, followed then to the corners of the 'Polynesian Triangle', with Hawaii around 900 CE, Rapu Nui, or Easter Island, in 1000 CE and New Zealand in 1200. Movement in the other direction through the Indian Ocean reached Madagascar from 50 to 500 CE. The full extent of these migrations is shown on the map opposite. Skilled sailors were the first to invent a maritime sailing technology, mainly in the form of catamarans, outrigger boats and crab claw sails. The linguistic connections between Polynesia, Madagascar and Southeast Asia were recognized in the Western colonial era by European authors, like the Dutch scholar

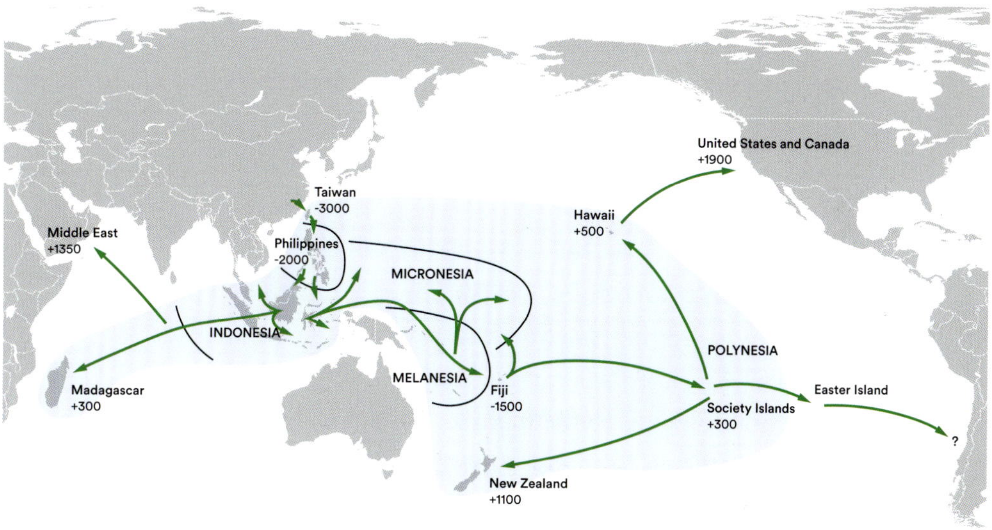

Migrations of the Austronesian Peoples

Adriaan Reland and his compatriot Cornelis de Houtman, a merchant seaman (Blust, 2013). In time, the Austronesians also became known as the 'people of the Southern World' and 'ocean people'. The basic language was spoken by upwards of 396 million people, or roughly 5 percent of the world's population, ranking them as the fifth-largest language group (Blust, 2016).

With regard to origins, there is now a broad consensus that original Paleolithic populations indigenous to island Southeast Asia were assimilated by incoming migrations of Neolithic Austronesian-speaking peoples from Taiwan and southern China around 5000 to 4000 BCE. This assimilation was occasioned by the Austronesian's technical ability to sail considerable distances, denied to Paleolithic populations who could only cross narrow inter-island seas. The Austronesian Expansion is also called the 'Out of Taiwan' model, originally proposed by scholars such as Peter Bellwood (Bellwood, 1979). An alternative 'Out of Sundaland' hypothesis from others, like Stephen Oppenheimer and Wilhelm Solheim, proposed that the homelands of the Austronesians were within Southeast Asia and its Sundaland land mass, derived during the last glacial period (Solheim, 1985). It is also sometimes referred to as the 'Nusantao' hypothesis from the Austronesian words *nusa* for 'south' and *tao* for 'people'. This was also supported by mitochondrial DNA evidence for Southeast Asian groups pre-dating the Austronesian Expansion. However, this has recently been repudiated using whole-genome sequencing showing that the Austronesians did originate among aboriginal Taiwanese. It also confirms the north-to-south dispersion among the Southeast Asian Islands and even to the Cham people of coastal Vietnam. This can also be observed in their basket-hulled boats, much as the Neolithic jade carving skill can be seen in the New Zealand Maori greenstone pendants, along with body art in a number of places among the Austronesian ocean sweeps.

By late 500 CE, what is now Vietnam was ruled by the Chinese early Ly Dynasty. With consolidation of the Sui Dynasty in China, the Ly first acknowledged and then rebelled under Emperor Wen of Sui and were conquered (Twitchett and Fairbank, 1979). In 605, the Chinese pushed further south, invading the Champa kingdom. Then, with the overthrow of the Sui by the Tang Dynasty, the northern portion of Vietnam fell under a protectorate to pacify the south, and Chinese infrastructure and schools were built once again. Then, in 687 CE, the Vietnamese Ly rebelled once again to be finally suppressed in 723 CE, by a large Tang Dynasty army. In 767 CE, the northern Chinese coast was invaded by a Srivijayan army that was also defeated. Then sometime later in 863 CE, the Tang were ousted from Songping, their capital, withdrawing to the north. A strong counterattack in 864 CE, led by an experienced Chinese general, recaptured the city and northern Vietnam. By 880 CE, power was transferred to local Sino-Viet elites who governed in the name of the Tang Dynasty. Then after more power struggles, the region became something of an independent state, as Vietnamese history began to come into its own with the Dai Viet (Dutton, 2012). Further over to the west, the Pyu city-states emerged in the 2nd century BCE, lasting until the 9th through the 11th centuries in Burma, today's Myanmar (Hall, 1960, pp. 8–10). They were founded by the southward migration of the Tibeto-Burman speaking Pyu people and the earliest inhabitants of Burma. The city-states were comprised chiefly of five walled cities and smaller towns. These included: Beikthano, Maingmaw, Binnaka, Halin and Sri Ksetra further in the south. They were located in three irrigated areas of the Mu River valley and the confluence of the Irrawaddy and Chindwin Rivers. Pyu culture was also heavily influenced by trade with India, importing Buddhism, as well as other material and organizational concepts (Aung-Thwin, 2005, p. 24). This millennium-old civilization came down in the 9th century through invasion from the rising Pagan Kingdom (Myint-U, 2006, pp. 51–52). The map on p. 23, top, shows the spatial distribution of Southeast Asian territories around 100 BCE.

During the ensuing centuries, other kingdoms, empires and regimes formed in both mainland Southeast Asia and across maritime Southeast Asia. As noted, the Pagan Kingdom formed around the Pyu people, unifying the territory in what would later become modern-day Burma and Myanmar, primarily around the Irrawaddy River. Beginning in 849 CE or thereabouts, the kingdom took its name from the settlement of Pagan, retaining the Buddhist influences imported from India. The Dai Viet emerged out of southern China, as noted earlier, continuing to exert influence and power southward, later in the form of the Vietnamese Empire. Champa of the Cham people held sway on the southern coast from around 300 CE until annexation by the Vietnamese in 1832 (Ngo, 2002). They had also adopted Hinduism from neighboring Funan to the west, centered around the Mekong River Delta. Nowadays many inhabitants of the area are Muslim. The Buddhist Srivijayan Empire arose around 600 CE, based on Sumatra and particularly in the city of Palembang in today's Indonesia (Cœdès, 1968). It was the first unified kingdom to dominate much of the Malay people and the Malay Archipelago. Primarily it embraced the Malay Peninsula, the islands of Sumatra and western Java. It had had earlier contact with China to the north and Tang Dynasty monks and explorers. During the 7th to 11th centuries, it was the hegemon in Southeast Asia, with rivalries with neighboring Mon-Khmer and Champa territories across the sea. By 1374, it was put down by the rising Hindu Majapahit regime to the east in maritime Southeast Asia. For their part, the Khmer were a Buddhist empire, centered in today's Cambodia, but ruling much of mainland Southeast Asia up to parts of contemporary Hunan Province in China. The Khmer arose in the 9th century out of the former Funan and Chenia regimes in much the same southern locale of mainland Southeast Asia (Chandler, 2008). During its heyday in the 11th through 13th centuries, Angkor was one of the largest pre-industrial urban centers in the world, with its famous temples serving both Hindus and Buddhists in turn. Decline of this empire apparently occurred because of the conversion among Hindus and Buddhists, incessant internal power struggles, and also a breakdown of infrastructure for precious irrigated agriculture. The map on p. 23, middle, shows the main state of play of Southeast Asian territories around 1000 CE. Moving on, by about 1400, the Majapahit were entrenched in what is now contemporary Malaysia and substantial parts of Indonesia. The Khmer occupied Cambodia and the Cham southern parts of Vietnam, which was otherwise firmly held by the Dai Viet. Thailand emerged in the 13th century, occupying substantial parts of mainland Southeast Asia until the end of the Ayudhaya Kingdom in 1767 and later into the present. The Lao Kingdom, by 1540 incorporating Lan Na to the west and Lan Sang north of Cambodia and the Khmer, shared boundaries with the Ayudhaya Kingdom of Thailand. The Philippines, by contrast, was roughly divided north to south by Sinicized, Indianized and Islamic regimes.

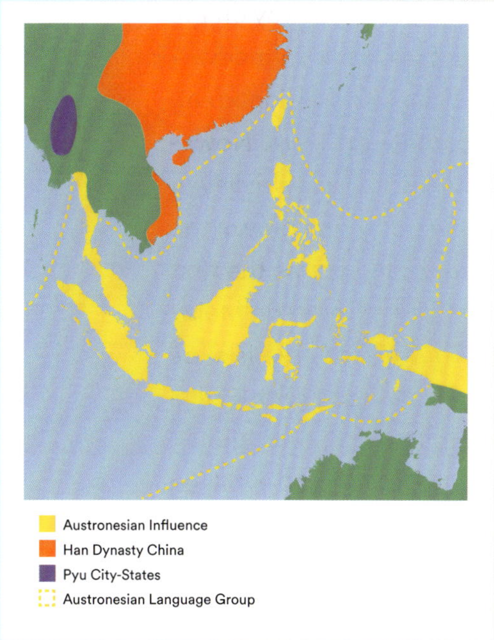

Southeast Asian Territories
c. 100 BCE

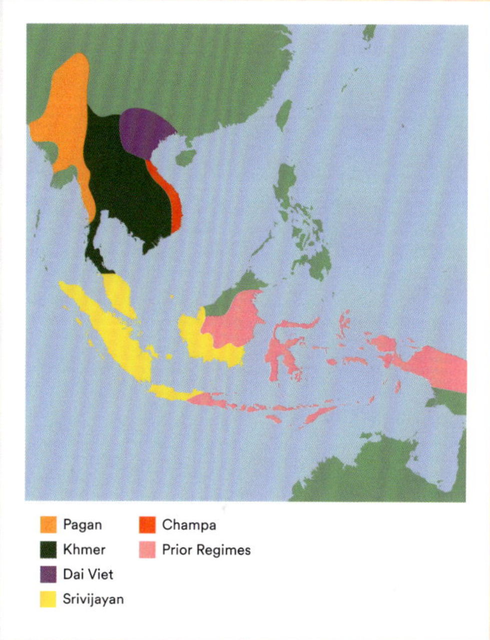

Southeast Asian Territories
c. 1000 CE

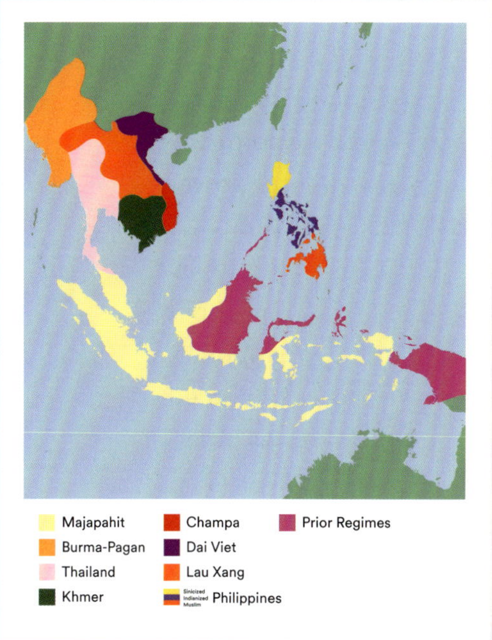

Southeast Asian Territories
c. 1400 CE

All these territorial distributions are shown on the map on p. 23, bottom, of Southeast Asia at around 1400. Islamic influence is considered to have spread through merchant activities of Arab Muslim traders as early as the 8th century, although spreading more generally by the end of the 13th century, especially in places like Sumatra (Ricklefs, 1991). This also involved scholars and missionaries, in addition to traders, as well as conversion of local elites. Due to the military power of the Malacca Sultanate, established since the 14th century in Malaya, Brunei, and the southwest Philippines, Islamization in Southeast Asia accelerated during the 15th century. This also coincided with the decline of the Hindu Javanese Majapahit Empire, as Muslim traders gained the upper hand in regional trade. Then, by the end of the 16th century, Islam was the dominant religion in Java, Sumatra and much of today's Indonesia. Rather than obliterating earlier Hindu and animist customs, however, they became embedded into Islamic tradition (Murphey, 1992).

Emergence of Modern States

The first phase of European colonization of Southeast Asia took place throughout the 16th and 17th centuries, after the arrival of the Portuguese, Spanish and Dutch and, later, the British and the French traders. This was also the period during which modernization was introduced to the region, including industrialization and secular politics (Andaya and Andaya, 2015). In the late 15th century, the Portuguese discovered a sea route around Africa and on to India and then through the Sunda and Malacca Straits into the Southeast Asian archipelago of islands and beyond into the South China Sea. They first landed in Timor in 1515, solidifying their presence by 1556 and creating it as a colony in 1702 (Newitt, 2005). They also founded a settlement at Macau in 1557 and began trading with China, as well as exploiting the spice trade among the myriad of islands in what is now Indonesia (Rowe and Kan, 2014). Elsewhere the Spaniards had been exploring the Philippines since the early 16th century. Actual conquest began in 1564 and soon brought the community of islands into a unified administration, lasting until 1821 or thereabouts (Agoncillo, 1990). Unlike the Portuguese, trade between Spain and the Philippines was made via the Pacific Ocean to Mexico and then across the Caribbean and Atlantic Ocean to Spain. Freed from Spanish domination, through the 17th and early 18th centuries, the Netherlands was an advanced and wealthy nation. They also had designs on the Spice Islands of Southeast Asia, a sole source of pepper, cloves, nutmeg, cinnamon and mace, so highly prized in Europe and the

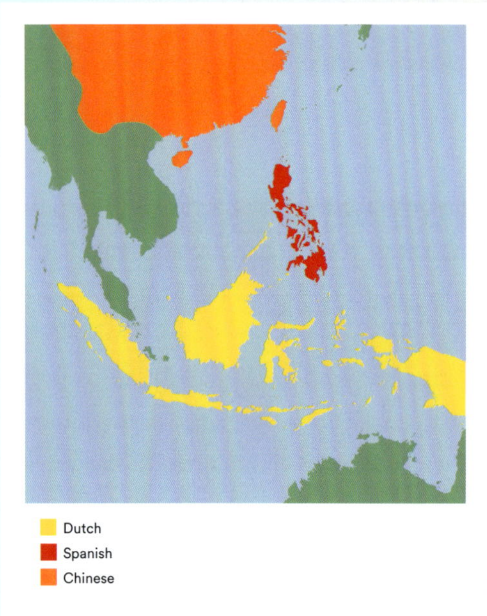

Colonization of Southeast Asian Territories c. 1600

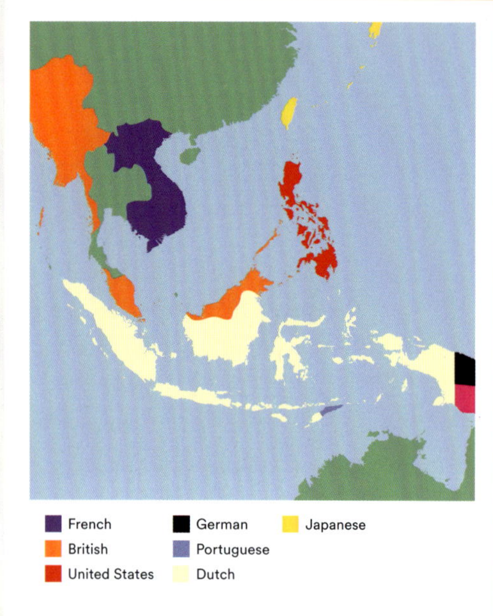

Colonization of Southeast Asian Territories c. 1900

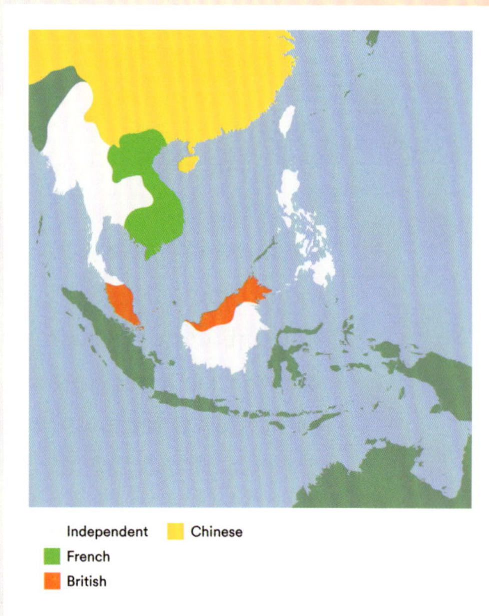

Colonization of Southeast Asian Territories c. 1950

primary ingredients of medicines, perfumes, food flavoring and meat preservatives. The first Dutch sortie took place from 1595 to 1597 and was instrumental in forming what became one of the first global corporations and quickly ended the Portuguese dominance in the region. Indeed, Ambon, chief among the island areas to the east, was captured from the Portuguese by the Dutch in 1605. Unlike the Portuguese, however, the Dutch pursued their trade through private investors rather than through the crown. In 1602, the Vereenigde Oostindische Compagnie (VOC, United East India Company) was chartered on the Amsterdam Stock Exchange. Also known, before going bankrupt in 1800, as the Dutch East India Company, by the late 17th century it was the most powerful company in the world, with its own warships, private army and some 50,000 employees. It quickly secured a monopoly over the valuable global spice supply, often through bloody struggle and violent force, led by the likes of Jan Pieterszoon Coen, its Governor-General. Representing the venerable 'Council of Seventeen', the leaders of the world's first joint-stock company, he also established Batavia in Java as the VOC headquarters (Brown, 2009, pp. 7–56).

British influence in Southeast Asia took place in several venues from 1824 to 1946 or thereabouts, beginning in Burma, now Myanmar. Three wars ensued between the British and Burma. The first in 1824 to 1826 was over the expansion of the Burmese dynasty into adjacent British-held territories in India. The second, in 1852, was provoked by British claims to teak forests in lower Burma, and the third, for two weeks in 1885, ended with the proclamation of the British Province of India in 1886 (Harvey, 1992). Modern impacts extended to the separation of Buddhist religion and state, the demise of the monarchy, direct British rule and secular education, among others. In 1937, Burma was separated from India and became a colony, prior to independence in 1948. In British Borneo, another venue of influence, three states were involved initially. They were Sarawak (1841–1946), North Borneo or Sabah (1881–1946) and Labuan off the coast of Sabah in today's East Malaysia (1846–1946). Both Sarawak and Sabah moved on to become Crown Colonies in 1963, with Labuan joining earlier through the Straits Settlements in (Wright, 1988). The adjacent Kingdom of Brunei was a British Protectorate from 1888, finally gaining independence in 1984.

Much prior to that time, from 1485 to 1528 or thereabouts, the Bruneian Empire had flourished before declining into the 19th century. British Malaya and the Straits Settlements as they were called, another British venue of influence, began with the ceding of Malacca to the British East India Company by the Dutch, along with Singapore in 1824, Penang earlier in 1800 and Dinding in 1874. Very similar to the Dutch VOC, the British East India Company was founded in 1600 as a joint-stock company, originally named The Governor and Company of Merchants of London Trading into the East Indies (Dalrymple, 2019). Its first voyage was in 1601 under James Lancaster and it was fiercely competitive with both its Dutch and French counterparts throughout the 17th and 18th centuries, especially over trade and the Spice Islands. Indeed, four Anglo-Dutch wars were fought between 1652 and 1784, with the British winning the first and the last and the Dutch the other two conflicts. The rivalry culminated in the Anglo-Dutch Treaties of 1814 and 1824, with Dutch dominance waning from around 1713 onwards (Lawson, 1993; and Brown, 2009). Not unlike the Dutch VOC, the British East India Company was abolished in 1874 due to financial problems and its administration absorbed into the British Raj (Bowen, Lincoln and Rigby, 2003). Finally, the Straits Settlements as a Crown Colony, along with Labuan, became the Federated Malay States between 1946 and 1948, eventually becoming Malaysia in 1963, followed by the expulsion of Singapore into an independent state in 1965 (Rowe and Hee, 2019, pp. 10–24).

French influence in Southeast Asia and particularly Indochina began with Jesuit missions in the early 17th century and then shifted militarily to the Cochinchina Campaign of 1858–1862, also protecting the work of the Paris Foreign Mission Society (Brocheux and Hémery, 2010). This began with a successful attack on what today is Da Nang in 1858, followed by the capture of Saigon in 1859 and concessions by the Vietnamese in 1866 through the Treaty of Saigon. This was coupled with Cambodia seeking and acquiring French protection and neighboring Siam's recognition of it in 1867. Following victory over China in the war of 1883–1885, the French gained control over northern Vietnam. With the addition of Laos in 1893, French Indochina was essentially formed and comprised of Annam towards the central-south of Vietnam,

Tonkin in the north, Laos and Cambodia. It lasted until 1954. Further encroachment also resulted in concessions from Siam to the western side of the Mekong River in 1904. The French East India Company (Compagnie Française pour le Commerce des Indes Orientales) was founded in 1664 to compete with the British and Dutch companies of similar ilk and was chartered by King Louis XIV of France (Wellington, 2006). Though flourishing briefly from 1670 to 1675, it was devastated in the French economic crisis of 1720 and unable to sustain itself. Finally disbanded in 1769, though reinstated in 1785, it was dissolved in 1790 and liquidated in 1794. As this timeline suggests, it had no impact on Indochina, where, much later in 1940, the Vichy government of France gave access to Japan, followed by Japanese occupation. After World War II, France then came into conflict with the communist Viet Minh, who sought independence. The ensuing First Indochina War ended with the decisive French loss at Dien Bien Phu. In the Geneva Conference of 1954, France relinquished all claims to territory on the Indochinese Peninsula. Both Laos and Cambodia also claimed to be independent, at much the same time (Brocheux and Hémery, 2010).

Imperialism by European powers and later by the United States continued through the 19th and 20th centuries in several conspicuous ways. Among these, the use of 'indirect rule', which had been a practice through the various East India companies, gave way to 'direct rule' of territories and colonial possessions. The British, for example, formed the Straits Settlements in 1876, the Dutch established the Dutch East Indies in 1800 and the French their various Protectorates in what they called Indochina. Later, in 1898, the Americans secured their hold on the Philippines after victory in the Spanish-American War. In almost all cases, so-called 'colonies of economic interests' were formed and reinforced. Generally, this practice took the form of leveling high taxation on local consumption of goods, including shifting production away from independent sources. In addition, intensive exploitation of natural resources was a primary reason for colonial hegemony. In this regard advantage was taken of colonies as forms of 'commodity frontiers', whereby the surface topography of occupied territory was exploited for cash crops in high demand such as rubber and rice, as well as substrate conditions for commodities like tin and other minerals.

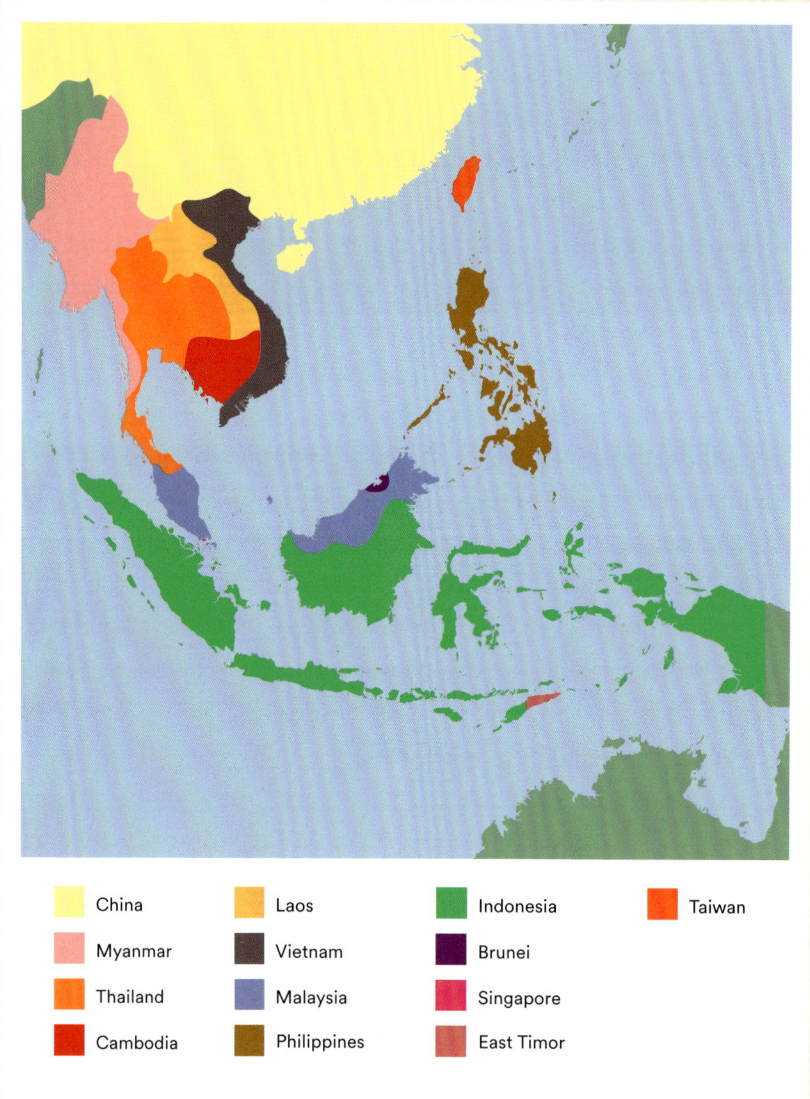

Map of Contemporary Southeast Asian States

Rubber planting, for example, was imported by British interests into Malaya and Singapore from seeds taken out of Brazil around the late 1870s by explorers there, and then redistributed from the Royal Botanic Gardens at Kew in London. Certainly, by around the 1940s, Britain dominated the world rubber market, with something like 90 to 95 percent of the world supply coming from Southeast Asia. Today it remains the world's dominant region not only for the production of rubber but also tin (Fortunel, 2013). Geographically the 'tin belt' extends some 2,800 kilometers by about 400 kilometers from China, Myanmar and Thailand to the Malay Peninsula and to the Indonesian Tin Islands, particularly Bangka Belitung Islands off the northeast coast of Sumatra. The use of tin is very old, dating back in the area to the beginning of its Bronze Age in 3000 BCE. However, at the turn of the 20th century, the invention of the automobile, pneumatic tires and food preservation in tin cans made both rubber and tin highly demanded resources (Ross, 2014). Finally, colonization, direct rule and imperialism were justified to any skeptical audiences at home with emphases on concepts like '*mission civilisatrice*' (civilizing mission) for the French and responsibilities of the 'white man's burden' for the British. In short, to colonize, after all, was to do good by introducing modern political ideas, social reforms, industrial methods and new technologies and to generally uplift the lives of locals (Hammond, 2000).

For its part, Dutch rule was both direct and dualistic, consisting of a Dutch hierarchy of officials, with Javanese aristocracy acting as intermediaries between the peasants and the European civil service. In 1830 they introduced the 'Cultivation System' to help replenish Dutch coffers in the face of losses due to the 1824 Anglo-Dutch Treaty, among other hardships. In effect this allowed them to exert strong control over the types of crops that were grown and their export value. Liberal revolt in the Netherlands resulted in a softening of these and other controls by 1870, on both humane and economic grounds. Then, with Queen Wilhelmina's prompting of 'Ethical Policy' in 1901, the idea of a debt being owed towards the colony was put into effect. One of the outcomes, however, was a rise in pan-Indonesian nationalism, with the founding of the first native political society in 1908 and the formation of the Islamic Union in 1911. Following on the heels of World War I and the Treaty of

Versailles, unrest and rising nationalism in Indonesia as in other parts of Southeast Asia began to sow the seeds for post-colonialism (Harper, 2021, pp. 317–360). This led in turn to a reversal of permissive attitudes around 1927 or thereabouts, into a more repressive imperial tone (Ricklefs, 1991; and Dick, 2002). After the signing of the Anglo-Dutch Treaty of 1824, the British began to centralize governance of the Straits Settlements. By 1819 Stamford Raffles had left eastern Java and founded Singapore in the remains of Temasek, the fiefdom of the Sultan of Johor, which then acted as a capital (Turnbull, 1972; and Rowe and Hee, 2019, pp. 50–60). Around 1909 this policy direction was reversed with decentralization towards placing greater trust and decision-making emphasis on local sultans. This had a similar rationale to the Dutch dualist policy of governance through alliances; the latter consolidated the idea of Federated States of Malaysia, which was to persist. Then later, in the 1930s, a period of economic depression ensued in the region, as elsewhere in the world.

By the late 1880s, the French began their 'civilizing mission' in Indochina, though with a focus on production, profit and labor. Small subsistence farms were reorganized, for instance, into large and more profitable plantations. Rice and rubber became staple cash crops, alongside opportunistic extractions of minerals such as coal, tin and zinc. Their internal tax system was pivoted strongly in favor of salt, rice alcohol and even opium use. As a by-product of the 'civilizing mission', local people loyal to France were recruited into administrative positions, again as a case of alliance building. If anything, the French were parsimonious in their deployment of French nationals (Evans, 2004). Upon victory in the Spanish-American War of 1898, the United States did not recognize the First Philippine Republic, which had been struggling against Spain since 1896. This led to war, won by the United States in 1902, although not fully until around 1913. As a territory under American control and governance, the Philippines gained the status of a Commonwealth in 1935, under President Manual Quezon, also gaining a higher degree of local autonomy. Demonstrably, this resulted among other actions in women's suffrage, the beginnings of land reform, and Tagalog becoming a national language (Agoncillo, 1990; and Dolan, 1991). With World War II and Japanese occupation in 1942, the Second Philippine Republic was declared, though this time as a puppet state.

	Buddhist					Hindu	Islam	Ocean	Architecture	Other		
	Srivijayan	Mon / Bamar	Khmer	Tai / Lao	Chinese	Majapahit / Oku	Malay	Austronesian	Pre-Modern + Modern Emphasis Contemporary Emphasis	Population in Mill. (%)	Western + Other Colonization	Independence
Vietnam		○	●	○	○				Buddhist Temples	97.8	1867	1954
									Homes	(14.4)	Fr.	Fr.
Cambodia			●		○	○			Buddhist Temples	16.6	1867	1953
									Comm. Homes	(2.0)	Fr.	Fr.
Laos			●	●					Buddhist Temples	7.1	1893	1949
									Homes	(1.0)	Fr.	Fr.
Myanmar		●							Buddhist Temples	53.5	1824-85	1948
									Russian + Spine	(8.0)	Br.	Br.
Thailand			○	●			○		Buddhist Temples	66.5	NA	NA
									High Rise	(9.8)		
Malaysia					●		●	○ Borneo	Colonial	32.7	18th C.	1957
									H. Rise, Mosques	(4.8)	Br.	Br.
Singapore	○				●		○		Colonial, Houses	5.7	1946	1965
									H. Rise, Rec.	(0.9)	Malay.	Malay.
Indonesia	○					○	●	●	Vern Budd. Temp.	268	18th C.	1949
									Homes	(39.4)	Dutch	Dutch
Brunei					○		●		Mosque	0.5	1888	1984
									Public	(0.07)	Br.	Br.
East Timor							○	●	Stilt Houses	1.3	16th C.	2002
									Dili Cathedral	(0.19)	Port.	Ind.
Philippines					○	○		○	Ch. Venn, Vern.	106.7	18th C.	1946
									Public	(15.7)	Sp.	USA
Polynesia (NZ)								○	Astro Types	0.7	1500BC	1945
									Chapel, Houses	(0.1)	NA	Aus. NZ.
Taiwan					●			●	Chinese, Shop	23.6	1683	1949
									H. Rise, Verandah	(3.5)	Ch.	ROC.

Salient Characteristics of Southeast Asian and Austronesian Nations

Throughout both these and pre-modern times, significant migration has occurred into Southeast Asia of 'Overseas Chinese', referring to those outside of the People's Republic and Taiwan. Indeed, the Chinese diaspora, as it is often called, has been pegged at 50 to 70 million people, mostly concentrated initially at least in Southeast Asia (Kuhn, 2008). Today this ethnically Chinese population stands at 75 percent in Singapore; 23 percent in Malaysia; 14 percent in Thailand, though of long-standing descent including parts of the royal family; and 10 percent in Brunei. As will be elaborated in chapter 4, the first settlers into the Malay Archipelago came around the 10th century CE, largely from Southern China and Guangdong and Fujian Provinces. Since that time, there have been successive waves of arrivals, though after the 1950s and into the 1970s with places of origin becoming more varied and from all over China (Khoo, 1998; and Kuhn, 2008). During the Ming Dynasty, for instance, migration occurred on the heels of exploration of the South China Sea and the Indian Ocean. Then larger waves of immigration took place during periods of unrest and privation during the Qing Dynasty in China, like the Taiping Rebellion around the middle of the 19th century, and later during the dynasty's further disintegration (Van Dongen and Liu, 2018). Fundamentally, the motivations were economic hardship and civil unrest in China and the attraction of better opportunities to the south. High concentrations in the Malay Archipelago, including contemporary Malaysia, Singapore and Brunei, can probably be ascribed to historical trends and differing attitudes between rival British and Dutch interests. Singapore was a 'free port' from its inception and, therefore, open to all, whereas the Dutch sense of their territories was almost completely exclusive. Throughout, Chinese immigrants also tended to maintain a relatively distinct community identity, reinforced by local institutions such as the Malaysian Chinese Association in Singapore. Unfortunately, this also led, in part at least, to civil unrest and ethnically based conflicts as in the 1969 riots in Malaysia and those more recently in 1998 in Jakarta, the Indonesian capital. At least one distinctive group emerged: the Peranakan. This is an essentially ethnic group defined by their descent from the first wave of southern Chinese settlers. Culturally, theirs is a hybrid of ancient Chinese and local strains going back even into much earlier Austronesian roots. Also involved is interracial marriage, but with the caveat of often considerable variation in the cultural forms, depending upon family origins and senses of identity. Sometimes the Peranakan are referred to as 'Straits Chinese', with obvious reference to the settlements along the Strait of Malacca and where many were and are concentrated. However, this equivalence is not reciprocal, as Peranakan also inhabit other areas of Southeast Asia, including Indonesia, and can involve other racial mixes. In strictly vernacular terms, though, a distinction can be struck between Peranakan, implying locally born, from Sinlah, meaning a 'new guest' to the region (Khoo, 1998).

By 1941, if not earlier, the colonial arrangement of Southeast Asia had begun to change appreciably, as Japan prosecuted its plan for its 'Greater East Asia Co-Prosperity Sphere'. It took time to transpire, however. Certainly, later during the second half of the 19th century, Japan began to aspire to become a 'first-class' modern nation. The First Sino-Japanese War in 1894–1895 netted it control over Korea, and through the Treaty of Shimonoseki, the ceding of the Liaodong Peninsula and Taiwan in China as colonial possessions. Further success in the Russo-Japanese War of 1904–1905 resulted in further territorial gains in Manchuria and northern China. The Mantetsu or Southern Manchurian Railway Ltd. was formed in 1906 as a large and well-funded semi-private corporation by the now Empire of Japan, yet another one of these globally oriented companies involved in nation building (Young, 1999). As the 'Dark Valley Decade' set in on Japan during the 1930s, it sponsored rising nationalism, militarism, and the eventual suspension of the Imperial Diet, the parliament, with Japan joining Nazi Germany and Fascist Italy in the Tripartite Pact and Axis Alliance in 1940. Some time before, in 1931, the so-called 'Mukden Incident' was perpetrated by the Japanese Army in what is now Shenyang, China, precipitating occupation of Manchuria and declaration of the Japanese puppet state of Manchuko. Further incidents and bellicose tactics prompted the start of the Second Sino-Japanese War in 1937. Against this background, the Greater East Asia Co-Prosperity Sphere was jelled and declared in 1940 by Yosuke Matsuoka, the Japanese Foreign Minister. Its purpose was clear. It was to 'liberate the people of the Orient from the shackles of Western Europe' and provide Japan with complete hegemony over a broad regional territory (Yellen, 2019, p. 4).

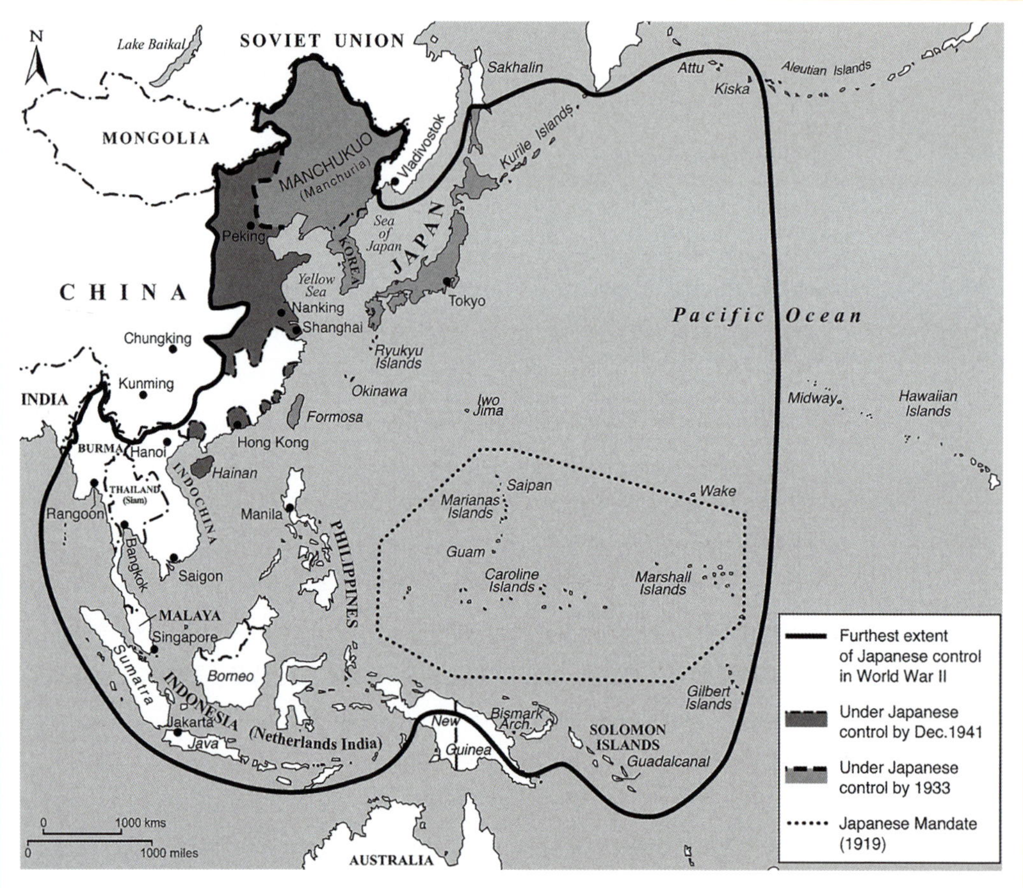

The Greater East Asia Co-Prosperity Sphere, 1942

What happened later is a matter of history. Pearl Harbor in Hawaii was attacked in December of 1941, drawing the United States into the Pacific War. Major areas of China were occupied by 1942, including Shanghai, Nanjing and Beijing. In 1941, the Axis-aligned French Vichy government in Indochina made bases available to Japan. With some early resistance, Thailand stayed out of the fray. But between 1941 and 1942 most areas of Southeast Asia previously under British, Dutch and American hegemony were occupied and controlled by Japan, as shown on the map of 1942, opposite. In short, at least the first part of Foreign Minister Matsuoka's declaration had come to pass (Yellen, 2019, p. 1).

The treatment of local populations by the Japanese was usually brutal, despite the pretense of perpetrating conflict in order to liberate them from colonial masters. In particular, the Chinese were persecuted in places like Singapore, whereas an attempt was made to enfranchise others such as the Malays and the Indians. Initially, in the Dutch East Indies the Japanese were welcomed as liberators. This situation changed significantly, however, as millions of Indonesians were forced into labor. Nevertheless, other somewhat better outcomes also followed. Bypassed by Allied troops, the Dutch East Indies was still under Japanese rule at the time of its surrender in 1945. Through Japan's facilitation and politicization down to the local level and provision of a voice for nationalist leaders like Hatta and Sukarno, the Indonesian National Revolution came about in 1945 before final recognition of independence by the Netherlands in 1949 (Ricklefs, 1991). Singapore was renamed Syonan, or 'Light of the South', and became the hub of Nampo, the southern portion of the Greater East Asia Co-Prosperity Sphere. There the Japanese envisaged a transformation from a trading *entrepôt* into a highly industrialized self-sufficient port city. Early entry by powerful Japanese monopolies and *zaibatsu*, such as Mitsui and Mitsubishi, took place. There was also strong emphasis placed on technical and vocational education. As in Indonesia, one legacy of Japanese occupation was certainly a lack of respect for former colonial occupiers and the realization that Singapore must rely on its own resources and never be occupied and exploited again (Chew and Lee, 1991, pp. 85–114). As the war began to turn in favor of the Allies, the Greater East Asia Conference was held in Tokyo in 1943

(Yellen, 2019, pp. 141–160). Prior to this, Japan had granted 'independence' to Burma and to the Philippines, as well as expressing respect for Thailand's sovereignty and independence. During the conference, the tone of rhetoric about the Co-Prosperity Sphere shifted appreciably from one of subordination and control to one of independence and equality. Nevertheless, in most other demonstrable regards the old imperial, colonial and territorial order remained clear and present (Yellen, 2019, pp. 205–216).

World War II's end in 1945 ushered in a slew of dramatic political changes in Southeast Asia that quickly led to the mosaic of independent nation states shown earlier by the map of contemporary states. The Philippines quickly negotiated its independence from the United States in 1946, ushering in a state significantly influenced by the institutional framework of its former colonizer. The 'bases era' transpired as it assumed a pivotal role in American designs on Asia, including the headquartering of the Central Intelligence Agency and allegations of 'crony capitalism' favoring American businesses. Though resisting communist-led rebellions in the late 1940s and '50s, like those in Malaya and Indonesia, the ruling regime changed dramatically with the ascension of Ferdinand Marcos as President in 1965 (Mackerras, 1995, pp. 315–320). At much the same time, President Sukarno was forced to resign from power in Indonesia assumed in 1949, as noted earlier. He was seen to be too closely aligned with an attempted coup and the leftist Partai Komunis Indonesia (PKI, Indonesian Communist Party), resulting in replacement by General Suharto and a Western-oriented military dictatorship (Mackerras, 1995, pp. 349–367). Burma's independence from Britain was promised with the signing of an agreement in 1947. It was also marked by several communist and ethnic-based insurgencies. This persisted in what has sometimes been referred to as the longest civil war (Lintner, 2005, p. 1). Taiwan became the refuge for supporters of the Guomindang, the Chinese Nationalist Party, fleeing from the Chinese Civil War, which ended with victory by Mao Zedong's communist forces in 1949. The Guomindang quickly established the Republic of China in opposition to the much larger People's Republic of China on the mainland. The First Indochina War began after the end of World War II and lasted until the defeat of the

French in 1954, as noted earlier. This ushered in the communist Viet Minh government in Vietnam and also the 'un-stitching' of the French colonial gloss of 'Indochina', so tellingly described in recent fiction by the hero – a Vietnamese – to his colleagues – a Laotian, a Cambodian and a Chinese from Saigon's Cholon quarter (Nguyen, 2021, p. 118). Laos, though proclaimed to be independent by Japan during the war, entered into civil strife in the Laotian Civil War of 1959–1975, won by the left-oriented Pathet Lao against the Kingdom of Laos and leading to formation of the Lao People's Republic. After becoming an autonomous state within the French Union in 1945, with its own constitution and political parties, Cambodia, not unlike neighboring Laos, was torn by a civil war, lasting from 1970 to 1975, between the Khmer Rouge or Communist Party of Kampuchea and the Kingdom of Cambodia. The conflict was won by the former, leading to the People's Republic of Kampuchea of 1979–1989. After the atrocities of Khmer Rouge dictator Pol Pot and his henchmen, partial restoration of cultural and religious freedoms ensued (Kiernan and Hughes, 2002).

As noted, the Federation of Malaya was enacted in 1957, securing independence from Britain. This was followed by self-governance for Sarawak and North Borneo in 1963 and the proclamation of Malaysia also in 1963. Today, it is comprised of thirteen states and three territories, with each state having its own elected legislative assembly. Based on historic Malay Kingdoms, a king is elected to a five-year term, appointing governors and assuming other constitutional duties. Politically, until recently, Malaysia was governed by the United Malays National Organization (UMNO). Singapore, for its part, was self-governing in 1959 from Britain and for a period of barely two years became a part of the Malay Federation. It was summarily ejected in 1965 to become the Republic of Singapore, led by the powerful People's Action Party, originally under Lee Kuan Yew (Chew and Lee, 1991). Still later, Brunei finally gained independence from the United Kingdom in 1984, though maintaining its monarchic status. East Timor was declared independent of Indonesia in 1975, reannexed in 1976, and administered by the United Nations from 1999 until achieving full independence in 2002 as the freely elected Democratic Republic of East Timor.

Versions of Grounded Path-Dependent Modernization

In recent years, challenges to the perceived Eurocentrism and unilinearity of themes regarding modernity have arisen. According to the likes of Charles Taylor there are at least two ways of understanding the rise of modernity, otherwise defined as cultural, social and economic change. The first is the difference between present-day Western society and that of Medieval Europe. The second is change from earlier times to today involving 'development', with the demise of traditional forms of society in favor of more modern ones (Taylor, 2001). By contrast the 'acultural theory of modernity', describes transformations in terms of culture-neutral operations that obtain regardless of specific cultures, like the growth of reason and scientific consciousness, development of secular outlooks, the rise of instrumental rationality and clear distinctions between fact finding and evaluation (Parsons, 1968). For Taylor, to rely on acultural theory is to miss out and fall into a distorted view where everything belongs to one Enlightenment package. Others like Dilip Gaonkar (2001) make similar observations, arguing instead for 'alternative modernities', culturally framed. For Jürgen

Habermas (1996, pp. 35, 52–53) modernity is an unfinished project, as the break with tradition resulted in a differentiated view of the world among the spheres of science, morality and art, each with its own foundations and formulations. Certainly, among terms like 'modernity', 'modernization' and 'modernism', though from different provenances, there arises a cluster of concepts about newness, change and the dual renditions of both positive and negative attributes. Indeed, adherents of 'multiple modernities' argue that forms of modernity are so varied and contingent upon cultural circumstances that the term 'modernity' itself must be used in the plural (Arnason, 1997; and Eisenstadt, 2005). Also, in addition to crises, modernities can be created by way of symptoms of success (Beck, 1992). Further, recent path-oriented variants of more conventional modernization theory are based on more grounded empirical observation. Accordingly, modernity is shaped by historical path dependency of trajectories of technological advancement, outside influence and economic growth and decline. In fact, even when subject to quite similar overall forces of modernization they can exhibit different trajectories. This also coincides with 'rational mastery' and 'individual autonomy' defined in multiple interpretations of modernity (Fourie, 2012). In addition, amid the maelstrom of changes, trends, fads and fashions to be had in 'being modern', certain hegemonic states can be and are often attained. In effect, they are core states of relative stability that appear at specific conjunctions in the development and evolution of the modern world. Moving from one to another, as it were, 'turning points' can be seen to occur defined by the likes of Deleuze and Guattari (1987) as moments of deterritorialization giving rise to the erasure of sufficient differences that distinguish one era from another, followed by reterritorialization that creates another era or epoch. Similar phenomena and outcomes are suggested by Miriam Levin and her colleagues (2011) and by Niall Ferguson (2005). With regard to the topic of 'modernity' in this volume, an interpretative stance is taken favoring 'cultural modernity', well-grounded, even empirical depictions of it and the appearance of 'hegemonic moments of production' and 'turning points' in orientations. More broadly, these can also be seen to coincide with four defining features of modernity. First, there is emancipation usually manifested by extensive secularization. Second, there is renovation with adoption in fields like architecture of technical innovation.

Third, there is often at least the promise of democratization and the making of opportunities accessible to everyone. Finally, there is expansion especially in economic well-being and the tendency to make modernity hegemonic as a way of life (Canclini, 1995, p. 264f.). Moreover, these features will be the case when viewing moments of architectural production under the influence of a multiplicity of cultural roots, quests for identity, as well as programmatic requirements, implied by the preceding narrative.

To begin with, a sharper focus on the contemporary period of, say, the past 25 to 30 years of architectural production can be obtained from cliometric analyses ranging across the present nation states of Southeast Asia from around 1950 onwards. These graphical plots of the relative intensities among selected characteristics germane to architecture and urban building reveal periods of internal hegemony and relative prosperity. More specifically, these are identified in the graph opposite, and the nation-by-nation details are given in the book's appendix. Each hegemonic period is defined by a relative convergence of time-dependent data profiles in an upward direction, suggesting improvement in prosperity. Of course, within Southeast Asia there are considerable differences in wealth, ranging from Singapore, one of the richest nations on earth with a Gross Domestic Product (GDP) per capita of around USD 63,363 in 2018, down to poor Myanmar with only USD 1,387 per capita. Overall, the average for the region is around USD 13,508 and slightly above the world average of USD 11,433. The regional median is to be found in the Philippines at USD 3,290 per capita, hardly wealthy. For external comparison, estimates for the People's Republic of China and the United States are USD 10,841 and USD 65,064 per capita, respectively (World Bank, 2020). The vertical arrangement of hegemonic periods in the graph reflects ranges of wealth per capita, with Singapore at the top and Myanmar at the bottom. Among them and as shown in the appendix, most have had two hegemonic periods since 1950, including the initial spurts of post-colonial development and then later at the beginning of the 21st century. The three nations of Malaysia, Thailand and Vietnam also had identifiable middle periods, though probably largely for reasons of political stability in relation to moments of instability.

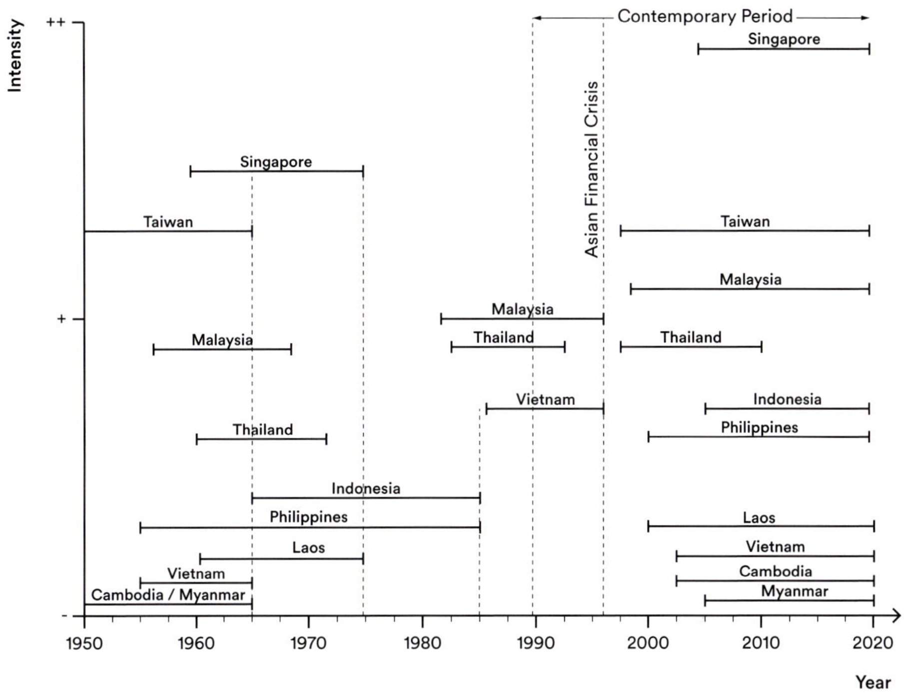

Periods of Relative Prosperity and Hegemony of Southeast Asian States

At the risk of a certain amount of oversimplification, internal profiles or trajectories can be summarized as follows for each nation in Southeast Asia. Singapore, by far the wealthiest, moved in an orderly way under the direction of the People's Action Party (PAP) from inception in 1965 well into the 1990s. By charting a pathway forward of being clean, green and a haven for foreign investment, as well as secondary and tertiary industrial development, the city-state managed to achieve first-world standards for its compliant population. Taiwan's early development under Guomindang tutelage slowed in 1965 with withdrawal of U.S. support. The island state still lived under martial law until 1987, with political reforms in the 1990s ushering in the recent period of democratic governance that began with the first elections in 1996. Becoming a federated state in 1957, Malaysia was socially frayed by the late 1960s with race riots and other disturbances. From 1981 onwards, with Mahathir bin Mohamad in firm control of UMNO, the country began to flourish until it was hit by the Asian Financial Crisis of 1997/1998. Since then a period of continued development has followed, though with less consistency in governance. Thailand's relatively stable constitutional monarchy, which had seen the country through without colonization, began to experience political instability and military intervention from around 1972 onwards. It also suffered during the Asian Financial Crisis as elsewhere in Southeast Asia and recently entered an autocratic period with a change in royal ruler. Indonesia began under the strong leadership of Sukarno in 1949, lasting until 1965 when he was replaced by General Suharto, as noted earlier. This military regime lasted until 1998, buoyed up at times by the USA before giving way to recent relatively peaceful transitions. Similarly, the Philippines came of age nationally during the dictatorial Marcos regime from 1968 to 1986, to be replaced by Corazon Aquino on the heels of the People Power Revolution, and others up to the present strongman, Rodrigo Duterte, elected in 2016. Laos, still relatively poor and agrarian with a GDP per capita of USD 2,800 or so, transitioned from French Indochina in 1959 before becoming the communist Lao People's Democratic Republic in 1975. Neighboring Cambodia, also adopting a socialist government though suffering horribly under the Khmer Rouge from 1979 to 1989, later became modern. Vietnam, also poor with about USD 2,750 GDP per capita, won nationhood from the

French in 1954, as noted earlier, before going to war with its southern cohort and the USA between 1965 and 1975. After some recovery though also war with its western neighbors, it entered the Doi Moi Reform period in 1997 and revived relations with the USA and other parts of the world around 2005. Finally, Myanmar, the poorest nation in Southeast Asia at USD 1,400 or so GDP per capita, having earned independence from Britain, as noted earlier, came under harsh military dictatorship in 1962 before entering a brief period of democracy from 2011 to 2021 followed by a return to brutal military rule.

Given the relatively uneven post-colonial developmental national profiles, contemporary architectural production has also been uneven in its timing and intensity in Southeast Asia. The recent bunching together of relatively upwardly inclined hegemonic periods in related socio-economic and urban dynamics suggests concentration of contemporary architectural activity during the past 25 or so years. This has often involved modest beginnings in domestic structures and community service facilities. Much of the production appears to be reactive to what was created in the past and often without the same monumentalizing and leveling impact. The adoption and re-use of older structures and of abundant local heritage has also figured strongly during the recent global rise and competition for leisure-time and tourist pursuits. On par though, rootedness in pre-modern cultures, colonial periods and reckoning with the more recent past is also profoundly evident. Moreover, over recent time as an architectural reckoning both with the past and the future has unfolded in the present, the extremes of one orientation with the other seem to have moderated.

Organization of the Book

As noted earlier, the basic conceptual framework of this book is around the development of contemporary architecture in Southeast Asia under relatively separate root conditions converging in the contemporary projects themselves. Following this introduction, chapter 2 focuses on indigenous vernacular architectural traditions and particularly those associated with the Austronesian peoples. Accordingly, attention is drawn to typal precedents in the forms of hut dwellings, longhouses and village configurations. Figural references are made to skeletal frames with stilt buildings and prominent flowing roofs in the manner of crab claw sails and other paraphernalia of oceangoing outrigger vessels. Against this background, numerous contemporary projects will be presented and discussed, paralleling these typal and figural references. Chapter 3 will then switch to early dynastic movements into Southeast Asia mainly from India in the west and China in the north. In essence these embraced Buddhist, Hindu and Islamic influences on architecture and settlement. Again, contemporary projects will be described and discussed principally with these points of reference in mind. Then in chapter 4, Western colonization, primarily by European maritime powers and throughout most of Southeast Asia, will be the theme and primarily deal with importation and local adaption of architectural forms and styles from colonial homelands. Here, contemporary projects will be reflective of these traditions, particularly with reference to trabeated forms to be found in earlier tropical neo-classical architecture and tropical Art Deco works. Finally, in chapter 5 the unfolding sequence of architectural production will focus on post-colonial architecture. Often these are the monuments to post-colonialism executed by fledgling nation states and leading to contemporary projects that adopt similar approaches, like neo-brutalism for instance, or they are more fully reactive and even reactionary in the manner, say, of the earlier Jengki Style in Indonesia. They may also be projects dealing with tropical conditions and so-called green buildings, as well as new housing programs in the form of contemporary high-rise towers. In all, across chapters 2 through 5, some 70 contemporary projects will be described and discussed. Further appendix material will include data regarding the development of nation states since 1950, as well as biographical notes about prominent architects mentioned throughout this narrative.

Austro–nesian Indigenous Vernacular

Chapter 2

An introduction to the Austronesian peoples has already been made including their origins by way of the 'Out-of-Sundaland' hypothesis or now the more favored 'Out-of-Taiwan' model. Nevertheless, the indigenous vernacular architecture and patterns of settlement are sufficiently long-lived and entrenched to be considered as arising in Southeast Asia and not necessarily always from somewhere else. Moreover, within the Indonesian archipelago as well as elsewhere in the region, the predominant characteristics of this architecture and settlement show sufficient conformity and similarity to allow for and even require collective discussion. Among these characteristics a number stand out. They include carved gable roof finials, almost without exception, and very prominent roofs, including those with saddleback ridgeline profiles and beehive shapes, as well as other ornamentation particularly of pointed rooftops. A substantial number of structures involve piling with floors above grade the undersides of which often form shaded platforms for a variety of activities alongside enclosed interior spaces above. Within the repertoire of timber frames, piles and copious thatched roofs there is a relatively consistent pattern of building types. These include 'origin-houses' (e.g. *tongkonan*), perhaps the most ceremonious of them all, alongside clan houses, head houses, village houses and longhouses, depending upon use, site and other often collective circumstances. Further structures to be found are granaries for food, tombs and even temporary structures in support of particular functions and special celebrations. Then there are more modern hybrid arrangements with, for example, saddleback-roofed *toraja* houses in Indonesia, on top of or beside relatively conventional homes with all modern conveniences. Other details are also relatively consistent in the forms of stone seats, painted walls and particularly painted ring beams around the middle stratum of buildings above the piles and below the roofs.

Clearly, many of these characteristics provide shelter from the elements of the tropics. Indeed, many like raised floors and breezy underfloor spaces and pitched roofs are well suited to tropical climates and so-called 'passive' approaches to habitable control. They often involve material selection and layouts that are protective of excessive degradation, such as woods with oils that resist termites, an absence of nails and other joinery materials and techniques that hamper resilience, and even the capacity to manually lift and move whole buildings. Like a lot of indigenous architecture, the praxis of making and building from readily available material is highly developed, time-tested and very suitable. All these qualities, however, do not converge on a thorough explanation or even outline of why the buildings look the way they do. Shape and appearance, after all, are also tied up with social and symbolic space, as the likes of Bernard Rudofsky, Amos Rapaport, among others, have pointed out (Rudofsky, 1964; Rapaport, 1969; and Waterson, 1990, pp. xv–xix). The house, among other building types, often draws its symbolic values from scale, materiality and associated imagery, rather than from a preponderance of places where people live. The American single-family house in a garden is as much a symbol as anything else, because it is not about need as many people do not live that way nor can expect to do so. With regard to Austronesian indigenous architecture, answers to this kind of question need to trace origins, social and technological as well as cosmological considerations.

Typal Precedents

Among the building types of Austronesian cultures, there are particular kinds of houses such as dwellings and ritual sites, as well as arrangements of several types together forming a particular place. Many 'origin-houses', marking the place of origination for kin groups, are of the latter kind. Among the Torajans, an ethnic group indigenous to Sulawesi in today's Indonesia, these origin-houses may remain largely unoccupied and are regarded more as ritual sites than practical dwellings. They are maintained often with considerable effort by a titular family who proceed to live nearby or next to the *tongkonan,* as it is called, in comparatively modern and well-serviced circumstances. Sometimes ritual offices will be vested in origin-houses in order to conduct ceremonies and maintain ritual contact with ancestors. Similar situations are to be found among the Toba Batak of Sumatra. There an origin-house may form a meeting place, set opposite to a tribal chief's residence (Waterson, 1990, pp. 43–59). Though not occupied as dwellings, these origin-houses are not literally empty. They are where heirlooms of clans are kept and maintained, and where the ritual ceremonies observed by clans take place, as well as communal meetings.

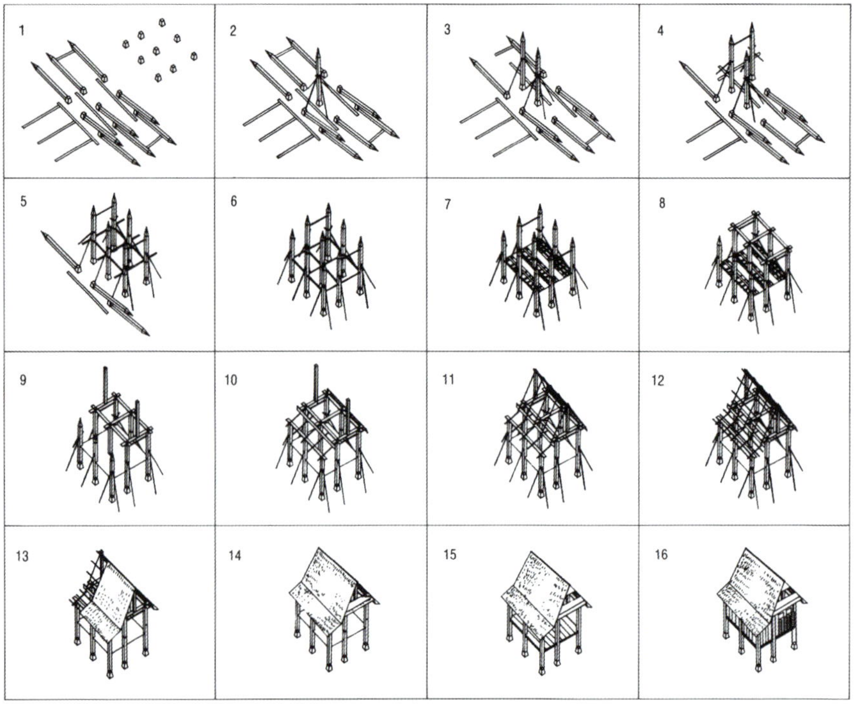

Mode of Construction

Toraja Origin-House next to Owner's House

Architecturally, the origin-houses are often grand and, in the case of the *tongkonan*, crowned by large, upwardly sweeping saddleback roofs, with gable-end facades that are elaborately carved and decorated. Inside, among the heirlooms elaborate carvings can often be found, sometimes in rare woods. Origin-houses also border on being temples, particularly with regard to ritual functions.

Moving forward in time of Austronesian migrations, the New Zealand Maori meeting house (*wharenui*) and ceremonial center (*marae*) are also an ensemble of building and open space. There, the terms *marae aatoa,* or 'marae proper', embrace a meeting house, dining hall, public facilities and usually a flat open space for meeting assembly and conduct. Typically, the *wharenui* faces the *marae aatoa*, though collectively they may also be known as the *marae*. Similar to the origin-houses of Indonesia, references to meeting houses may also vary, from *wharetupuan,* for instance, referring to an ancestral house, to *wharenui,* i.e. literally a meeting house. In almost all cases they are synonymous with sub-tribes and are symbols of kinship groups (Metge, 1976). Most *wharenui* are rectangular planned buildings with steep gabled roofs and front verandahs, often with large bargeboards adorned with carvings. Usually, the relative size and profusion of decoration is a sign of prestige, though the *wharenui* did not really come into being until the 19th century. The verandahs can be 4 meters deep, with a door located to the left of center, usually with a decorated lintel above, and a window to the right of center (van Meijl, 1993). In ritual practice, meeting houses involve a cosmic timelessness for assessing the conditions and contents of the past through the present and into the future. The representation of time spatially follows a pattern of the past being up front, with the future way in the back. In essence, Maori time was linked to natural events and not to generalized abstractions of quantifiable periods. History, in effect, is relived and, therefore, reference to ancestors is of considerable relevance (Salmond, 1975).

More generally among Autronesian people, houses take a number of forms and often embody ritual aspects as noted already. The Rotinese house, for instance, belonging to Rote Island on the southwest edge of Timor, is sometimes regarded as a memory palace, with elaborate

Maori Wharenui and Marae

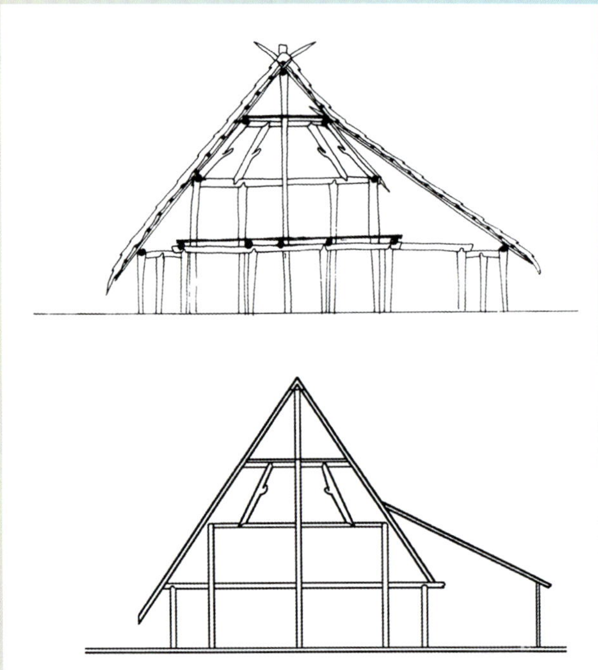

Section of a Rotinese House

naming of all the building components and spaces in between (Fox, 1993a). The prominence of a house is assessed according to its size and, therefore, the number of posts lifting it off the ground. The cross-section is dominated by a tall gabled roof structure, with a wide perimeter skirting around its base, all supported on posts and piled into the ground. As with much Austronesian housing, the floor is raised the equivalent of one story above grade, providing shaded space for house-related activities and meetings. Depending upon a dichotomous or trichotomous interpretation, the Rotinese house has a lower ground level, an upper level on the floor constructed above grade and then a loft in the peak of the gable as the most private part of the house. South is regarded as superior to north and, generally, east is regarded positively and associated with 'the head' and 'the outside'. By contrast, west is seen less positively, as 'the tail' and about 'the inside' (Fox, 1993a).

Traditional Toba Batak houses also employ tall, upwardly sweeping saddleback roofs, with elaborately decorated and carved woodwork on the spacious and slightly inclined front-gable ends. Among groups like the Karo, they also deploy massive high-hat roofs. Again, all houses are built on piles with open ground areas and transition to the raised main floor area. Roofs are typically thatched. Similarly, the Minangkabau houses are also made out of wood, with the exception of the rear longitudinal wall, which is simply a plain lattice woven in a checkered pattern out of split bamboo. They are a cultural group living in western Sumatra, Indonesia. Women are the property owners and despite today's dominant Muslim influence, the society is matrilineal. Often men are guests in the houses. The substantial roof of a Minangkabau house is made of a truss and cross-beam structure, and is thatched from palm trees (*ijuk*). Roof finials often resemble buffalo horns in their pointed configuration, alluding to the Minangkabau name (Dawson and Gillow, 1994, pp. 74–80). In short, throughout the Indonesian archipelago as well as elsewhere where Austronesian culture has settled, the single house form has comprised a number of functions and ritualistic observations. It has been associated with communal meeting, rituals of ancestry and commemoration, companion to outside activity, and dwelling place for individuals and families. The prominence of the owner or title holder and the size and embellishment of the house has varied according to and

Elaborate Batak Decoration

Minangkabau Royal Palace

across these functions. The chief's house, for instance, has been used as a communal meeting place, and a ritual site, whereas commoner houses or huts have not.

Beyond the single house form, there are also longhouses to be found, particularly in northern Borneo or today's Sarawak, Malaysia. Among groups like the Iban, for example, longhouses consist of federations of independent families. They are, in effect, territorial aggregations of distinct groups. They are not community pavilions, however, but privately owned semi-detached dwelling units, without formal hierarchy or hegemonic organization. A bit like a contemporary condominium association, each individual family is subordinated to collective goals. This corporateness is expressed architecturally through the hearths and posts that make up the single collective structure. Among the Iban, for instance, *bilek* refers to each family's domestic space, typically involving three intergenerational groups. These are assembled next to each other through partitioned spaces. An extensive and lengthy unpartitioned space in front of the *bilek* faces out towards a river, the general site condition of the longhouse (*rumah*). This is referred to as the *ruai* and runs the length of the building and is usually expressed as a long verandah or porch. Assemblage of the individual *bilek* within the longhouse is also usually of two forms. The first emanates from a source (*pun*) located at the center of the row of units and moves symmetrically towards both ends (*ujog*). The other is a single alignment of *pun* and *ujog* from one end of the longhouse to the other. As noted, all longhouses face a river, a part of which is also set aside for bathing (Sather, 1993). Additional structures, such as granaries and barns used to store food, generally follow the construction patterns and styles of houses. Often granaries were placed in a conspicuous and surveilled location in front of the house. Typically, they were built on heavy poles often sloping slightly outward to support the load of grain. Though smaller in size than the houses, the granary floor was built higher out of respect for the rice goddess. The exposed tops of all vertical posts were capped to protect the grain from rodents. Barns also mimicked the structural and cladding qualities of houses and were used entirely for utilitarian purposes. As mentioned, temples were often in the form of large houses and as dwelling places for the spirits (Waterson, 1990, p. 199f.).

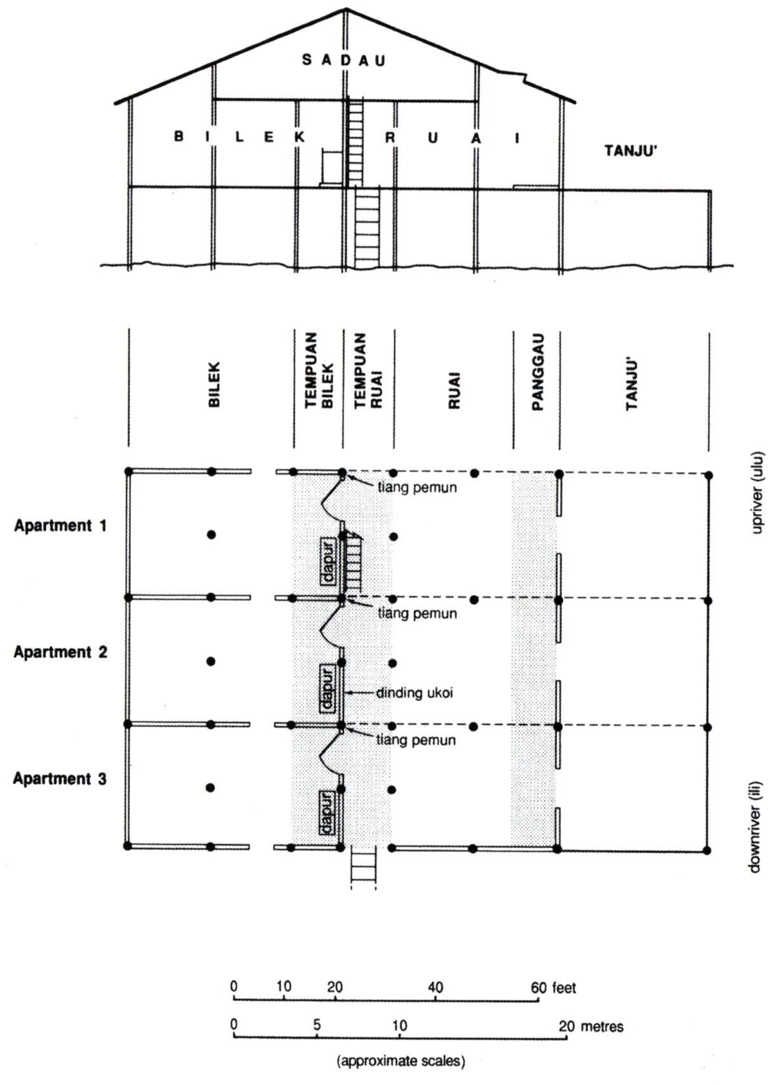

Longhouse Section and Plan

Dagal Longhouse in Sarawak

Maori Granary

Figural References

Among the prominent components of Austronesian building and architecture, there were at least three features. The first was the pile foundations and skeletal wooden frames arising from them that formed the structure of buildings. Sometimes huge ironwood piles, over a meter in diameter, were used and even arranged in a V-shaped pattern to better resist earthquake stresses. All this gave rise to the ubiquitous elevation of main floors of buildings above grade, often with an occupiable shaded open space beneath. These piled structures appear to date from Neolithic times (Waterson, 1990, pp. 1–7). There the origins might date back to Indian influence of not placing structures directly at grade and with references also made to Japanese buildings like the Yaiyoi structures of southwestern Honshu of around 300 BCE (Benedict, 1975; and Domenig, 1980). A second conspicuous component of Austronesian indigenous building was the presence of large and almost all-encompassing roofs often clad in thatch. In this regard there are at least three main types of roofs, including the saddleback roof, the high-hat roof and the beehive roof. One technical explanation for the first two, derives from the progression of form from primitive tree-shaped assemblies of poles set in the ground and overlapping at the top, then on into gable roofs of different configurations and overall shape profiles.

Tongkonan Saddleback Roof House

High-Hat Sumbanese Clan House

Beehive Atoni House

The saddleback roof, for instance, is curved in the longitudinal direction, often sweeping upwards sharply at either end. The Toraja origin-house described earlier is typically of this form (Domenig, 1980). The other is the tall gable structure forming the high-hat roof form, with its usual perimeter skirting around the outside. Both are shown in the illustrations on p. 61, and both cover buildings that are rectangular in plan. The tall and rounded beehive roof buildings, by contrast, arise from circular plans; here the roof constitutes more or less the entire building. More generally in the East Indies there was the *joglo*, a very tall roof form squared off at the top and flared out at the base, the *limasan* form that was similar but less tall and more squared off at the top as a gable, and the *kampong* form of intermediate height but rising to a point (Dawson and Gillow, 1994). The undergirding wooden skeletal structure is shaped by cross-bracing bent toward the middle like, for instance, the Isneg houses of northern Luzon, the Philippines (Scott, 1966, p. 188).

Others refer to the imagery of boats and in particular the boats of the Austronesian peoples. They do so by citing linguistic parallels as well as referring to depictions of objects such as Dong Sou drums of Vietnam (600–400 BCE) and to rattan screens from Lampung at the eastern end of Sumatra, Indonesia, adjacent to the Sunda Strait (Vroklage, 1936; and Dawson and Gillow, 1994, p. 34). This boat symbolism and especially large building roofs can also be borne out through the profiles of the ancient sailing canoes and outriggers of the Austronesian ocean peoples (Doran, 1981), in particular, the Oceanic spritsail vessels, sometimes referred to as 'crab claw sail' craft because of the curved profile formed by winds within such a sail. There is a resemblance to large saddleback-roofed houses. Among well-known sailing craft of this kind (*wangka*), the proportion of the vertical height of the sail to the canoe hull was of the order of 4.5–8.5 to 1. Most, if not all, Austronesian houses have analogous proportions of roof height to lower main-floor height in excess of 4 to 1, far larger than other ratios among other kinds of houses, usually of the order of 1–1.5 to 1. Other boat analogies also refer to the curvilinear shapes of the prows and sterns of oceangoing canoes. Similarly, in the Maori culture the *wharenui* has been likened to an upside-down canoe (Van Meijl, 1993, p. 214).

Crab Claw Spritsail Craft

Curved Prow and Stern Canoe, Taiwan

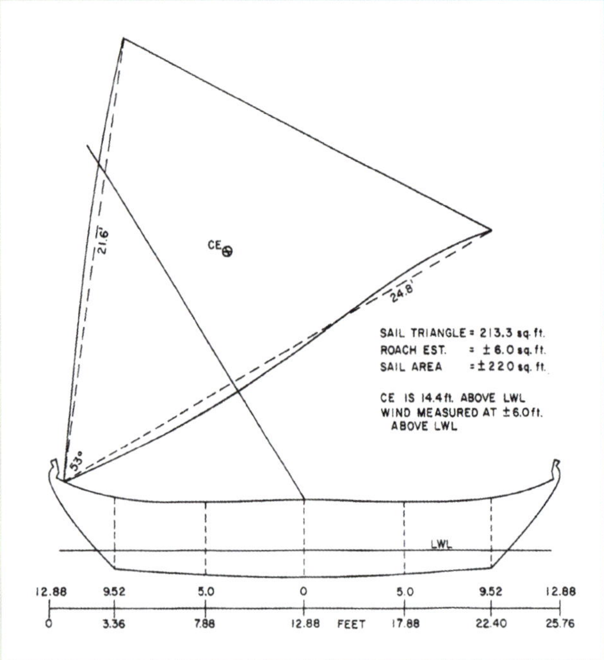

Proportion of Hull to Sail on Spritsail Rigged Craft

A Toba Batak Village

The third component concerns decorative elements. Conspicuous here are the crossed gable finials on top of the roofs of many structures. In many instances they are a direct reference to the importance of buffalos in many Southeast Asian societies. Then there are the painted and decorated ring beams encircling the main level of buildings. This clearly reflects almost all the belief systems of the indigenous Indonesian archipelago, where the concept of a three-tiered cosmos is shared. In this, the middle level is occupied by humans, in between the upper world of the heavens and the lower realm of animals. In addition, decorative patterns of unbroken lines of good fortune abound, often around the eight cardinal points. Richly carved sculptural installations in origin-houses, for example, often adorn the interior spaces of heirlooms.

Though extensive, even by earlier European standards in, say, the Spice Islands, the layout of settlements was rural in their arrangements and patterns, lacking clear boundaries and strong distinctions from the farm and jungle landscapes around them. They were, in appearance anyway, sprawling and invisible to a degree that did not distinguish them as separate domains from the nature around them. Despite the high and large roofs of buildings, the interiors of even noble origin-houses were relatively small, enclosed and without windows. While the exteriors were often imposing, the interiors were not. Certainly, the prominence and decoration of building roofs was a mark of social standing and high prestige. The semi-enclosed space beneath the main floor of a building, such as a house, formed a sheltered space for meeting, informal contact, household work and the like, as suggested earlier. Most people did not spend extensive amounts of time inside. The concept of houses as bodies was relatively commonplace, with the roof ridge as the cranium and the wall posts and piles as feet. This was complementary to the three-tiered cosmological reading presented earlier. With the sea so important to ocean peoples and to islands, 'boat' and 'boatload' linguistic references to smaller social units arose, such as the term *barangay* in the Philippines, the Tagalog word for 'village' (Waterson, 1990, p. 93). Also, as noted earlier, tribes and social units within them were both patrilineal and matrilineal, even to the extent of husbands in Minangkabau society being regarded as guests and visitors to houses all owned by women.

Contemporary Projects

Drawing on this background, contemporary project ranging over the past 20 or so years reflect both formal and figural aspects of Austronesian building and architecture. Not surprisingly, they are not built within the traditional cultural heritage of bygone years and consequently do not embody old belief systems and cultural values. Examples are drawn from almost all the nation states of Southeast Asia, though mainly from the island communities of Indonesia, Polynesia and Taiwan. In addition, examples are grouped according to building and settlement types, as well as according to other constructive and morphological arrangements like skeleton frames and non-rectangular arrangements common among Austronesian buildings.

Huts and Longhouses

Te Wharewaka o Poneke (Wharewaka Function Centre) in Wellington, New Zealand, occupies a central location on the waterfront once occupied by the Te Aro Pa, or fortified Maori village up to the 1880s. This was one of the largest *iwi*, or tribal communities, among several

Collection of Austronesian Structures

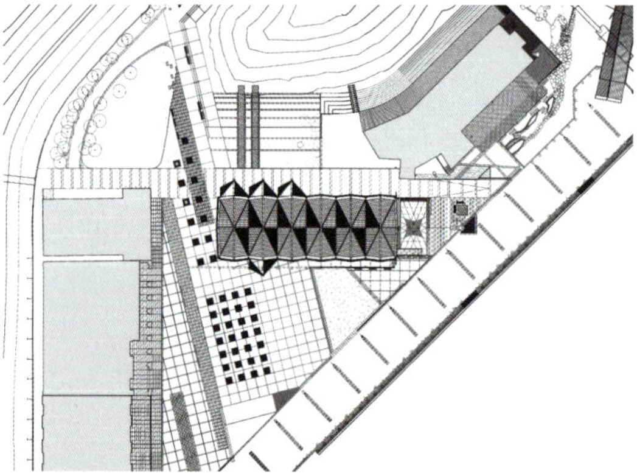

Wharewaka Function Centre, Wellington, New Zealand, 2011

that occupied the once fertile waterfront that is now the center of Wellington. Another to the north was the extensive Pipitea Pa, now covered by landfill, along with commercial, warehouse and wharf buildings. On a headland jutting into the harbor and defining the Whairepo Lagoon to the west, Te Wharewaka is also next to the larger Te Papa Tongarewa (Museum of New Zealand). The building by Architects Plus was completed in 2011 and is in the form of a traditional *wharenui*, though draped with an architectural interpretation of a Maori cloak (*korowai*), creating a structure of triangular metal components, much like the large feathers of a *moa* cloak, which can be manipulated to create shading for indoor and adjacent outdoor spaces. The plan is rectangular, of the order of 63 meters in length by some 20 meters in width. It has three floors, including a basement for public toilets and a kitchen, as well as a ground floor and first floor of meeting and function rooms, display of several lengthy canoes (*waka*) and a café. The front of the *wharenui* faces northeast as is customary and faces a well-defined paved open area of a *marae*. The entry facade, again with the customary wide verandah, is defined by a strong gable-roofed alignment of bargeboards, with patterned surfaces echoing wood carving. The door with a decorated lintel is located to the left of the center post yet again, as customary, with a generous window opening to the right. The *marae* almost buts up against Taranaki Street, which provides access and merges with the Great Harbour Way beside Te Papa Tongarewa. The other building on the peninsula is The Boatshed, which is also the home of the Wellington Rowing Club. Landscapes on the easterly and westerly sides of Te Wharewaka are well developed as hardscapes and vegetated areas and accommodate outdoor inhabitation and some dining. The lagoon side also serves as a headquarters for guided canoe tours in the harbor (ArchDaily, 2012). Directly in front of the *marae* is a large bronze statue of Kupe Raiatea, the legendary Maori explorer of around 1300, or so, with his wife Hine Te Aparangi, who is reputed to have given New Zealand its Maori name of Aotearoa, or 'the land of the long white cloud.' They are both accompanied by a statue of tohunga Pekahourangi (Biggs, 1957). As a multi-purpose function center and display area, Te Wharewaka well serves the purpose of introducing visitors to aspects of Maori customs and life. It also does so in a manner that is contemporary and yet formally and historically respectful.

The Tanghalang Maria Makiling National Arts Center in Laguna, the Philippines, north of Manila, is an open-air theater that has a seating capacity of around 2,500, including the outside bleachers. It was completed in 1976 and was designed by Leandro Locsin. It is a part of the Cultural Center of the Philippines, a government-owned and controlled corporation created by Ferdinand Marcos in 1966 to preserve and promote Philippine arts. Sited squarely on top of Mount Makiling, the theater is surrounded by other venues including an executive house, a two-story clubhouse and a chapel. The 13.5-hectare site is also home to the Philippine High School for the Arts. A dormant volcano, Mount Makiling is also a forest reservation (Girard, 2021). Locsin's design for the theater is a direct reference to the nipa hut or *bahag kubo* type of stilt house, indigenous to parts of the Philippines and also iconic of its indigenous architecture. In this particular contemporary manifestation it has a robust brutalist concrete base of support for the above-grade structure, monumentalizing the stilts of the traditional nipa structure. It is crowned by a soaring pyramidal roof, symmetrical on all four sides of its square plan and covered in red clay tiles. The central part of the roof is flat and accommodates the central lighting of the theater below. Significant portions of the roof structure are exposed as in the original nipa huts and support wood panels lending excellent acoustic qualities to musical performances. Orchestral works are generally performed in the round, with the sheltering presence of the hulking corner supports as a backdrop. Though greatly amplified in scale and monumental expression, the theater also literally mirrors the nipa hut both in timber roof structure and above-grade support, even if tile replaces the nipa, which in Tagalog refers to palm tree thatch commonly used in traditional indigenous architecture.

Two secondary schools offer good examples of contemporary versions of the longhouse type. The first is the Bann Huay San Yaw Post Disaster School in Thailand of 2014. It was one of nine schools out of some 73 that were badly damaged by the Mae Lao earthquake in the Chiang Rai area of northern Thailand, which registered 6.3 on the Richter scale. After the earthquake, a non-profit, Design for Disaster, launched a program with the support of the Engineering Institute of Thailand and the Consulting Engineers Association of Thailand.

Tanghalang Maria Makiling National Arts Center,
Laguna, the Philippines, 1976

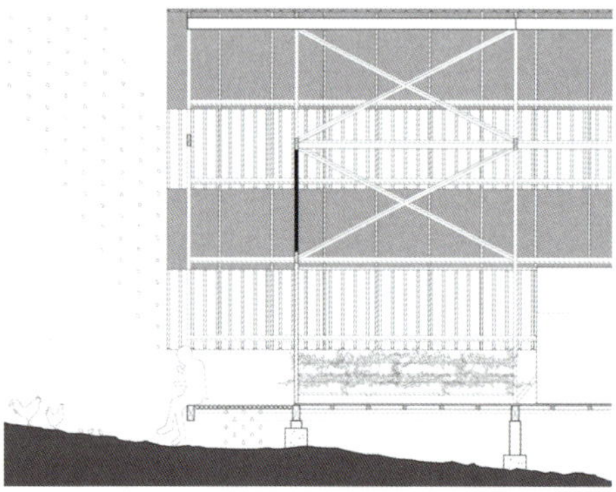

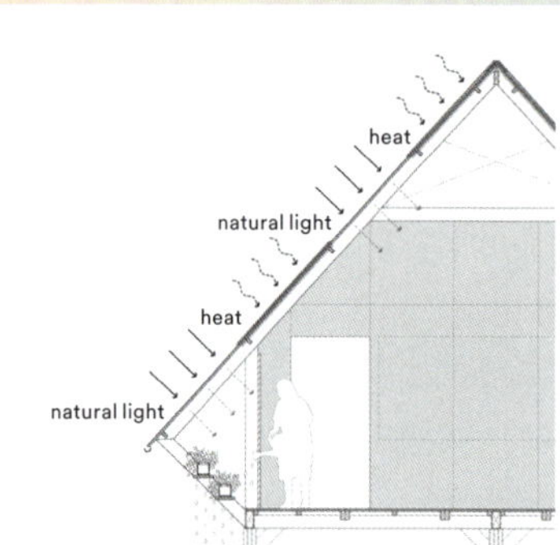

Bann Huay San Yaw Post Disaster School, near Chiang Rai, Thailand, 2014

Vin Varavarn Architects were assigned to the Bann Huay San Yaw School. Three classrooms were to be provided for secondary school students from tribal families. Overall, the school was to be earthquake resistant and easily constructed by local workers. It was also to be low-budget and compact to save on land use. Most of the materials were to be lightweight to reduce horizontal movement caused by earthquakes. A single structure was built, comprised of three classrooms with foyer spaces in between to provide necessary sound insulation and a space for students' shoes. The building is rectangular in plan and measures roughly 33 meters in length by 8 meters in width. The entrance is directly into the two foyers at the center of the building and the serial arrangement of classrooms. The overall building section is pentagonal and thus similar to a traditional longhouse, but with two additional bracing elements at the bottom left-hand corners. All the necessary structural elements were designed to be exposed and to express feelings of security and safety, as well as to reduce finishing costs. The large gable roof, which is also customary, allows the classrooms to be skylit but with moderation by bamboo shading devices distributed on the roof's surface. Openness of the structure allows for adequate cross-ventilation and the entry doorways are made from movable panels in the roof at the top of short stairways. The entire structure is mounted on cylindrical metal posts on exposed concrete footings. It is placed on a sloping site, one end of which allows provision of a semi-outdoor multi-functional space. Within each classroom, desks are arranged along the perimeter and bamboo shelves are provided on the outside in order to house colorful pot plants, tended by students, and also to act as guardrails for student safety. A careful protocol was devised involving 16 steps of construction from the erecting of foundational posts to the completed building, much in the manner of traditional longhouse framing and erection. The deliberate and relatively generous provision of common spaces between the classrooms, around the entry and at both ends of the building, also follows in the manner of vernacular longhouses (ArchDaily, 2019).

The second building is the Secondary School in Roong, Cambodia, of 2014 by Architetti Senza Frontiere Italia. Built in the Takeo Province of Cambodia, a reputed cradle of Khmer culture, it is some 50 kilometers south of Phnom Penh. It was sponsored by the Association Mission Possible, which began operation in Cambodia in 2005, promoting health and education projects in particular. The basic typology is relatively common in rural areas like Roong and coastal Cambodia, like Koh Rong. The Secondary School was placed on its site to also anticipate further extensions, with the bathroom segment at one end of the linear array of classrooms and acting as a pivot point for future expansion. The overall building is 62.8 meters in length and 10.2 meters in width. It is comprised of six enclosed classrooms and two semi-enclosed spaces. A 3-meter-wide corridor along one side provides a common space for gathering, social interaction, play during the rainy season and sociability, much as the *ruai* of the longhouse discussed earlier did. It also acts as a semi-open verandah, with a 5-meter height to the top of the hipped roof of the structure. Large bamboo slatted panels inside the verandah allow for cross-ventilation, as well as visual contact from the classrooms to the common space, again as was the custom between the *bilek* and *ruai* of traditional versions of the longhouse. Experimental use was made of sun-dried soil blocks and bamboo beams, used also in collaboration with Habitat for Humanity. The block walls were plastered with a clay plaster to which a red color pigment had been added. The serial arrangement of classrooms and semi-open spaces provides lively variety to the supporting walls along the outside of the corridor-verandah (Archilovers, 2014). A second phase was added in 2017–2018, with two additional classrooms and two laboratories. This project is very similar to the High School in Ngwe Saung, Myanmar, of 2014 by a+r ARCHITEKTEN in co-operation with the German NGO, Projekt Burma. The major difference is that the High School is two stories in height, with an extensive screen sheltering the upper floor common space or *ruai* equivalent. Like the Roong Secondary School it was made almost exclusively from local materials and employed local craftsmen in its construction. In this case it was made from traditional 'brick nogging structure' comprised of timber frame construction with masonry infill on a concrete base. Sun protection was provided with an ornamental bamboo mesh. Suspended ceilings made of bamboo and glass wool provide good acoustics (ArchDaily, 2014).

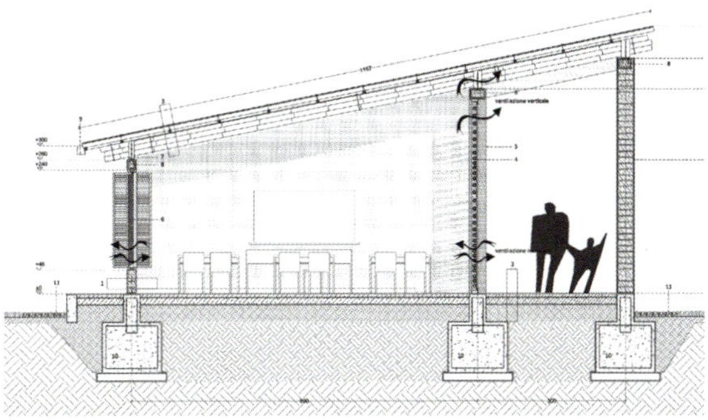

Secondary School, Roong, Cambodia, 2014

Finally, the fifth building complex in this series is the Alfa Omega School in Tangerang, Indonesia, by RAW Architects, completed in 2019. Architecturally, it is something of a hybrid of a traditional longhouse and three-level indigenous houses. Designed to accommodate 300 students, it is built in a challenging environment of swampland in the Province of Banten in western Java, next to Jakarta. It forms a sequence of spaces that commences with a shallow ramp up to the school and along a corridor with a prominent zigzag bamboo roof leading to an anteroom and thence into the school complex proper. The relatively independent school buildings are each in three layers set on top of 2.1-meter concrete stilts or piles. The first layer above this foundation is a steel-framed structure infilled with curvilinear brick masonry walls. On top is a lightweight upper floor topped by a large and gabled thatched bamboo roof. The four main school buildings are further organized into four square classroom modules. These resemble somewhat the cellular structure of traditional longhouses, with occupiable common space around the classrooms sheltered from above. The four buildings are oriented to merge in a pinwheel-like fashion, sometimes seen as a hand with fingers outstretched, on a main court and an amphitheater. These add to the complement of communal space. It is the prominent thatched roofs and the middle levels on stilt foundations that most recall traditional housing types. All were built by local craftspeople and the majority of materials were sourced nearby. In short, it was a collective process as in the early days, completed by local masons and welders from the area (Astbury, 2019).

Village Configurations

The Jean-Marie Tjibaou Cultural Center of 1998 by Renzo Piano celebrates Kanak architecture, by one of the Austronesian peoples. Located on the Tina Peninsula, some 8 kilometers from central Nouméa in the French territory of New Caledonia, it is named after Jean-Marie Tjibaou, a leader in the Kanak Independence Movement who was assassinated in 1989. The complex was created by order of the French President, its naming after Tjibaou coinciding with its opening in 1998. Parenthetically, although there has been tension between Kanak inhabitants that make up over 40 percent of New Caledonia's population,

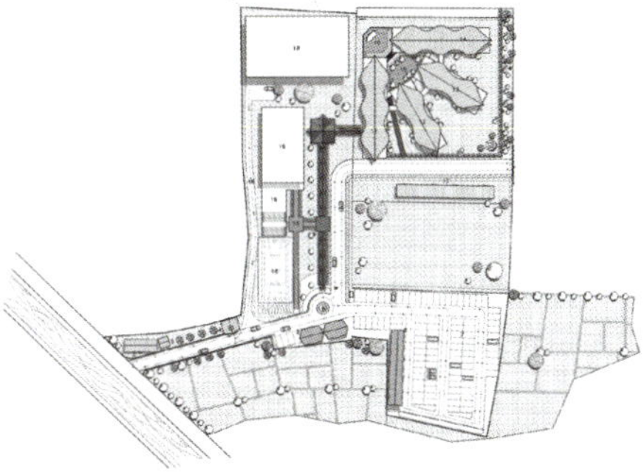

Alfa Omega School, Tangerang, Indonesia 2019

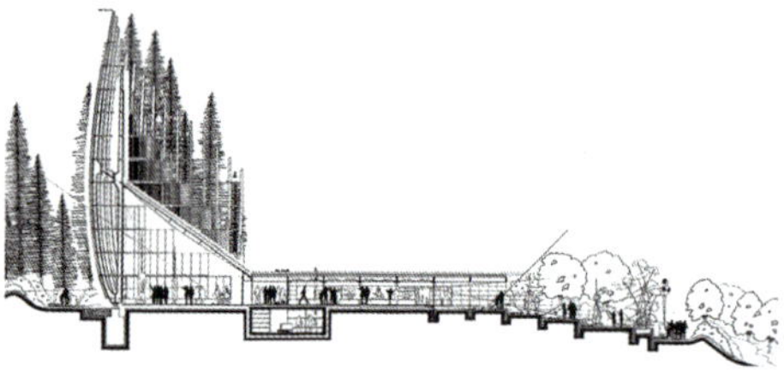

Jean-Marie Tjibaou Cultural Center, Nouméa, New Caledonia, 1998

two referendums under an accord allowing transition to independence have failed, with another scheduled for 2022. Among South Sea and Polynesian nations, New Caledonia is relatively well off with a GDP per capita slightly higher than New Zealand's. The center was the result of a competition won by Piano in 1991, with construction taking place between 1993 and 1998. The complex is 8,550 square meters in area and comprised of ten curvilinear units called 'huts', arranged in three village-like clusters along 250 meters of the ridge of the peninsula. Each cluster is centered on a tall hut some 28 meters high and representing the traditional 'great hut' or 'chief's house' of the Kanak that typically anchored a row of huts amid a well-treed environment offering shade to the gathering space created by the double-sided hut row. This is further reinforced by the presence on the periphery of tall Norfolk pine trees. The tall and curved structures represent the tall conical-shaped image of Kanak dwellings with circular plans and large thatched roofs. As in original circumstances, huts vary in size, with rectangular interiors housing performance and exhibition spaces, as well as offices and services. A covered walkway following the slight curve of the peninsula links the hut ensembles, downwind and downhill. The entire complex is approached through landscapes by way of introduction and as was customary for a Kanak settlement. The overall layout also takes full advantage of the prevailing easterly wind and controls sunlight with an outer face of the curved hut segments in direct contact with the windward side facing the stormy ocean but with the leeward side facing the serenity of the lagoon. The tall curved and ribbed vertical structures of the huts were made from durable iroko wood fixed on steel frames and prefabricated in France and then assembled on site (Blaser, 2001; and Murphy, 2002).

The University of Technology Petronas of 2005, by Foster and Partners, is a campus built on a 400-hectare site in the new township of Seri Iskandar in Perak, Malaysia, a former tin-mining region. It is wholly owned by Petroliam Nasional Berhad (Petronas), the Malaysian oil and gas multinational corporation, and serves technical education and research needs of that company as well as others. The completed first phase is 85,000 square meters in area. The overall layout was in the form of a five-pointed star comprised of semi-circular arrangements of

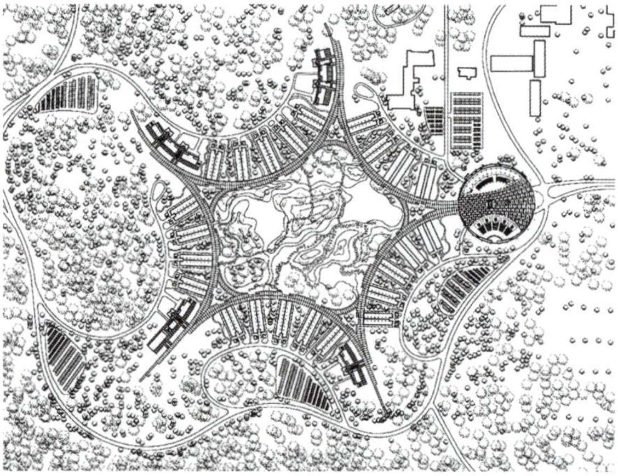

University of Technology Petronas, Perak, Malaysia, 2005

separated buildings, partially covered by a high and expansive canopy with a walkway beneath. This, in turn, responds well to adverse climatic conditions of heat and torrential rain during the monsoon season. Among the freestanding buildings and in the walkway, public space is airy and well modulated (Johnston, 2007).

Studio TonTon in Tangerang, Indonesia, belongs to an architectural firm of the same name and has evolved over time as the studio expanded, from initially 12 people to 25 persons. With a practice originally founded in 1999, Antony Liu was joined by Ferry Ridwan in Studio TonTon in 2007. Their office is situated on a rectangular site about 30 meters wide and backed up to a golf course; both long sides have been lined by tall bamboo trees to screen out the neighboring properties. Entry to what has become a small campus is through a relatively narrow opening on the street and with a water feature screening out noise. Subsequent additions are joined on one side of a long central space by an open but roofed corridor, providing access to linear studio spaces. Several structures also along one side sit on Y-shaped steel supports, echoing the natural trees on the site. A material palette of glass walls and lightweight, white-painted frames introduce uniformity, openness and transparency among the staff as well as the studio principals. Although ultra-modern in material aspect, the overall relatively casual linear layout, with studio and other spaces on either side of a continuous semi-paved open space, has all the formal qualities of a vernacular indigenous village common to the area. In addition, the careful curation of the trees and other vegetation on site also followed customary practice (Studio TonTon, 2018).

Located in the most densely populated area of Ho Chi Minh City, Vietnam, the site for the House for Trees by Vo Trong Nghia Architects is a landlocked suburban block accessible only via a pedestrian lane, as indicated in the olique aerial view. It is a two-bedroom house for a family of three arranged and constructed in five volumes. This area of the city has only a 0.25 percent coverage by greenery and as a response the house seeks to reconnect the residents with a natural environment. It does so by envisioning the five building volumes as planters with 1.5 meters' depth of soil on the roofs and sufficient space

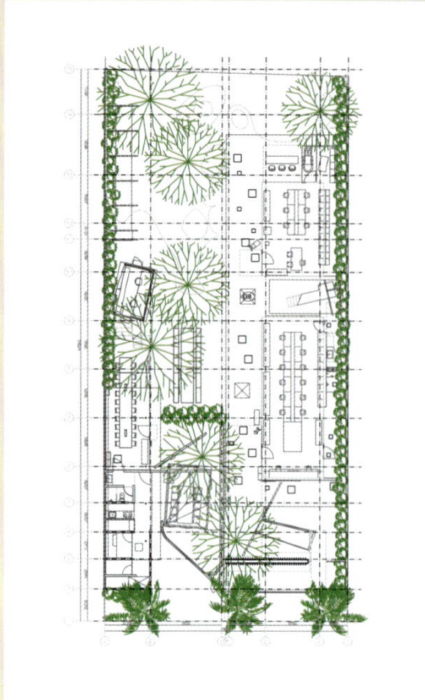

Studio TonTon, Tangerang, Indonesia, 2013

House for Trees, Ho Chi Minh City, Vietnam, 2014

Cassia Coop Training Centre, Kerinchi, Indonesia, 2011

to also accommodate stormwater, thus mitigating local flooding. With a relatively small footprint of 112 or so square meters, the volumes are loosely arranged around a central court, with smaller interconnecting gardens between the volumes. Large glass doors and operable windows ensure that the dwelling has abundant light and ventilation. The blurred boundary between outside and inside links the garden with the living areas (Stevens, 2014). With regard to broader cultural architectural references, both the courtyard arrangement and boxy dwelling components are reminiscent of Sinic or Chinese court houses with their pavilions and the importance placed on trees in urban circumstances.

The Cassia Coop Training Centre in Kerinchi, Indonesia, of 2011 by TYIN tegnestue Architects is for historically exploited cinnamon farmers in Sumatra, which provides some 85 percent of global production. The building houses a variety of programs ranging from training to health care, as well as a generally safe and healthy workplace in contrast to earlier conditions. Taking advantage of two local construction materials and methods, the building consists of two brick wall enclosures organized around a central courtyard and covered by a large roof supported on Y-shaped timber columns. This arrangement allows a cohesive complex to be composed from the limited dimensions of unbraced brick walls, and for an adequately sized building to be constructed from otherwise small material segments. Construction was done by the architectural group and local workers (Hudson, 2012). Again, the quadrangular courtyard form has ample precedents in the region and each lengthy space under the expansive unifying roof also recalls more local longhouse configurations.

Fabric and Skeletal Constructions

The Chapel of Futuna in Wellington, New Zealand, of 1961 was designed by John Scott, the first Maori graduate of the University of Auckland's Architecture Program. Now protected by the Wellington District Plan, it once belonged to the Futuna Retreat in Karori, a suburb to the west of central Wellington, founded by the Society of Mary, a French Roman Catholic order from Lyon, which arrived with Bishop Pompallier to New Zealand in 1838. The chapel is dedicated to Peter Chanel, a missionary

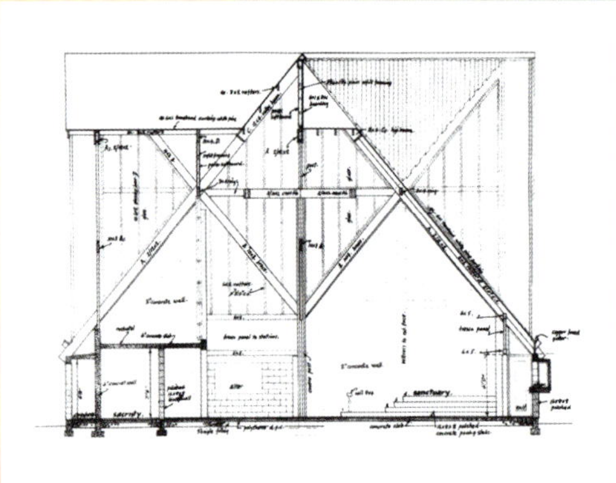

Chapel of Futuna, Wellington, New Zealand, 1961

who was martyred on the Pacific Island of Futuna in 1841. It is cited as one of the first, if not the first, examples of local architecture to combine both Maori and Pakeha (non-Maori New Zealander) elements. The steep gabled roof, the center posts, the prominent bargeboards (*maihi*) and the deep entry porch, all draw on the Maori tradition of the *wharenui* discussed earlier. By contrast, the rough stucco finish, the geometric forms and the slender exposed roof struts and rafters recall modernist traits and those of New Zealand houses of the 1960s and '70s. This composite of architectural languages was not seen before. The building was constructed by Marist Brothers, apparently only with the aid of an electrician. The main roof was originally tiled in asbestos plates, subsequently replaced by metal tiles. Dramatically skylit by vertical strips of stained glass, the patterns recall aspects of Maori contemporary art (Walden, 1987).

The Ngibikan Village Reconstruction of 2006, in the Yogyakarta region of the southern portion of central Java, came on the heels of a devastating earthquake that saw some 140,000 homes destroyed and, tragically, 5,700 deaths. With financial assistance from a local newspaper and in collaboration with villagers, architect Eko Prawoto developed a timber structural framework, inspired by the local *limasan* typology of housing with its eight main pillars, a characteristic prominent gable roof and broad peripheral overhangs. This can probably be most usefully understood as portal frames constructed from wood and braced by short timber segments and, therefore, easy to construct and to erect. The structural frame, now flexible and seismically resistant, could then be infilled with materials at hand, including earthquake debris. Non-professional builders were also deployed including local villagers, thus vesting them in the recovery effort. Covering an area of around 43,250 square meters, 65 houses were built in the short span of only 90 days (Shim, 2011).

The New Church of Kadon Parish, Kadon, Vietnam, of 2014 was designed by Thu Huong Thi Vu and Tuan Dung Nguyen for the traditional Churu people, the ethnic group living in Lam Dong Province within Vietnam's central highlands. In essence, it is a multi-use community center, classroom complex and church. In the architects' description, it is a 'roof

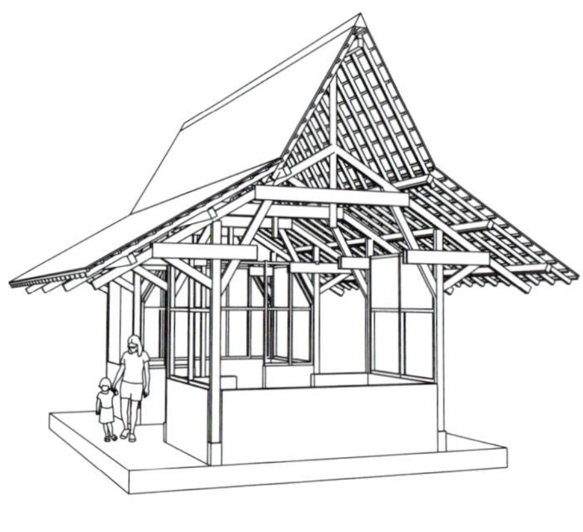

Ngibikan Village Reconstruction, Yogyakarta, Indonesia, 2006

for the people'. Located at the center of the village of Kadon, it is a large rectangular covered space of some 60 meters by 35 meters, with its long axis oriented north-south and with a tall gable height of 11 meters. In its church arrangement the building can accommodate 3,000 people. It also has operable wall panels that can be closed off to form rooms, such as classrooms and areas for ethnic celebrations. In contrast to the large roof, the walls are constructed from two layers of timber batten screens, allowing both visual and physical connection to the outside. The timber battening also extends to the underside of the eaves of the large roof. Supported on slender steel intermediate columns, the project was constructed by local builders. The spacious interior is luminous in its sheer expansiveness (Herrmann, 2016).

The National Gallery of Singapore project of 2016 by Studio Milou consists of a minimal architectural intervention that symbolically unifies the two historic late-colonial buildings of the Supreme Court and the City Hall and transforms them more or less beneath a wave of light. As the illustrations on p. 91 show, this renovation focused on the space below, above and between the two buildings, creating three public spaces spanning the entire height and length of the new combined building. Functionally, it created an organization and circulation appropriate to the new art gallery program. This approach also allowed the two existing buildings to remain architecturally intact and to be sensitively renovated. The new additions' unifying element is a steel and glass roof, or 'wave', which extends the length of the combined building, creates a new public plaza on the roof and drapes into the in-between space signifying the new gallery entrance with the Padang Atrium. This roof, in turn, is porous to allow in filtered light and is supported on tree-like steel columns reminiscent of early Austronesian structures. Housing the world's largest collection of Southeast Asian art, the gallery hosts both permanent and temporary collections. Its central location on the Padang in Singapore underlines the importance of the gallery (Chiang, 2007).

New Church of Kadon Parish, Kadon, Vietnam, 2014

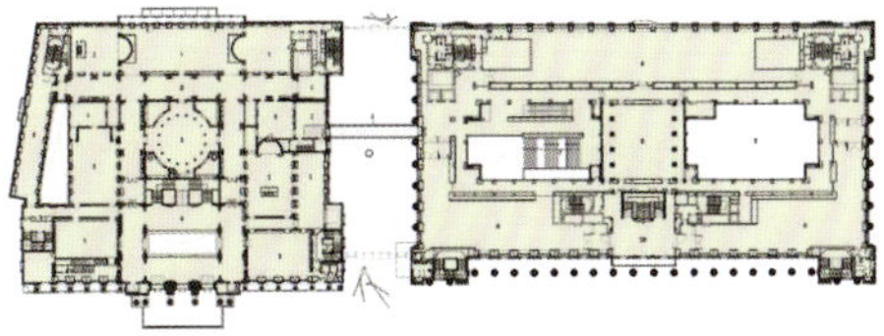

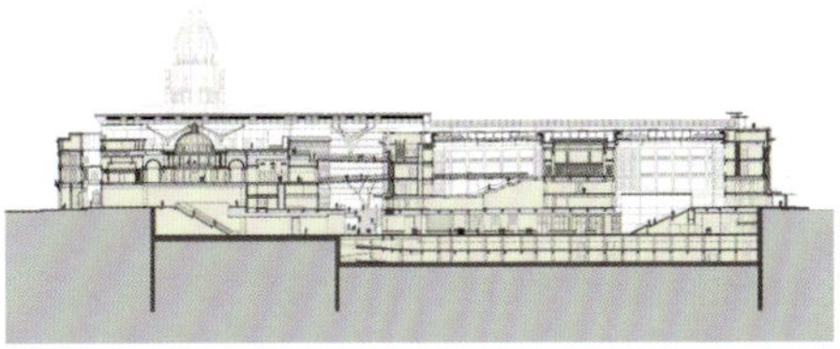

National Gallery Extension, Singapore, 2016

Tainan Art Museum, Tainan, Taiwan, 2020

Another case of an art gallery comprised of two separate buildings linked together is the Tainan Art Museum of 2020 by Shigeru Ban, with Shi Zhao Yong. Ban's new structure joins the former Police Department Building dating back to 1931, originally designed in Art Deco style by Sutejiro Umezawa. Located in Taiwan's former capital, Ban's scheme reacted to the lack of public open space in the city center site. He did this by creating a loose arrangement of boxes and a topography of publicly accessible rooftop gardens offering respite for museum visitors and city citizens. This arrangement of volumes is then placed under a pentagonal fractal roof suspended on large steel structures, developed in collaboration with Kyoto University, to provide necessary shading in the sub-tropical climate of Tainan. This roof and the loose arrangement of boxes is also described as a reference to the five-petaled Phoenix blossom that is the city tree of Tainan (*Delonix regia).* In addition, a less formal museum layout is created, without a clear front and approachable from all sides. Alternatively, the large pentagonal roof reflects traditional architecture on its independent structure with smaller enclosed spaces inside, as described earlier. The building is also set on a plinth, again like some traditional architecture (Crook, 2020).

Non-Rectangular Organic Arrangements

The Stella Maris Catholic Church in Pluit, Jakarta, Indonesia, of 2012 was designed by Budiman Hendropurnomo of Duta Cermat Mandiri, Jakarta. This office was established in 1987 and is affiliated with Denton Corker Marshall (DCM) in Melbourne, Australia. Pluit, the site of the church, is located in northern Jakarta by the sea and is an administrative village inhabited primarily by ethnically Chinese inhabitants. Located below sea level and, hence, prone to flooding, the village is now equipped with a pumping system for use during the rainy season. In fact, it was during the flood of 2002 that the old church was damaged and subsequently dismantled to make room for the new one. The specific site is next to a canal running west from Waduk Pluit, one of the main inlets from the sea. Due to this danger of flooding, the main worship hall of the church was placed on the first floor, with the ground floor used as a semi-open car park. This also reflects the above-grade disposition of main floors among traditional vernacular buildings

Stella Maris Catholic Church, Pluit, Indonesia, 2012

discussed earlier. Designed to accommodate up to 1,100 worshippers, the new church is larger than the previous building and designed to accommodate rising numbers of churchgoers. It also incorporates balconies in the shape of canoes for a mezzanine capacity of up to 500 people. The building is constructed of local materials, externally in the form of 4 by 12-centimeter stone slabs. It is arranged parallel to the long side of the commercial site beside the canal in order to provide fuller internal spaciousness. The ceiling of the new worship space soars to a height of over 16 meters and is clad with horizontal planks of teak wood mounted on galvanized steel frames. The visual effect is to virtually cover every surface of ceiling and wall. The overall monochrome impression symbolizes simplicity and again reflects similar impressions among traditional buildings. The oval shape of the church both inside and out serves several purposes. First, with the building on the corner site it addresses the church's visual presence. Second, it continues associations with boat imagery, again growing out of indigenous traditions as discussed earlier. Third, it simultaneously echoes the shape singularity of traditional buildings dominated by very large roofs relatively continuous with walls, as well as the use of curvilinear plan forms (Merrillees, 2015; and Siregar, 2015a).

The Learning Hub of Nanyang Technological University in Singapore of 2015 by Thomas Heatherwick presented an opportunity to rethink the layout and architecture of a traditional university. Commonly referred to as the 'Hive' or locally as the 'Dim Sum Basket building' due to its characteristic shape, it also reflects organic shape compositions of traditional indigenous architecture. The building consists of 16 towers, four of which are vertical circulation cores and the other twelve are classrooms and roof gardens. Tapering towards the base, the classroom towers rise eight stories and are easily read as connected relatively plain volumes on the exterior, somewhat in the manner of the large roof-wall shaped buildings of indigenous architecture, though upside down. All the towers face inwards towards a central public space, which is naturally ventilated and used as breakout space for spontaneous meetings between students and faculty from diverse backgrounds. According to the architect's description, the cocoon-like plan of the vertically stacked classrooms is intended to create spaces with no corners

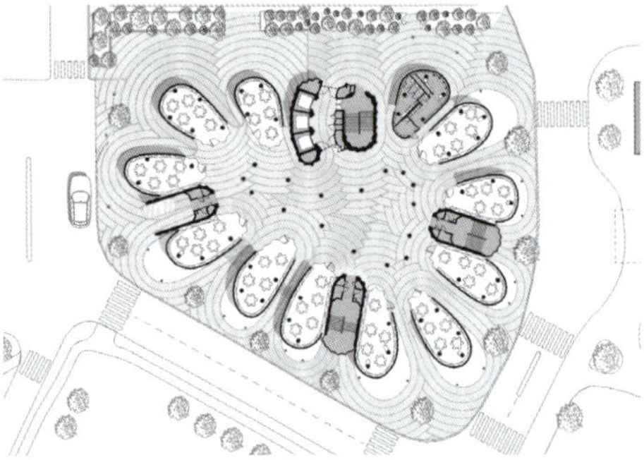

Learning Hub, Nanyang Technological University, Singapore, 2015

and to facilitate collaboration. Significant focus was also placed on the building's energy efficiency, especially with the use of natural ventilation reducing the ubiquitous use of air-conditioning. The concrete stairs and lift towers between the classrooms are embedded with casts of drawings by British artist Sara Fanelli that depict images from science, art and literature and are intended to trigger thinking processes and creativity. The slightly elongated plan arrangement of the individual towers facing each other and a public open space echoes vernacular village layouts common to the Malay Archipelago, as discussed earlier. In addition, the cast images in concrete represent a decorative program not dissimilar from earlier indigenous buildings also from the Malay Archipelago and particularly their 'ring beams' and entry carvings (Mark, 2015).

The Cooled Conservatories at Gardens by the Bay in Singapore of 2012 were designed by Wilkinson Eyre within the 2006 winning master plan by the British firm of Grant Architects. Located in the central area of Singapore adjacent to the Marina Reservoir, the two domed greenhouses dominate this garden of national significance and tourist site. They were both designed as large and enclosed structures without internal supports, like many similarly shaped though much smaller indigenous buildings. They also provide relatively precious and focused interior spaces like origin-houses of old. In addition, they aim to minimize environmental footprint and are equipped with photovoltaic cell and rainwater devices. The latter collect rainwater from the dome surfaces and articulate it into the cooling system associated with the adjacent iconic Supertrees. Of the two, the Flower Dome, at 1.2 hectares in land area, is the largest greenhouse in the world. It is comprised of some seven gardens, which merge into each other in interesting ways, featuring plants found in Mediterranean areas, as well as semi-arid areas like Australia and South Africa. The Cloud Forest, also energy-efficient and showcasing sustainable building technology, is an enclosed entertainment space. It is 0.8 hectares in area, replicating the cool, moist conditions found in tropical mountain regions some 1,000 to 3,000 meters above sea level. At its center, it features a 42-meter-tall 'cloud mountain' accessible by elevator or on foot. It also houses the world's tallest indoor waterfall (Rowe and Hee, 2019).

Cooled Conservatories at Gardens by the Bay, Singapore, 2012

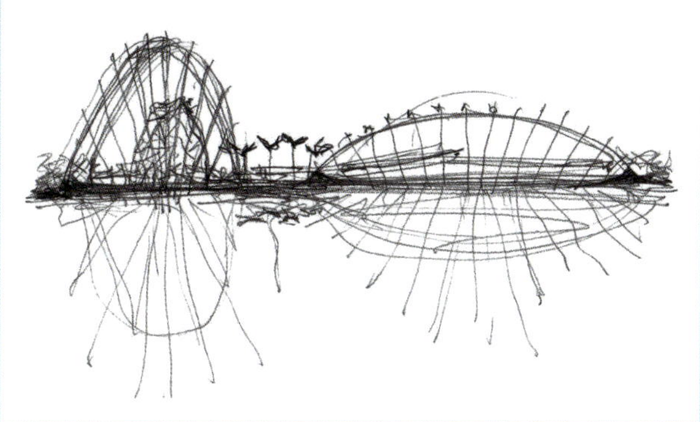

The Taitung Aboriginal Gallery in Taitung, Taiwan, of 2016 is by Bio-architecture Formosana, with Ying-Chao Kuo and Ching-Hwa Chang as architects-in-charge. Located on the southeast coast of Taiwan, Taitung was settled by aboriginal tribes such as the Amis, Paiwan and Puyuma, well before the Han Chinese encroachment in the 17th century. In effect, it is one of the homelands of Austronesian culture, dating back almost 6,000 years. Today the gallery is a self-conscious exploration of contemporary Austronesian architecture. The large roof in a wave form and with a varying pattern of blue tiles represents the ocean and, therefore, the Austronesian 'ocean peoples' as explained earlier. It also achieves large spans allowing activities to be housed beneath, while also recalling the expansive roofs of indigenous architecture. An arrangement of cargo containers comprises the spaces below the large roof, with air-conditioned individual units used as shops and studios. Walkways in between the containers are naturally ventilated and aided by airflow from the sides. The complex also conveys the feeling of a village environment. Surrounded by Austronesian trees and plants, the larger site gives something of an experience of a native rainforests (Architect, 2017).

The Multimedia Nusantara University Building of 2013 by Denton Corker Marshall and Duta Cermat Mandiri again, located in the Jakarta satellite town of Gading Serpong, Indonesia, is comprised of several multi-storied, organically shaped buildings resembling the organic forms of traditional vernacular buildings described earlier. These shapes derive from the clever deployment of a curved double-skinned facade system over and around nine to ten floors of academic space inside. This skin, in turn, consists of modular aluminum plates with small pores on the surface that act as a sunscreen for the entire building, much as the vernacular beehive roof did for traditional dwellings. Shading was further enhanced by the 70-centimeter-wide terraces between the windows and the secondary skin. This space is also used to facilitate building maintenance, and the surface pores allow fresh air into the building, improving internal air circulation and quality. While resembling the rounded figures and profiles of indigenous vernacular buildings, the organic shapes continue and reflect nature and topography by extending to the green roof that shades the semi-basement areas.

Oval voids were introduced into this roof to provide natural light below into the car park. The elliptical shape of the floor plates of the classroom and academic facilities inside the double skin continue and enhance the bubble or beehive-like configurations. This quality is exaggerated even further with lower floors pinching in, so to speak, on the bulbous figures. In short, while the ensemble of organically shaped building figures clearly draws upon the past vernacular of Indonesia, the interiors and materiality of the buildings are ultra-modern and contemporary (Siregar, 2015b).

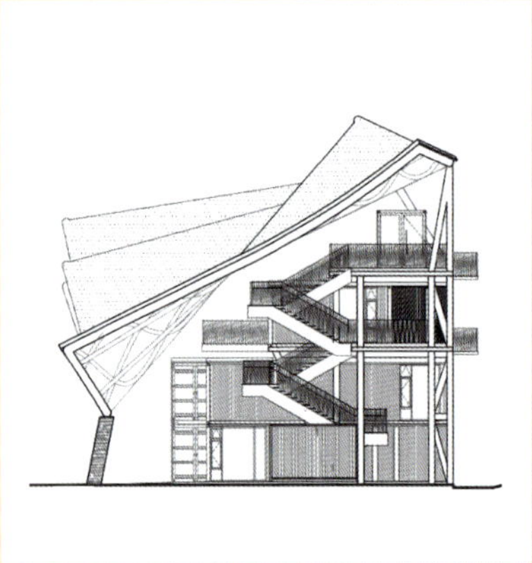

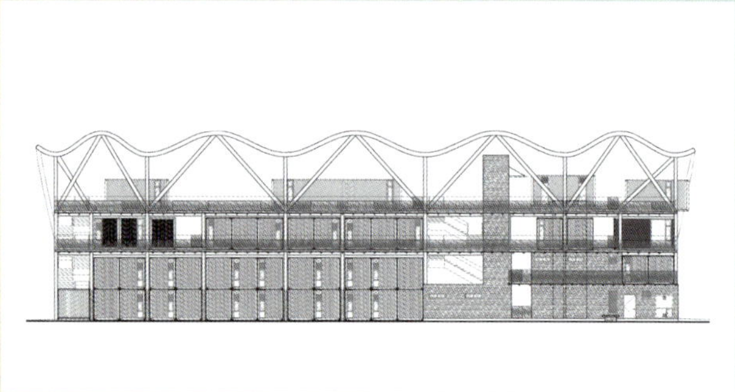

Taitung Aboriginal Gallery, Taitung, Taiwan, 2016

Multimedia Nusantara University Building, Gading Serpong, Indonesia, 2013

Early Dynastic Variations

Chapter 3

As described in the introduction, during antiquity the region now known as Southeast Asia was occupied by a mosaic of communities ranging in level of social integration from bands to chiefdoms. The latter commanderies exhibited high degrees of self-sufficiency and distinctive artifactual traditions, and they exploited ecologically complementary natural environments (Wheatley, 1983, pp. 43–94). These mosaics were also sometime referred to as mandalas, or as relatively loose political organizations, particularly in mainland Southeast Asia (Acharya, 2021). These communities were tied up with the diffusion of Indianization from the west and Sinicization from the north, largely in successive waves that moved first through mainland Southeast Asia, as noted earlier, and then into its maritime archipelago and over indigenous, often Austronesian, inhabitants, so to speak. The Indianization occurred largely through a complex combination of Buddhism and Hinduism by way of traders supporting their economic interests, adventurers seeking power, and through the proselytizing of priests (Cœdès, 1968, pp. 14–35). Moreover, the sheer thrust of Indian power at the time in its various forms should not be underestimated. It was a significant part of an economic block in the world with the largest gross domestic product from the 1st to the 19th century, accounting for roughly three times the European and American equivalent in 1800 (Bairoch, 1976; and Federico, 2002). Urban imposition in Sinicized territories was exercised most strongly in lowlands with development in and around the Red River of Vietnam and the commandery of Jih-nan in the 5th century CE. The Buddhist Srivijayan Empire of the 7th to 12th centuries was the first unified regime to dominate the maritime archipelago, seemingly from around Palembang in eastern Sumatra (Cœdès, 1968). It was followed by the Majapahit Javanese Hindu Empire from 1293 to 1527 with a peak around 1330 to 1389, stretching from Sumatra in the west to New Guinea in the east. Alongside them on the mainland were the Champa and the Khmer. Then came Islam, beginning with Arab merchants in western Sumatra as early as the 9th century CE, although not in full ascendency until the 15th century. In fact, the Sultanate of Brunei was founded in 1402. The pervasive expansion of Islam involved three processes. Early on in Sumatra there was the emergence of new politics. Later, in Java there was a succession of rulers from Hindu political powers, and elsewhere it also involved the conversion of members of the ruling class to Islam (Wheatley, 1983, pp. 419–449). In addition, there was the geographic diffusion of the wet-padi rice culture, also involving spread from the west and the north, as well as establishment of specific settlements like the Co Loa Citadel in contemporary Hanoi, Vietnam, in the 3rd century BCE, well within the Sinic cultural reach at the time (Chang, 1976). Still later, there was the faint beginning of the Chinese and Indian diasporas mentioned in the introduction.

Settlements from West and North

A large and early Buddhist site is the Borobudur Temple in central Java, dating from the 7th century CE and built by the Sailendra Dynasty. A Buddhist structure in the Mahayana tradition, it is the world's largest of its kind. It consists of nine stacked platforms of diminishing size, the first six of which are square and the final three circular in plan. It is capped by a central dome or stupa, reflecting Gupta art out of India. In keeping with Srivijayan custom of the time, it blends indigenous ancestor worship with the Buddhist concept of obtaining Nirvana. At the time, the Sailendra Dynasty's power encompassed all of the Srivijayan Empire, extending into southern Thailand and part of the Philippines. Following the 14th-century decline of Hinduism and the Majapahit Empire, it was abandoned and fell into disrepair as the Javanese converted to Islam. Covered with volcanic ash and inundated by jungle it was reprised by Stamford Raffles, the British Lieutenant-Governor of Java, in 1814. Subsequently, a number of restoration projects were undertaken and between 1975 and 1982 the Indonesian Government pursued and gained its recognition as a UNESCO World Heritage Site. From 1973 onwards it has again been a place of Buddhist worship.

Borobudur, Java, Indonesia

Planes and Steps in Plan at Borobudur

When viewed from above, it reveals the pattern of a giant tantric Buddhist mandala. The lowest and widest platform measures 118 meters on each side. The upper level is crowned by a single tall stupa surrounded by 72 smaller stupas. Taking the overall form of a stepped pyramid, there was early speculation that it may have existed in a large lake, like a floating lotus plant. This interpretation, however, has not been borne out by archaeological research. As a stupa, Borobudur is intended as a shrine for the Buddha and not simply a temple. With a vertical cosmology subdivided into 31 planes, the three levels of the stepped pyramid reflect the three realms of Buddhist cosmology: the world of desire (*Kamadhatu*), the world of forms (*Rupadhatu*) and, finally, the world of Nirvana, non-existence of self and enlightenment (*Arupyadhatu*). Detailed decoration in the form of narrative bas-reliefs on the levels also reflects these realms. The building itself is on stone foundations taken from nearby quarries (Gómez and Woodward, 1981; and Soekmono, De Casparis and Dumarçay, 1990).

Also built on a massive scale was Angkor Wat in Cambodia, the most extensive religious structure in the world to date, with a land area of 162.6 hectares. It was originally constructed as the personal mausoleum of the Khmer King Suryavarman II, though becoming dedicated to Vishnu, one of the principal Hindu deities in the early 12th century, then being converted into a Buddhist temple towards the end of the same century and remaining that way. In effect, it also became the state temple of the powerful Khmer Empire. Constructed on a flat site, with the central temple complex in the middle of a square island set into a wide moat, the composition of towers, symbolizing the surrounding mountains and ocean, rises symmetrically towards the center. It in turn is comprised of three rectangular galleries with pavilions placed at the corners on a cruciform terrace, structured as illustrated by the plan on p. 111. Apparently, the western orientation, rather than to the east as was customary, derives from its origin as a mausoleum. The outer wall is 1,024 meters by 802 meters and 4.5 meters high. The moat is 190 meters across, with the temple complex reached from west and east by two causeways. Unlike Borobudur, stone blocks were quarried about 40 kilometers away and transported to the site. The profuse arrangement of bas-reliefs also contributes to the identification of the

Stupas on top of Borobudur

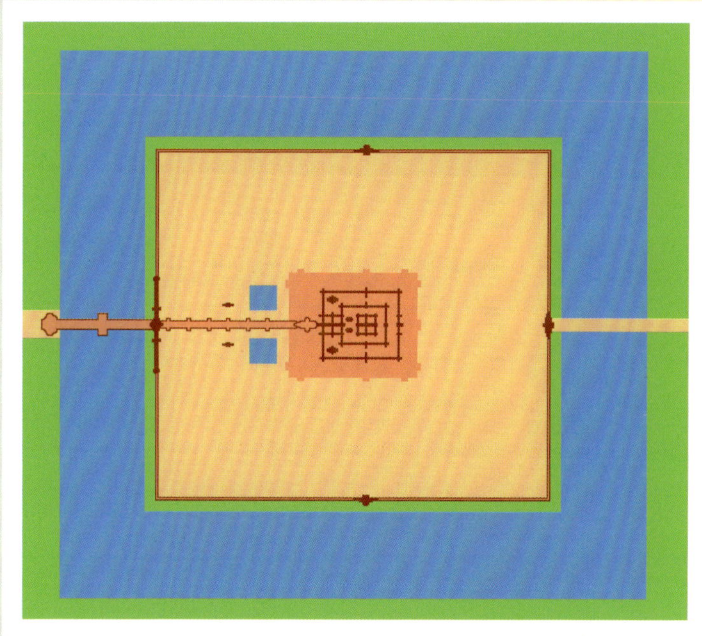

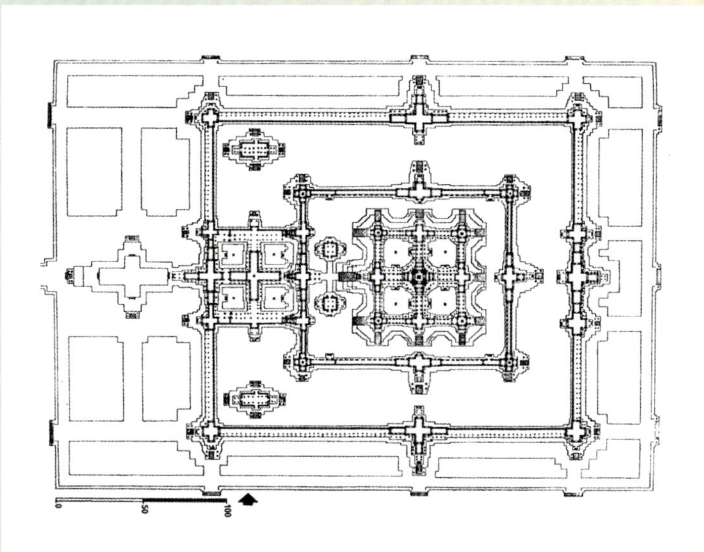

Plan of Angkor Wat, Cambodia

Plan of Angkor Thom, Cambodia

Mahayana Buddhist Temple in Bayon, Cambodia

temple as classical Khmer architecture. Restoration began as early as 1908, continuing into the 1970s before stopping during the Khmer Rouge era. It was finally listed among UNESCO World Heritage Sites in 1992, though removed from the list of sites in danger in 2004 (Albanese, 2006; and Higham, 2014). Angkor Thom was the last enduring capital of the Khmer Empire and was established in the late 12th century by King Jayavarman VII, covering some 9 square kilometers in area. At the center was Bayon, the state Mahayana Buddhist Temple, also reverting to Hinduism in the mid-13th century with the worship of Brahma, the Hindu god. The building is referred to as belonging to the baroque style of Khmer architecture. It is again highly decorated and rises symmetrically in ascending tower-like form (Albanese, 2006). By about the middle of the 15th century, Angkor was abandoned (Cœdès, 1968, p. 235f.). Nevertheless, both Borobudur and Angkor Wat, among other temple complexes in Southeast Asia, display differences with Indian examples. First is a concentration on axial planning and strict adherence of orientation according to cardinal directions. Second is the association of sacred architecture with royalty and the consideration of the king as divinity in human form. Third there is the uniting together of isolated structures into extensive architectural complexes like through the concentric courtyards at Angkor Wat. Finally, there is the identification of the cosmic mountain Meru, among other cosmological references, with sacred temples (Michell, 1988, p. 159f.).

As mentioned in the introduction, walled enclaves among the Pyu city-states of Myanmar, like Beikthano, were named in this case after the Hindu god Vishnu. It was also probably the first capital of a politically uniform state in Burma or Myanmar. Further Indian-derived Hindu structures, such as the Ceto Temple complex in Java, were a mixture of stone pavilions with hipped stone-tiled roofs and characteristic tall carved split-gates along the main thoroughfare. In fact, tall masonry split-gates adorned the entrances to Majapahit palaces, which also had large gabled roof structures reminiscent of earlier indigenous vernacular architecture. Sinic structures, by contrast, tended to be quadrangular in layout, as in China, and generally more block-like in formal character. In general, this followed the long-standing tradition of bounded figures and quadrangles, dating back into antiquity. Reconstructions from records show rectilinear halls and quadrangular courtyard arrangements dating from the 21st century BCE to 256 BCE, comprising the Xia, Shang and Zhou Dynasties. Palaces from these eras also show halls with broad two- and three-tiered gabled roofs (Congrong, 2021). For many, the familiar courtyard house and compound dates from this period and particularly from ruins discovered at Erlitou, the Shang capital (Wu, 1999, p. 71). In their particularities, these forms also allowed buildings to respond readily to climatic, functional and other situational conditions by, for instance, modifying the size and geometries of inner courtyards (Ma, 1999; and Knapp, 2003). Later Muslim architecture, from around 1200 onwards, also appeared to make reference to vernacular styles, with for example tiered roofs on mosques, like the Tuo Kayu Jao Mosque in western Sumatra and similar buildings in Bali and in the Demak Sultanate of Java's northern coast. Interestingly, minarets were not originally an integral part of Indonesian mosques. In addition, several like the Kudus Mosque in central Java built in the 16th century followed a Hindu-Buddhist style of architecture common to the Majapahit Period (Miksic and Tjahjono, 1998).

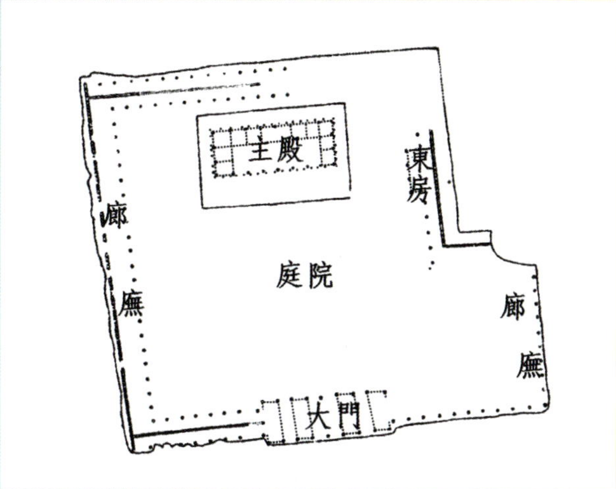

Erlitou of the Shang Dynasty, Henan, China

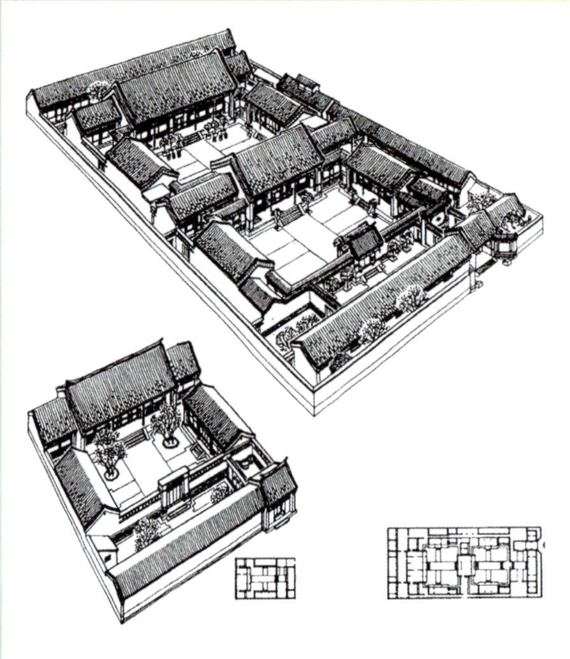

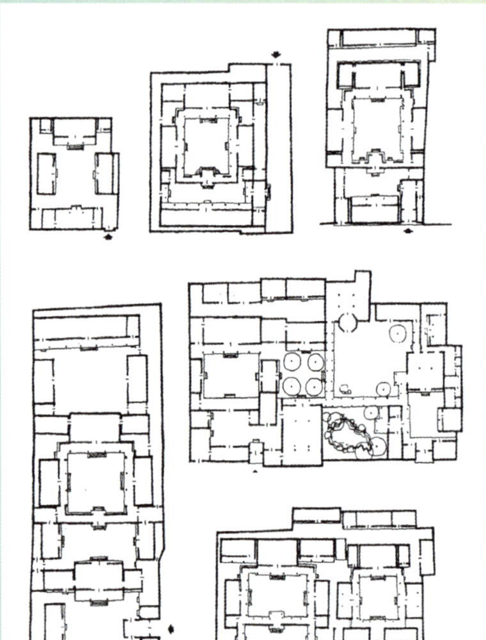

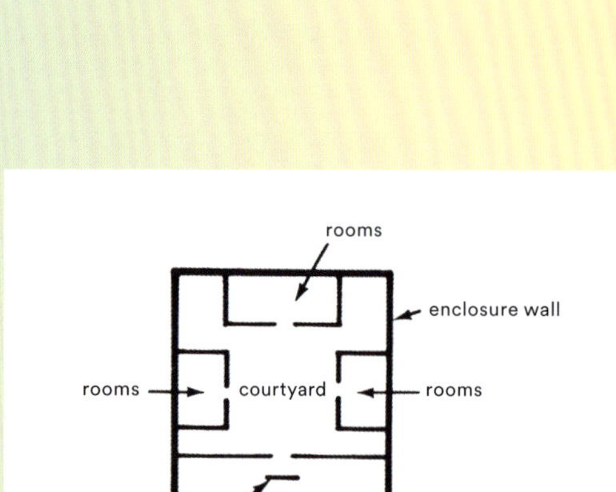

Quadrangular Sinic Structures

Pagodas and Temples by Other Names

Throughout this phase of what is being termed dynastic activity emanating from India, China and even the Middle East, there was the strong influence of religion, as indicated by the preceding discussion. Consequently, religious building of places of worship, contemplation, meditation, commemoration and prayer alongside royalty and chieftain kinships, was the main staple and most lasting presence. Apart from their earlier animist affiliations, many parts of Southeast Asia became subject to Hindu, Buddhist and Muslim doctrines and cultural infusions. Moreover, with this came an inevitable succession of representative building types in the forms of temples, stupas, pagodas and mosques, along with other auxiliary accommodations commonly associated with each religious persuasion in the realms, for instance, of collective living quarters like monasteries, and educational facilities like madrassas. Temples generally adhere to the primary definition of places of worship, though this may also be ascribed to stupas and *wats* in the case of Cambodia. Though different in particular form, they always faced to the south or to the east and never to the north or to the west. Stupas were bell-shaped or hemispherical structures also often shaped upwards into points, that contained religious relics of some kind and were sites of meditation. Distinct from temples, usually they could not be entered or have an interior in deference to the security of the relics. The Shwedagon Stupa on Singuttara Hill at Rangoon, now Yangon, in southern Myanmar was built between the 6th and 10th centuries CE and contained several relics attributable to Buddha, and stands as a reliquary stupa. At 99 meters in height and clad in gold it rose in a stately and very visible fashion above a broad plinth of numerous smaller tapered stupas and single-celled shrines. The upward rise of the main stupa began with circular bands of terraces of descending diameter, followed by a turban band and inverted alms bowl and more circular terraces up to crowning elements of lotus petals, banana bands and an umbrella crown capped with a diamond bud (Inglis, 1998, pp. 52–57). Pagodas can refer to either temples or stupas. As a collective building type, they are reputed to have originated with the Indian stupa, though in China and Japan they are typically tall multi-tiered structures with prominent eaves, rising to heights of odd numbers in segments from three to 13. In addition, as described earlier, Buddhist-Hindu conflations at the same place, like Angkor Wat for instance, were not uncommon in Southeast Asia.

Among temples especially emanating from India, there are three styles of building, stemming from the Gupta period between the 4th and 6th centuries CE. In most respects, they can be distinguished by the spatial and material qualities of major temple elements in play. For instance, there are the *gopuram* or entrance gates; the *vimana* or overall shape of the temple tower; the position of the *shikhara* or crowning element of the tower; and the *mandapa* or pillared hall for public rituals. The first type is the Dravidian or southern style and one that is conspicuously present in the pagodas of Thailand, Laos, Myanmar and Cambodia. Its distinguishing features are that it is materially usually rock-cut. It has large *gopurams*, a pyramidal *vimana* and a *shikhara* confined to the top of the main structure above the reliquary sanctuary. It is also surrounded by prominent fortress-walled enclosures comprising large annular courtyards. In addition, it is typically a center of religious, economic and educational life and is accompanied by a substantial *mandapa*.

Shwedagon Stupa, Yangon, Myanmar

Dravidian or Southern-Style Pagoda

Nagara or Northern-Style Pagoda

Vesara or Mixed-Style Pagoda

The Nagara or northern style, by contrast, is usually built from brick and has no substantial gate or enclosing wall. The *shikhara* was dome-shaped around an axis centered above the inner sanctuary and with the whole structure raised on a plinth. The third type was the Vesara or mixed style, poised as a combination between the Dravidian and Nagara styles, though reduced in height but not in the number of tiers in the tower. It was to be found in the Deccan or central area of India (Michell, 1988; and Michell, 1995). Nomenclature applied to Buddhist temples extended to *chaitya, vihara*, stupa, pagoda and *wat* as noted earlier. Typically, *chaitya* referred to a shrine, sanctuary, temple or prayer hall, whereas *vihara* referred to a monastery or facility for dwelling. Usually, in the Buddhist context, the latter referred to the living quarters of monks with an open shared space or courtyard, though the term *vihara* can also be found in Hindu contexts (Willson, 1999).

Muslim traders along the main trade routes between Western Asia and the Far East are thought to have been mainly responsible for the introduction of Islam to Southeast Asia, even if they were not the earliest contacts, as noted earlier. Their place of collective worship was the mosque or *masjid*, literally referring to a 'place of ritual prostration'. It is a place of worship for Muslims like components of temples and pagodas for Buddhists and Hindus; in fact any place of worship that follows Islamic rules of prayer can be said to be a mosque. Informal and open places of worship are sometimes called *masala,* while those for communal Friday prayers are referred to as *juma.* Mosques contain a *mihrab* or ornamental niche set in the direction of Mecca (*qibla*) within the prayer hall. The prayer halls, in turn, are segregated by the gender of worshippers and also contain a *minbar* or pulpit for delivering sermons. Most, though not all, have minarets or towers for announcing the call to prayer and symbolizing the presence of the mosque in its community. Along with other elements described below in more detail minarets were not always present along with Middle Eastern hypostyle prayer halls in Southeast Asia. Staying with monotheism, Roman Catholic churches were also to be found, especially on the heels of Jesuit and other missions from around the 16th century onwards. However, for the most part they were associated with the Philippines and Spanish colonization, a topic of the next chapter.

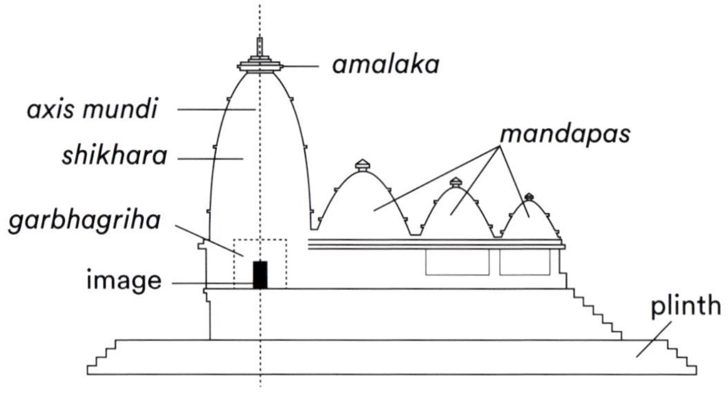

northern-style temple

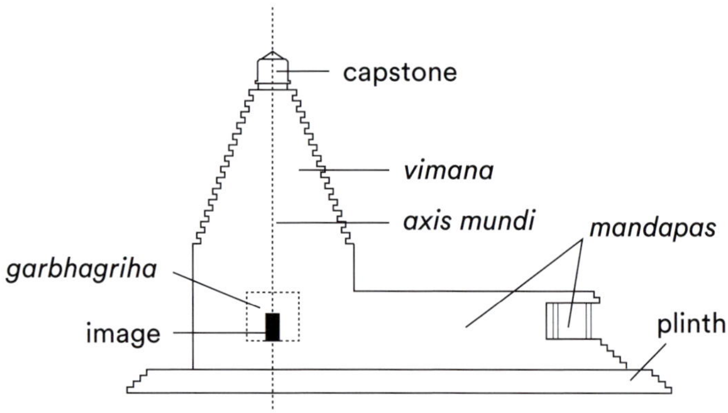

southern-style temple

Differences between Pagoda Styles

Mosque Layout

As can be seen throughout this narrative, the interchangeability and syncretic presence of Buddhism and Hinduism occurred throughout Southeast Asia, particularly with regard to built environments or pagodas. Moreover, it is quite different in this regard from the later exclusiveness of Muslim and Christian practices. This appears to be in keeping with a common trait among indigenous and local communities of moving on with their lives while adopting only what is required or seems necessary for the particular hegemonic regimes that come and go. It may also at least partially explain why formal aspects are markedly orthodox and conservative (Michell, 1988, p. 159; Higham, 2014; and Acharya, 2021). In part, it also seems bound up with very local senses of underdevelopment and political bondedness, as suggested by some of the origins of Southeast Asia's not highly evolved urban conditions (Wheatley, 1983). In addition, from a contemporary standpoint of architectural 'agency' existing in a wider network of actors and co-production, the situational correspondence of Buddhist and Hindu senses and cosmology gave rise to little motivation towards substantial divergences in architecture. They were all under more or less the same pagoda roof, as it were (Picon, 2020, pp. 139–145).

Gates, Pavilions and Other Elements

In *Yingya Shenglan*, his book about countries visited during Admiral Zheng He's historic voyages during the Ming Dynasty in the 15th century, Ma Huan, Zheng's interpreter, described a Majapahit settlement surrounded by a thick brick wall some 9.3 meters high and 310 meters around. The palace itself was two stories tall, each of the order of 9 to 14 meters in height, with wooden plank floors covered in mats and with a prominent roof covered in wooden shingles. The homes of commoners had thatched roofs of nipa palm leaves and each family had a storage shed raised above the ground. Most of this seems to have coincided with prevalent vernacular tradition, particularly as noted in the preceding chapter. Temple architecture was apparently in an eastern Javanese style with strong geometric qualities and tallness as well as slenderness in presentation. Two kinds of gates prevailed between domains in the city. One was the split-gate and the other was the *paduraksa* with its pyramidal capping. It also appeared as if late Majapahit architecture revived Austronesian megalithic elements such as stepped pyramids, instead of earlier more towering structures (Mills, 1970; and Dreyer, 2007). This is also borne out by the Ceto Temple complex of

15th-century Javanese-Hindu origin, situated, among others, on the slopes of Mount Lawu. In common with other late Majapahit Javanese art and architecture, it had diverged from Indian precepts even further than described earlier. These divergences were of at least two kinds. First, Hindu temples usually had square or rectangular bases but at least at Sukuh Temple the base was trapezoidal with three terraces, each one higher than the others. Also, there was no evidence to suggest that the top supported a wooden pavilion as was common among earlier palace architecture (Miksic, 1997, p. 223f.).

The split-gate is also referred to as a *candi bentar* and is a classical Javanese and Balinese gateway entrance commonly found at religious compounds, palaces and cemeteries. It is very tall and constructed of masonry, usually tapering to the top and presenting a striking silhouette when approached from below via a stairway. Its precise symbolism appears to be unclear although it is probably made this way to convey a sense of grandeur particularly by way of its concentrated enframement of the entry. Beyond on visual axis one usually finds a prominent element of the temple complex. The latter is not fully in view as one comes up to the gate, so the *candi bentar* also prepares the approaching person for the axial view. Gated precincts are common, especially among Balinese temples or *pura*. They are typically associated with the number 'three' as in 'three spaces' to be moved through from the outside world to domains that are increasingly sacred. This often takes the form of an outer courtyard followed by two inner courtyards. In addition, the sequence terminates in a multi-tiered pagoda with three, five, seven, nine or eleven tiers, where the higher number conveys greater importance. The very prominent Pura Ulun Danu at Bratan, for instance, has an eleven-tiered pagoda. Placed at the culmination of a major Hindu Shiva temple in Bali on the shores of Lake Bratan, it is, like all *pura*, an open-air place of worship within a walled compound. It also has a Buddhist stupa, returning to the mixed and syncretic religious use of many of such temples (Davidson, 2003). The importance of similar and even more ornate roof structures in Burma, now Myanmar, can be seen in the *pyatthats* of places like the Mandalay royal palace, with its nine-tiered and pointed roof. In fact, the *pyatthat* was a multi-storied roof with an odd number of tiers common to Burmese

Majapahit-style Candi Bentar (Split-Gate), Indonesia

Multi-Tiered Pagoda, Pura Ulun Danu Bratan, Bali, Indonesia

royal and Buddhist architecture that also typified the close link between kinship and Buddhist faith (Inglis, 1998, p. 21). More modern Buddhist contemplation and monastic centers, however, often eschew stupas and their pagoda derivatives in favor of simpler collections of a Buddha hall, a dharma pavilion for learning and truth-seeking contemplation, and sparse monastic living quarters. Nevertheless, natural accoutrements of sites are still prized and incorporated as preparatory places for contemplation. As the name suggests, the Buddha hall houses the figure of Buddha in one of his incarnations. The dharma pavilion is the place within which followers seek the plain, undistorted truth leading eventually to enlightenment and nirvana, often via *vipassana*, one of India's most ancient meditation techniques. Consequently, the pavilion's main architectural orientation is towards the creation of appropriate respectfulness. Typically, this involves a volume of space in three parts. The first is a space of compression at the entrance. The second is to lead visitors to have a clearer consciousness, usually via symmetrical forms and light from above. The third is clarity in form and the use of symmetry or a similar focus of one's 'inner journey', as it were. As noted, living quarters are provided for both laypeople and, separately, for monks. Dharma derives from the dharma wheel (chariot wheel) or *dharmachakra* in Sanskrit and is used to represent Buddhism much as the cross represents Christianity. Within this representation, the axle and center represent the perfection of Buddhist teaching (*dharma*), the rim represents meditation, concentration and mindfulness, and the hub represents moral discipline. The number of spokes may vary but the usual eight in number represent the eightfold path towards enlightenment (Murthy, 1966).

Illustration of a Dharma Wheel

By contrast, the earlier and preceding Srivijayan capital was supposedly established, as noted earlier, in the vicinity of Palembang in eastern Sumatra, Indonesia. This was first mooted by the eminent French scholar George Cœdès around 1918, who almost literally put 'Srivijaya' on the map, corroborated by others somewhat later (Cœdès, 1968, pp. 81–96; and Kelley, 2020). Much of this appears to have been based primarily on early Chinese sources from at least 700 CE, or thereabouts (Wang, 1958). It also seems to be corroborated by Arab traders who began to visit from the 10th to 11th centuries onwards. Unfortunately, so far there has been a lack of archaeological evidence, despite these eyewitness accounts, to substantiate the presence and substance of the Srivijayans in the area of Palembang (Bronson and Wisseman, 1975). Finally, although individual Chinese traders began to infiltrate Southeast Asia from their homeland, at least certainly on the heels of Zheng He's epic voyages, there was nowhere near the extent of the immigration and diaspora that occurred during the 19th century among the then European colonies (Wilkinson, 2012).

More squarely among examples of Islamic architecture there are at least ten or so elements of note. The first is probably the presence of domes (*qubba*) in the form of hemispherical structures often raised on rotunda structures or drums. First appearing in Mesopotamia, they proliferated throughout the Muslim world and through India into Southeast Asia. A second element is the use of arches, often with pointed configurations or in multiple arrangements in conjunction with columnar structures. The presence of *murquanas,* sometimes resembling honeycomb patterns, is a third element to be found, although less so in Southeast Asia, even though 'intricate work' is often on display. A fourth element is the minaret. These are tall towers, usually with balconies, that act as visual guides in settlements to the presence of mosques and also as focal points for the call to prayers. They may range in number from one to six minarets. Internally, the *mihrab* marks the direction of *qibla* and is usually a semi-circular niche in the wall of the mosque, symbolizing the direction of prayer. Arabesque patterns often abound, on both the interior and exterior of Muslim architecture. These patterns are of a geometric, floral or calligraphic character only. A seventh common element is the presence of a hypostyle hall, which is invariably rectangular or square in shape, often with columns in a regular gridded arrangement. There the function is usually to increase the spatial metaphor of an almost boundless space. The presence of open courtyards is an eighth element, often of considerable scale to host gatherings of numerous congregates and visitors and usually with fountains for performing obligatory ablutions.

Around mosques and other Muslim complexes are commonly found gardens, often in quadrilateral layouts and with water features. The aim is to offer respite and a sense of serenity, together with symbolizing the presence of a paradise on earth. Finally, there are *iwan* in the form of three-sided rectangular halls with one side open and usually with a vaulted roof. Elsewhere in Islamic architecture the entrance of the *iwan* (*pishtaq*) is decorated with friezes of calligraphy, and glazed and geometric tilework (Desai, 1970; and Brown, 2010).

Muqarnas

Mihrab

Elements of Islamic Architecture

Arches

Courtyard

Gardens

Hypostyle Hall

Arabesque

Dome

Iwan (Pishtaq)

Minaret

Contemporary Projects

Drawing on this background, contemporary projects range again over the past 20 years or so. Examples are drawn from about half the nation states of contemporary Southeast Asia. Though not surprisingly, many were in the wake of early dynastic influence as defined here from India in the west and China to the north. These are to be found in Myanmar, Thailand, Vietnam and, of course, Taiwan. Examples are grouped accordingly as being broadly Indianized or Sinicized in architectural orientation. In addition, mostly the dynastic influences central to this chapter – certainly from an Indianized perspective – were theocratic in direction, namely Buddhist, Hindu and Muslim, even if used sometimes interchangeably. Consequently, the following contemporary projects will reflect this orientation while also reflecting the Sinic propensity towards quadrangular building and prominent roof structures discussed earlier.

Indianized Variations

The Assyafaah Mosque in Singapore of 2004 by Forum Architects is a self-consciously contemporary mosque that aims to present an alternative to the Middle Eastern model. Operated by the Islamic Religious

Assyafaah Mosque, Singapore, 2004

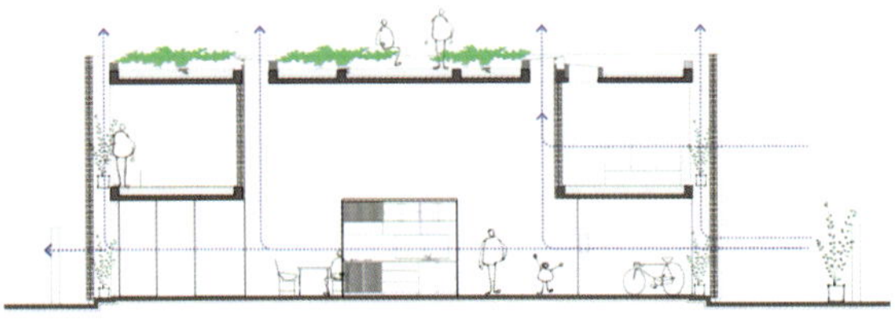

Termitary House, Da Nang, Vietnam, 2014

Council of Singapore (MUIS) and with Tan Kok Hiang as principal architect, it is located in northern Singapore. Key components of the mosque typology including the dome, arches and ornamentation are either foregone or imbued with new practical functions. These include the arch structures that redistribute loads from the upper floors so as to provide ample open space for the prayer hall, as well as all the arabesque rendered in a metallic lattice that provides natural ventilation to the prayer halls. Nevertheless, the grandeur of the prayer hall is preserved, rising four stories in height with a cantered *mihrab* wall and overlooked by the female prayer gallery. With a combined floor area of 3,490 square meters the mosque has a capacity for some 4,000 congregants. Other accommodations on site and integral with the mosque are 16 classrooms, ablution areas in the basement, administrative offices and a car park. Architecturally, each element also registers across the site, particularly in its street elevation. The nearby context is mainly of moderately high-rise residential dwellings and the entire mosque complex caters to the social and spiritual needs of Muslims living in the Sembawang area. Perhaps the most striking feature of the mosque is the creative reinterpretation of the traditional form of the arabesque, a universally recognizable symbol of Islamic art and architecture, as noted earlier. At the Assyafaah Mosque use is made of contemporary materials comprised of fine-faced concrete and aluminum elements for the arabesque screens (Aga Khan Award, 2007; and Necipoglu and Payne, 2016).

The Termitary House in Da Nang, Vietnam, of 2014 by Tropical Space is a small house of about 140 square meters in area on a residential street in this coastal city (ArchDaily, 2019). The name derives from the anthills and mounds built and occupied by termites that apparently served as an inspiration and more than a metaphor for sustainable living in a tropical setting. Termite mounds in northern Australia and parts of Africa, for instance, can rise to over 2 meters in height. Moreover, those built by the magnetic termite species are deliberately oriented north-south to avoid the midday sun. They also make use of solar chimney effects ventilating mounds in a form of passive cooling. Indeed, this approach has been applied in several buildings like the multi-storied Eastgate Centre in Harare, Zimbabwe, of 1996 by Mick Pearce, also where termite mounds are to be found (Baird, 2001). The other reference is clearly the red-brick and stone Hindu temples built by the Champa, recognized in the introduction as an Indianized civilization wedged between the Dai Viet to the north and the Khmer to the southwest. The magnificent My Son Sanctuary of stone-cut rock, or what's left of it, is relatively nearby and a UNESCO World Heritage site. Like both the temples and the mounds the Termitary House is a simple volume sitting on its narrow lot in the form of a brick-clad cuboid, some three stories tall. The facade facing the street as well as the others are comprised of red-brick screens with a fine grain of equally spaced solids and voids. This allows the house to remain relatively cool in the summer via the use of double walls of brick on the outside and glass and metal frames on the interior. The external patterning also recalls the elaborate sculptural surface forms and bas-reliefs of the My Son and other Hindu temples. Fundamentally also a courtyard house, there is a shared large space at the center with a cooking counter, dining table and entertainment area off to one side. This area also serves as the 'lobby' of the house with a living room on one side and a bedroom on the other. Stairs then lead to mezzanines of other bedrooms, an altar room and a small library. A flat roof covers the cubic volume and serves as a well-planted garden terrace, though with slender openings allowing light down into the main space (ArchDaily, 2019).

The Buddhist Temple in Thailand of 2012 by Kwanchanok Weschasart is a project that re-examines the temple complex in the context of contemporary life. More specifically it challenges its increasing commercialization and foregoing of ornamentation during inclusion with often adjacent programs of shopping malls in central urban conditions. Instead, it proposes a contemporary Buddhist temple complex away from the center that remains constant in essential components but changes in order to stay the same with regard to experiential meaning. In this proposal a composition of simple buildings is focused on a particular personal involvement of moving through the site and the resonance of that experience in the acquisition of *dharma*. Located in a suburban area of Bangkok, people entering the site are also entering a well-treed natural setting and participating in its peacefulness compared to the relative chaos outside in the surrounding area.

Buddhist Temple, Bangkok, 2012

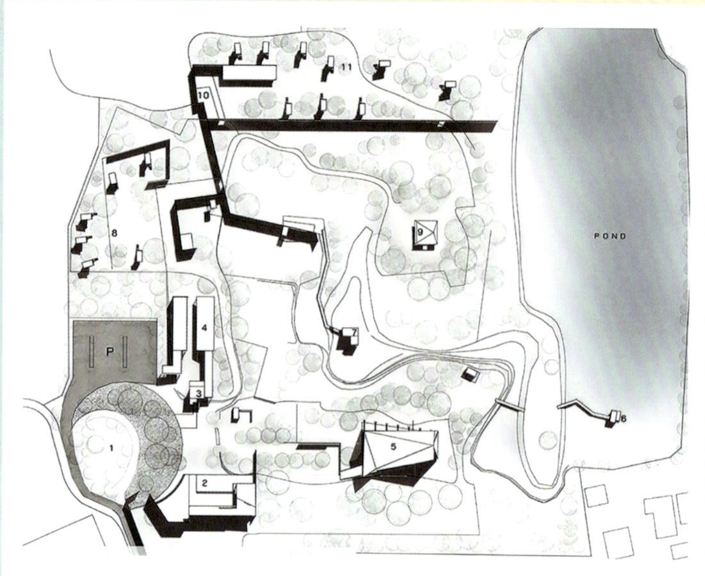

Buddhist Temple, Bangkok, 2012

In addition to the dharma hall and living quarters, the program includes offices, an alms hall and a small museum. There is also a curvilinear arrangement and a narrow path leading on to the dharma pavilion at one secluded end of the site. Throughout, the building components are simple and in a symbiotic relationship with the natural setting. Thus, they generate the prescribed religious significance mainly through their relative arrangement and positioning to one another. In this regard, for instance, a sense of compression is achieved through the forested pathway mentioned earlier, leading to the dharma pavilion and the focused realm of contemplation in its simple, enclosed interior (Murthy, 1966; and Sasiwongsaroj, Pornsiripongse, Burasith et al., 2012).

The Al-Irsyad Mosque in Padalarang, Indonesia, of 2010, also called Ridwan Kamil Mosque and designed by PT Urbane Indonesia, is likewise a self-conscious contemporary interpretation of a mosque. Located in western Java, it is generally shaped as a cube without a dome. The design centers on the central prayer hall, which is symmetrically disposed as a square within a circle of water. Modestly large at 8,000 square meters, it has a capacity of some 1,000 congregants. The strongly geometric figure of the prayer hall is surrounded by gardens and other facilities in a relatively informal pattern much like a village. There is a minaret off to one side and numerous trees demarcating paths and building boundaries. Again, an arabesque is on display, with the enclosing wall of blocks arranged to present abstracted Islamic text as a graphic pattern. This feature also supports natural ventilation of the prayer hall. The presence of *murquanas* in the ceiling light fixtures helps to recall intricate patterns in the space, though in a contemporary manner and as figurative stalactites. The architecture firm of PT Urbane Indonesia was founded in 2004 and provides services in architecture, interior design, planning and community design (ArchDaily, 2010; and Tjokrosaputro, 2011).

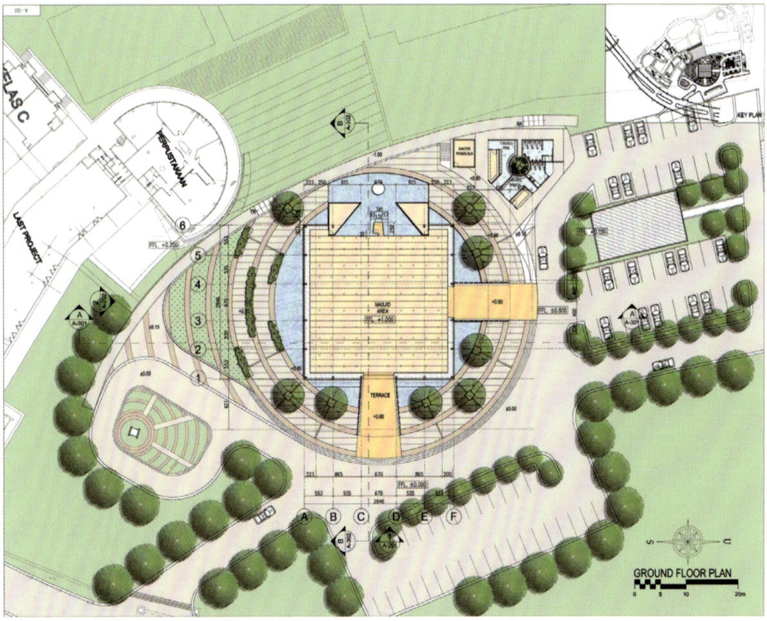

Al-Irsyad Mosque, Padalarang, Indonesia, 2010

The Zaya Thakedi Amata Zawdi Tharyar Aye Meditation Center in Yangon (2010–present) is by SPINE Architects under the leadership of two American-educated principals, Stephen Zawmoe Shwe and his wife Amelie Chai. Founded in 2004, this firm has grown substantially in size and stature, particularly because of its pursuit of contemporary architecture in Myanmar. The Zaya Thakedi complex is no exception and a good example of a new Buddhist monastery and contemplation center, largely through SPINE's donated talent, time and knowledge. It is located on a site occupied by an existing temple, as shown in the accompanying overall image. Among other components, the complex consists primarily of a dharma pavilion or ordination hall and monastic quarters in a garden setting, also containing an outdoor timber resting and contemplation facility. The dharma pavilion is circular in plan and rises three levels on piles from a pool of water and is entered on axis via a staircase. It is capped on top by a dome-like roof in eight tiled segments, echoing the familiar figure of the dharma wheel, the universal symbol of Buddhism that represents the eightfold path to enlightenment. The circular and domed arrangement is characteristic of older Buddhist sites such as the Dhammayazika Pagoda in Bagan, Myanmar, of 1196, among others. The three levels also correspond to the three levels of Buddhist cosmology noted earlier. Internally, the dharma pavilion is arresting, lit both from above and from horizontal openings in the sides of the circular drum-shaped overall structure. Directly behind the dharma pavilion are the monastic quarters or ward, arranged in couples of spaces entered from four prominent porches, again reflecting the numerology of the eight steps to betterment. The monastic quarters then extend back in a rectilinear formation of cells and associated living quarters. The outdoor timber structure is also raised on piles, characteristic of earlier forms of vernacular building as narrated earlier. It is located to the right between the pavilion and the monastic ward. Throughout, although the Buddhist symbolic and metaphorical references are clear, the architecture is modern in both the crispness and simplicity of form and construction materials. The horizontal walls of the first floor of the monastic quarters, for instance, bow out slightly in two directions from the entry porches, creating a pleasing undulating line to the horizontal facade. Similarly, the finishes of the dharma pavilion are figurally unencumbered. The overall site area of the entire

Zaya Thakedi Monastery, Yangon, 2010

Zaya Thakedi Monastery, Yangon, 2010

complex is almost 7 hectares. Buildings are arranged in a squared-off and symmetrical fashion around a central axis stretching from the original temple though the ordination hall and the center of the monastic ward (Murthy, 1966; Wu, 2015; and SPINE Architects, 2021).

Finally, the Foothill House of 2019 in Chiang Mai, Thailand's second city, is a 682 square meter holiday home in northern Thailand, designed by Site-Specific: Architecture & Research (SS:AR), a rather experimental studio founded by Chutayaves Sinthuphan. Like the traditional layout of Thai houses, the Foothill House is divided into functional areas, such as kitchen, services, living room, guest rooms and master bedroom suite. Each also has its own relatively specific form and they are connected via an outdoor communal area. More specifically, the house is a complex of five smaller buildings, each specially built and distributed across the rural site. In a collaboration between the architects and local craftsmen, prolific use was made of the local red brick that has been a part of Chiang Mai's culture for centuries. Indeed, a journey through the Foothill House reflects the materiality of each building, usually rendered in either brick or white stucco. Also, as noted by a commentator, as one moves the brick patterns become more intricate in mixes of solid and perforated patterns (Wilson, 2019). Each building has a distinctive size, shape and architectural presence. This ranges from the unusual, perforated wall enclosed master bedroom suite, with wide steps on one side leading up to a roof garden, to the plain white gable-roofed boxes of the garage and service areas. Again, as in traditional Thai house complexes, roofs are prominent and usually constructed in the form of steeply inclined gables or flatter, wide-eave configurations. The communal space linking the buildings together is paved, grassed and replete with shallow geometric pools. The stepped side wall of the master bedroom suite also forms a viewing platform for nightly projection on a nearby screen. All told, the silhouette of the five buildings evokes the image of traditional Thai housing, such as the House at King Rama II Memorial Park, with high-pitched gable roofs and a loose collection of building forms. In addition, the brick materiality and craftsmanship recall the Chiang Mai heritage of ancient Indianized Buddhist structures (Aasen, 1998; and Wilson, 2019).

Foothill House, Chiang Mai, Thailand, 2019

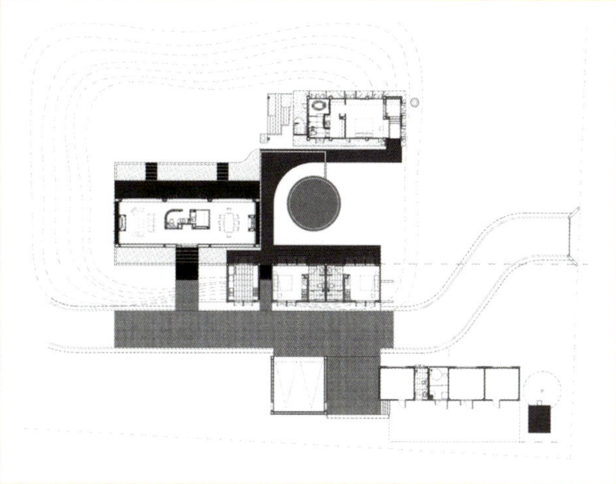

Sinicized Variations

The Hanoi Museum (Bao tang Ha Noi) in Vietnam of 2010 by the experienced German firm of von Gerkan, Marg and Partners is a freestanding museum in an artificial lake landscape in the Hoan Kiem district on the western side of the city, adjacent to a major ring road. Located next to the National Convention Center, the broader setting also supports outdoor exhibits, monuments and a traditional village. The museum was the subject of a competition in 2005 and is sizeable, at some 54,000 square meters in gross floor area. It is entered from ground level on all four sides aligned with the cardinal points, with an expansive circular void lobby and spiral staircase connecting the upper three exhibition levels projecting out into space with the ground level. The first and second levels are for exhibitions exclusively, while the third level houses rooms for conferences, offices, research facilities and a library. The top-heavy arrangement, which gives the impression of floating above the artificial lake below, is justifiable as a self-shading device, protecting the exhibition spaces from direct sunlight. Structurally, the top floor is supported by four cores, located at the four corners of the smaller ground floor and from which the intermediate levels are hung. The facades differ depending upon the direction faced. They are clad in semi-transparent green glass with Vietnamese ornamental patterns etched or worked into them. With an overall appearance of an inverted pyramid, the building is like a large, upturned roof. Nevertheless, it also resembles, in part, He Jingtang's China Pavilion at the Shanghai Expo of 2010, which began construction in 2007, looking like, at least for some, an ancient Chinese crown. More than that though, the Hanoi Museum appears to continue in much the same narrative vein as the Expo pavilion by rather emphatically representing Sinic architecture, also in an inverted pyramidal manner, but without actually imitating any particular earlier traditional structure (Welch, 2010; and Rowe, 2019).

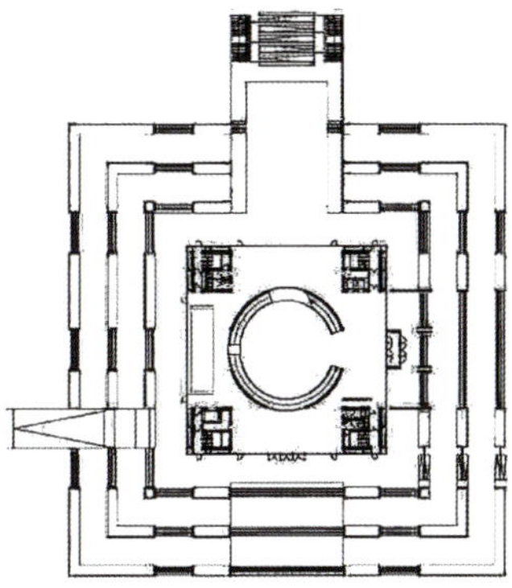

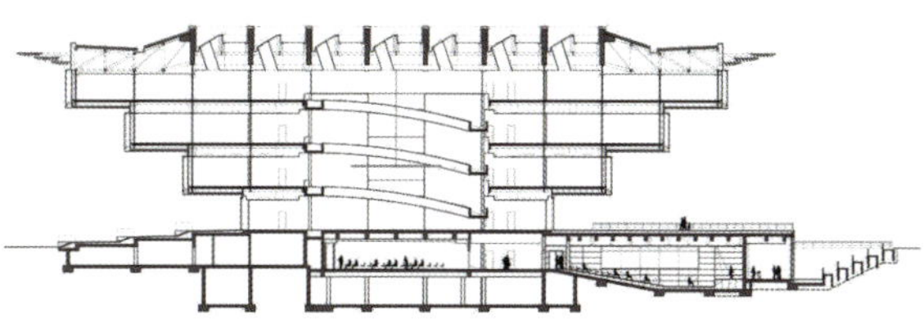

Hanoi Museum, Hanoi, 2010

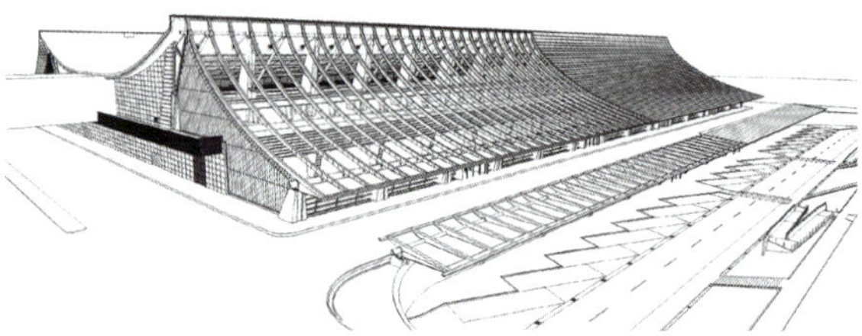

Taoyuan Airport Terminal One Regeneration, Taoyuan, Taiwan, 2013

The Taoyuan Airport Terminal One Regeneration in Taipei, Taiwan, of 2013 by Norihiko Dan and Associates covers an area of around 15,600 square meters on an existing terminal site. Originally constructed in 1979 by the engineer T. Y. Lin, it featured a pre-stressed structure that was state of the art at the time. It was also heavily influenced by Eero Saarinen's Washington Dulles Airport of 1958 to 1962, as a compact rectangular building with an elegant and prominent upswept roof. Some 30 or so years later, though, the Taoyuan Terminal One was operating well over capacity and had become outdated. In short, regeneration was a matter of expansion and retrofitting. More specifically regeneration was aimed at establishing a new national gateway for Taiwan and expanding the terminal without removing the existing structure. The expansion was a considerable boosting of capacity from 5 million passengers annually to 15 million passengers. In order to preserve and assimilate key features of the old into the new structure, an ingenious scheme was devised that hung two draping surfaces off the existing outward-leaning columns, effectively extending the building outwards in two directions and also acting as additional needed seismic bracing. The two additional surfaces were louvered but transparent, allowing light into the deeper plan of the extended new building. In outward appearance, the structure clearly makes reference to the 'big roof' projects during the People's Republic of China's period of 'socialist content and national or cultural form' if not before, i.e. during the Republican period of 'glorifying China's past while building in a modern manner'. The two-sided expansion is gracefully draped with a double-folded and tiled roof, as in older times. On the interior, the result is a spacious and dramatic space, easy to navigate for both departing and arriving passengers alike, befitting a new national gateway (Rowe and Kuan, 2002, pp. 87–107; and ArchDaily, 2015a).

The Wat Ananda Metyarama, a Thai Buddhist temple in Singapore of 2014 by Czarl Architects, is an addition to a venerable shrine located in the Bukit Merah area adjacent to the extensive Singapore General Hospital complex in the center of the city. In fact, the original old shrine was built in 1925 and is now the oldest Theravada Buddhist temple in Singapore. The new block of around 1,526 square meters was added to the hilltop site in a basic V-shaped plan form that screens the rest of the site off from the nearby Bukit Merah Flyover. Throughout, the design makes reference to the narrative of the Buddha attaining enlightenment meditating beneath the Bodhi tree. Indeed, the clients of the project did not want the architecture to be linked to the tradition of Thai Buddhist temples but rather to be 'reflective' of them. In forming a frame at the edge of the site, the new structure defines a broad space on the interior for outdoor use for religious and communal festivities and with a dining hall on the first floor. From there, the program is arranged and distributed at various levels of the two arms of the V-shaped overall volume in accordance with an idea that traces the growth of a Buddhist consciousness – based upon discovery, learning, meditation and, finally, sermon and discourse. Hence, architectural volumes are fragmented and displaced in the form of cantilevered boxes on angular columns rising five to six levels, with a single basement. This fragmentation is further accentuated by a deliberate interplay of solidness and transparency throughout the building. For instance, the meditation hall on the fourth level is a loft space enclosed by openable glass panels. Sky-gardens and planters also help break up the volumes and allow for additional greenery on site. Overall, the program includes new monks' quarters, dharma classrooms, meditation halls and a museum in addition to the dining hall and communal space mentioned earlier. The overt orientation towards an 'urban tree building' further underlines the Bodhi tree analogy. More palpably, an abstraction of light filtering through the gaps of the Bodhi tree were mapped onto the facades to create an organic pattern of triangular windows. In addition, the multiple-level fragmentation of building volumes and program components recalls the usual separation of the parts of a Buddhist pagoda or temple complex, together with the preparatory spaces in between them (ArchDaily, 2014).

Wat Ananda Metyarama, Singapore, 2014

The VAS Office Building complex in Da Nang, central Vietnam, of 2015 by Kientruc O is located on the western edge of a band of development beside the Han River, which flows in from the coast at Da Nang Bay. The site is flat and a more or less typical and rather bland industrial office park. The building was designed for the Vietnam American Steel Company (VAS). The project proposed a workspace typology closely adapted to local climate and vegetation. Instead of a typical climate-controlled box, the design was composed of verdant courtyards, a loop of covered walkways, office spaces and supporting facilities like dining and restrooms. All are in close proximity to a garden with staggered wall, roof and glass planes creating ambiguous boundaries between inside and outside. The walkways are also naturally ventilated, thus reducing operational costs. Indeed, a core principle of the project was to provide transitional layers to achieve a soft and layered effect throughout the complex. Man-made and natural components were to be symbiotic where the interaction between them did not favor one over the other, simultaneously establishing a more intimate link and co-existence of human workspace and natural ecology. In achieving this, the project also drew upon the local architectural typology, particularly dealing with dwellings in natural settings and where gardens comprise common spaces for people to connect together. Fundamentally in play here is the bounded figure of Sinic architecture and the presence of a courtyard or quadrangular structure. In the VAS Office Building, this is clear in the large garden formed at the center of the complex. However, this is further modulated and embroidered, as it were, by interstitial cutouts together with smaller court insertions within the overall ensemble. This is further amplified by the prominent circular skylights in the roof that punctuate and animate floor surfaces. A glazed perimeter scrim then recombines the informality of this layout into a coherent whole of well-defined edges and entry to the complex (ArchDaily, 2015b; and Archilovers, 2016).

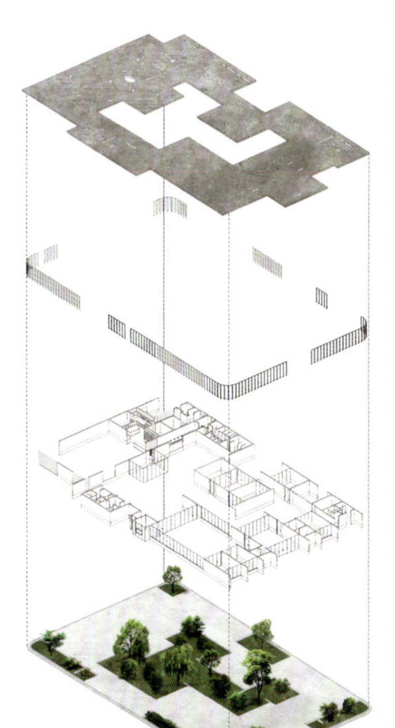

VAS Office Building, Da Nang, Vietnam, 2015

The Binh House in Ho Chi Minh City, Vietnam, of 2016 by VTN (Vo Trong Nghia) Architects, is a vertical, moderately high-density residence that aims to preserve the traditional Vietnamese and Sinic courtyard house lifestyle. Located in the crowded and dense Tan Binh district, it is inhabited by a family of three generations on a typically narrow lot, rising some half a dozen levels or so in what is essentially a three-storied house with 233 square meters of accommodations. Architecturally, one of the challenges was to create space for each generation so they could interact comfortably despite their differences. A basic strategy was adopted to locate gardens on top of vertically stacked spaces, bounded by sliding glass openings. This effectively achieved two purposes. The first was to improve the microclimate of the dwelling by naturally ventilating and lighting it. The passive ventilation scheme drew upon chimney effects caused by lopsided pressure differences in the vertical column of air in the building. The second was the alternating stacking of openings, allowing for a modicum of privacy together with visibility and potential connection among family members. In a broad layout, a bar of service functions and vertical access was created along the western side of the building lot, providing shading to adjacent areas. Then the three main stacks of space were aligned along the bar with open courts in between. Deep planter boxes capable of supporting large trees were dispersed within the building section. These vertical gardens could also be planted with vegetables supporting residents' daily needs. Sustainable materials of natural stone and wood along with off-form concrete lowered operating costs; to date no use of furnished auxiliary air-conditioning has been made. For Vo Trong Nghia, this Binh House is one of his 'Houses for Trees' series aiming to project prototypes for Ho Chi Minh City and in the same manner as the 'House for Trees' project depicted in the preceding chapter about contemporary Austronesian vernacular architecture. It is also in the spirit of the local Vietnamese typology discussed with regard to the VAS Office Building complex. Further, it resonates with apartment complex proposals by the likes of Ho Khue Architects in what follows, also in Da Nang, as well as commercialized products of firms like Viet Anh Home Design and their 'Pine Palace Tree Houses', as well as others in resort and out-of-the-way settings like Da Lat in the Central Highlands (Maire, 2018; and ArchDaily, 2020).

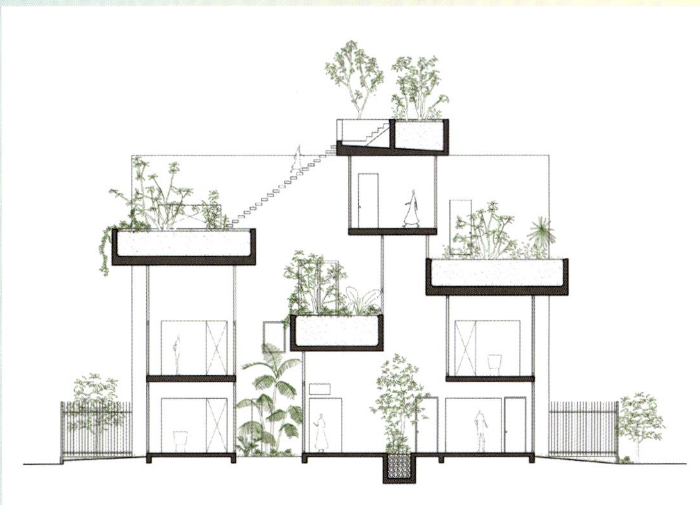

Binh House, Ho Chi Minh City, 2016

Binh House, Ho Chi Minh City, 2016

Finally, Green Peace Village in Da Nang, Vietnam, of 2019 by Ho Khue Architects is a five-storied apartment building of some 815 square meters in area on a very narrow and slightly irregular lot. Overcoming the typical, very crowded urban context of the city, it brings significant vegetated relief to the monotony of neighborhood dwellings. Comprised of three apartments on multiple floors, each has access from the narrow street frontage via stairs or a passageway and each has a dry balcony. Other on-site amenities include a fitness center, a coffee shop and a laundry room. The top floor also has a swimming pool and seating area. The main concept of the volumetric layout was apparently derived from terraced fields, common in Vietnam as in neighboring China. Unit floors are stacked on each other with the resulting stepped terraces proving natural light and ventilation. In addition, inner-side atriums are provided to further allow light and ventilation into the narrow lot configuration. The design process essentially involved the subdivision of each apartment vertically to make way for numerous roof and terrace gardens. Via the stairs between apartments one and two and the passageway between apartments two and three, additional space has been provided among the apartment blocks, again facilitating the flow of air and entrance of natural light. The result has been a green roofed structure across the different levels incorporating sizeable trees. The many stepped terraces also provide potential connections between dwellers. Conceptually, the complex is oriented towards a return to older, rural Vietnamese circumstances, where gardens formed the common spaces for people to gather and make contact. The warm feeling of simple village life is also embraced by the use of indigenous burnt brick as the basic building material (Khue, 2019).

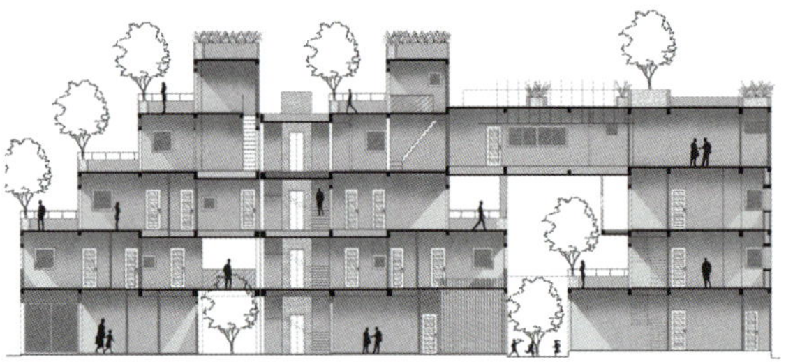

Green Peace Village, Da Nang, Vietnam, 2019

Western Coloniz-ations

Chapter

4

As noted, and discussed in the book's introduction, Western colonization in Southeast Asia took place over a reasonably lengthy period of time, starting more or less with the Portuguese but mainly with the Dutch and Spaniards around the 16th and 17th centuries. They were followed later by the British, largely at the onset of the 19th century and then by the French at mid-century and finally by the Americans toward the end of the century. For the Dutch and the British, these incursions were the product of corporate traders and, indeed raiders, like the Dutch East India Company (VOC) and the British East India Company, and took place before the respective national colonial interests took over and were expressed. From this onset, again as described earlier in the introduction, the aim was exploitation of local resources and trade in goods exotic and therefore valuable in the European context and elsewhere. It also involved accommodation of simultaneous power grabs by competing rivals and protection from those rivals in the form of defensive emplacements and, in places like Batavia and Malacca, the building of walled settlements. Almost without exception, in the beginning little attention was paid to endogenous cultures and manners of settlement or building. Rather what was built was aimed squarely at communicating the power and prestige of the colonizers. When adaptation finally did occur to local circumstances, it was usually made in the face of undeniable hardship and incrementally. Mostly this condition was occasioned by the tropical climate of the region but also in some locales by the presence of hazards like earthquakes or the lack of availability in needed materials and artisanal skills. Later, and as intrinsic exogenous influences altered internationally and in homeland settings, adaptation and use of endogenous approaches occurred more frequently and fluidly. In the architecture of the region this appears to have been prevalent by the time the earlier neo-classical styles of one sort or another had given way to Art Deco, Rationalism and Modernism of the 1920s and particularly the 1930s. Throughout though, a pervasive process of transplantation followed by adaptation, accommodation and even hybridization appears to have ensued. No doubt this might also be seen to have occurred in relation to encroachments by other roots of Southeast Asian architecture discussed in earlier chapters. However, it is also probably fair to say that the sheer gap in building practice, material and technology was more substantial under Western colonization, as was deployment of the cognizance of this difference by the colonizers involved (Nas, 2006, pp. 9–13; and Schenck, 2020, pp. 23–31).

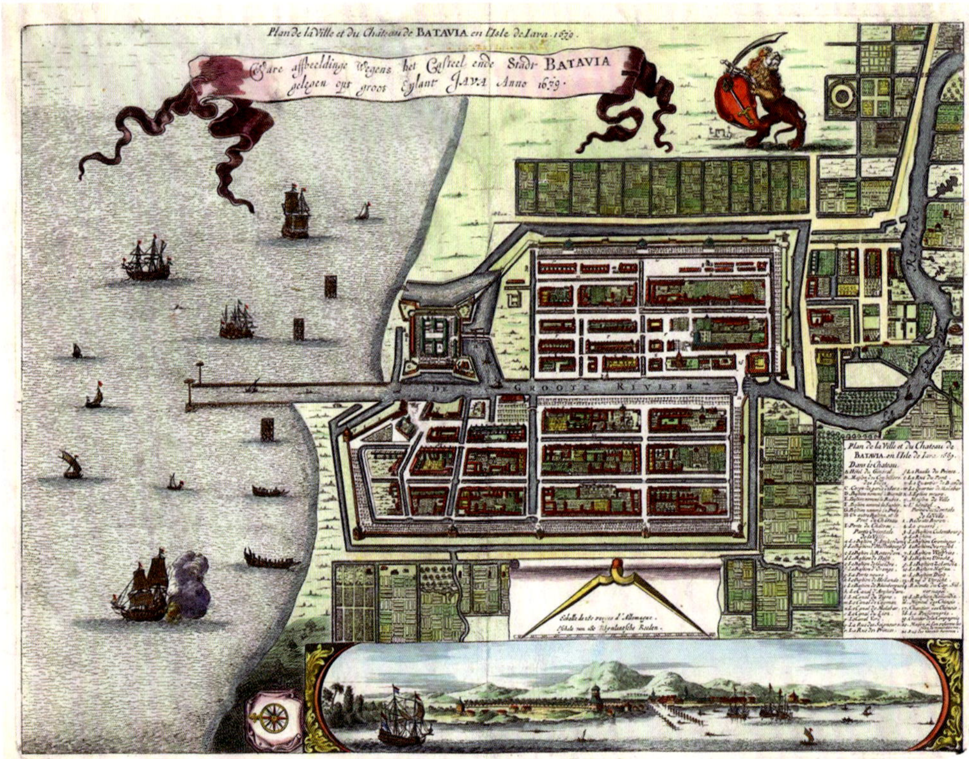

Plan of Batavia, Dutch East Indies, 1679

Transplantations from Homelands

More or less in the order of arrival, the Dutch in the hands of the VOC made little effort to adapt to the local tropical climate of the island archipelago. Throughout the 16th and 17th centuries they used masonry construction, primarily of houses and some public buildings, together with town and city walls. At their headquarters of Batavia, for instance, they constructed canals through low-lying terrain and laid out the settlement in a grid of blocks also subdivided by canals and surrounded by walls as protection, as mentioned earlier, from rivals like the British and from attacks by indigenous populations. The prevalent form of Dutch terrace house had small windows, as in the Netherlands, and was poorly ventilated. This condition along with the routine dumping of waste into the adjacent canals proved deleterious to public health, even as the Dutch viewed the traditional architecture of the islanders as unhygienic. In fact, it wasn't until the mid-18th century that these circumstances began to be rectified and colonial buildings began to incorporate local architectural elements and climatic adaptations. Later in the 1920s with the shift in architecture internationally and in the Netherlands to Rationalism, De Stijl and Art Deco, architects like Thomas Karsten incorporated indigenous Indonesian elements into rational European forms (Passchier, 2006; Widodo, 2006; and Coté and O'Neill, 2017).

TABLEAU de la Partie de BATAVIA, où s'est fait proprement le terrible MASSACRE des CHINOIS, le 9 Octob. 1740
AFBEELDING van dat Gedeelte van BATAVIA, alwaar eigentlyk de schrikkelyke SLAGTING der CHINEZEN geschied is, den 9 Octob. 1740

View of Batavia during the Chinese Massacre, 1740

The British also replicated the architecture of their mother country throughout their holdings in Singapore, Malaya and today's Myanmar. For them neo-classical Palladianism was the choice, particularly of European merchants in Singapore attempting to emulate the neo-Palladian manor houses at home. It also extended to more public buildings like the Singapore Institution by Philip Jackson of 1823 and Government House, The Istana, by John F. A. McNair of 1869. But, unlike the Dutch, they also adapted immediately to the local conditions. Neo-Palladian architecture was very much in vogue during the 17th and 18th centuries in England and even extended into other colonial possessions like Canada with, for instance, the Nova Scotia Legislative Building of 1819. Inspired by Andrea Palladio in Italy (1508–1580), it was an architecture based on symmetry, perspective and the values of classical temples, even though in Britain it was rather less ornate than in Italy. Also, scrutiny of several buildings in Singapore, like the Singapore Institution, Government House and the Istana Kampong Glam of 1843 by George D. Coleman for the Sultan of Johor, show that they did diverge from the English models with regard to climate and the lack of skilled labor. All had Palladian classical facades, were symmetrical in layout, had a clear delineation of floors and even occupied suburban sites as in the environs of Vicenza. Nevertheless, they were also less ornamented, more austere, arranged with Malayan porch verandahs and had linear plans as distinct from compact court arrangements, to facilitate cross-ventilation. In Burma, now Myanmar, the Ministers' Building and District Courts on Strand Road in Rangoon, now Yangon, by Henry Hoyne-Fox of 1895–1905 and 1911, respectively, are clear examples of transplantations from their British homeland. The District Courts building with its neo-classical facade and tall pedimented and columnar entrance, in particular, reflected this instantiation. Also, the luxury Strand Hotel in Rangoon of 1899 was built in a Palladian manner, even more elaborate than its cousin in Singapore. The later Victorian and Edwardian idioms also flourished as in the residence of Bogyoke Aung San, the father of Myanmar's independence movement (Summerson, 1980; Reed and Farber, 1980; Inglis, 1998; and SgArch, 2021). *Godowns*, or buildings dedicated to storage and warehousing, were also constructed, as elsewhere in the burgeoning trading sector of East and Southeast Asia. Typically, they were in the charge of *compradors,* or agents for foreign

The Istana, Singapore, 1869

Istana Kampong Glam, Singapore, 1843

Ministers' Building and District Courts on Strand Road, Rangoon, 1895–1905

Ellenborough Building, Singapore, 1877

organizations in the trade, a term derived from the Portuguese for 'buyer'. In Singapore, several achieved architectural merit like Edward Boustead's godown by George D. Coleman of 1830 and the sprawling Ellenborough Building by John Turnbull Thomson of 1847. The latter was a long two-storied structure with a continuous ground-floor sheltering walkway framed by rounded arches and with a double Doric columned neo-classical facade on the second floor, crowned by a sloping parapet roof (SgArch, 2020).

At the beginning of the French colonization of Saigon and the provinces around it in 1859, the colonists lived largely in indigenous bamboo structures before quickly initiating more lasting construction of hotels, villas and commercial establishments. The first Roman Catholic church was built of timber in 1863, though failing to last because of termite infestation. Shortly after this, in 1864, one of the first significant buildings was the Messageries Maritimes, with a three-story arcaded structure around its flanks in a fusion of French and Vietnamese construction and also ushering in the era of double-walled structures, later including the now prominent Ho Chi Minh Museum. From this rather modest beginning, however, ostentatious neo-classical styles of architecture, like the Governor-General's Palace of 1873, became the dominant style, as in France, clearly projecting the power and prestige of the colonial government. If anything, architecturally this style emphasized a Beaux-Arts methodology of symmetry, classical proportions and ornate surface decoration. There and in other parts of Indochina, French architects gradually succumbed to harsh climatic conditions by enlarging windows for ventilation, made possible by steel framing and the use of electric fans. As elsewhere in Southeast Asia, international architectural influences around in home countries began to impinge, bringing new directions to local buildings, such as Art Deco, certainly by 1927 or thereabouts in apartment buildings, followed by more orthodox modernism by 1931 and 1932 with Saigon's PTT Building, for instance. The large and elaborate State Bank of Vietnam probably marked something of an end to this period into the 1930s, as a strong neo-classical building but also with Art Deco and even Khmer decoration. Elsewhere, in the nearby Philippines, the Roman Catholic Church had been a dominant force shaping most of the church-related

Governor-General's Palace, Saigon, 1873

State Bank of Vietnam, Saigon, 1928

Manila Metropolitan Theater, 1935

The American Memorial and Cemetery, Manila, 1948

structures between 1571 and 1898. As another one of Spain's colonial possessions, it was subject to at least two distinctive major influences on its building and settlements. The first was the rigors of the 16th-century 'Law of the Indies' in physical planning and layout, together with the ornate facades of Baroque churches. As narrated earlier, this came to an end with the United States take-over of the Philippines from 1898 to 1946, even though the Americans continued a pattern of mimicry of Spanish Colonial buildings and attempts to hybridize local nipa huts into the form of hygienic tsalet houses. Almost from the outset, however, neo-classical architecture also appeared on the heels of Daniel Burnham's 1912 Plan of Manila and appreciation of, if not infatuation with, the 'City Beautiful' style of urban design and architecture back in the United States. The Manila Central Post Office of 1926 by Juan Marcos Arellano was one such work, as was his Manila Metropolitan Theater of 1935 although in the slightly later Art Deco style. Indeed, Arellano was probably the major local architectural contributor at the time, though other Art Deco structures included the Saint Cecilia's Hall of 1932 by Andres Luna de San Pedro. This was to continue through much of the colonial period and even into the years that followed with, for example, the American Memorial and Cemetery of 1948. There, on a prominent verdant 62-hectare site inside Bonifacio Global City, the memorial is located in the form of two semi-circular, flat-roofed trabeated enclosures centered on a chapel and altar in a short white masonry tower (Moore, 1968; Norindr, 1996; Alcazaren, 2005; Lico, 2008; Alacon, 2008; and Schenck, 2020).

Processes of Adaptation and Accom-modation

What followed almost across the board was both initial and further adaptation to climate and resource issues. This appears to have come about both by incremental practical reckoning with architectural need or through changes in colonial policy. Responses of a climatic kind typically involved roof elements becoming more conspicuous and sheltering. Double-walled facades, as already noted in Vietnam, became more common alongside the practice of surrounding buildings with verandahs. Large windows, taller floor-to-ceiling heights and uses of electrical-mechanical equipment also took place, allowed by evolving new technologies. Throughout, stylistic and even material references back to indigenous forms of building before colonization became more commonplace, often creating hybrid inflections to more normative colonial styles of architecture. By the mid-18th century in the Dutch East Indies, for instance, the Indies Style was advanced, incorporating local architectural elements. These included more longitudinal than compact layouts for better ventilation. Also, the *joglo* and *limasan* roofs described in chapter 2 were combined with neo-classical columnar configurations and deep verandahs. With the bankruptcy of the VOC and the arrival of Herman Willem Daendels as Governor-General, the Indies Empire Style (*Indisch Rijksstijl*) flourished as something of an imitation of Europe's Empire Style, involving eclectic use of antique motifs, symmetrical layouts, high ceilings and thick walls, often together with front and rear galleries flanked with columns. This last element was also an attempt to copy the local Javanese verandah (*pringgitan*). The Istana Merdeka in Jakarta of 1873 was a typical residential example, as was the slightly earlier National Museum of Indonesia of 1862 as a civic building (Milone, 1967; and Nas, 2006, pp. 10–13). A change in outlook to the Dutch Ethical Policy, noted earlier, around 1901, also shifted the balance towards incorporating indigenous architectural elements into otherwise European forms. As mentioned, the work of Thomas Karsten was distinguished in that regard. Indeed, he seems to have almost reversed the dominance of transplanted and local aspects by remaining highly sensitive to cultural traditions, functional zoning and activity areas, along with the imposition of adequate hygienic conditions. Especially in his mass housing project of Mlaten in Semarang beginning in 1919, as several well-informed commentators have interpreted, he saw this rebalancing as positively promoting a necessary public educational role towards better ways of living and for all concerned. The architecture of his Van Deventer School of 1923 and his large city markets, like Pasar Gede in Surakarta of 1929, also followed in the same spirit with prominent tiled roofs, high ceilings, spacious interiors, open corridors and bustling adjacent outdoor spaces (Coté and O'Neill, 2017, pp. 175–219).

Istana Merdeka, Jakarta, 1873

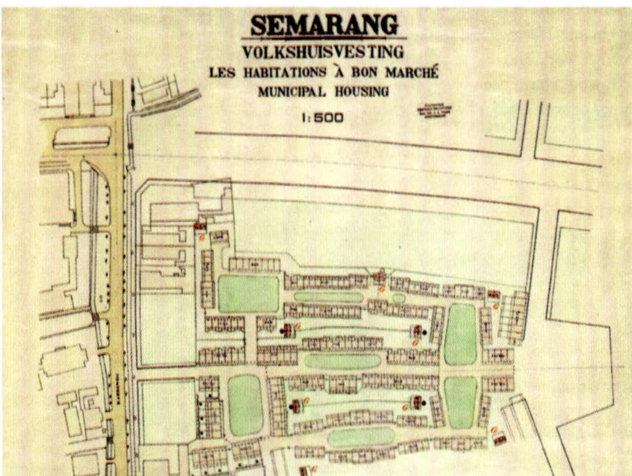

Kampong Mlaten, Semarang, Indonesia, 1923

Van Deventer School, Semarang, Indonesia, 1923

Pasar Gede Market, Surakarta, Indonesia, 1929

Similarly, in Indochina and especially through their 'associationist approach' to the colonial process in the 1920s, the French began accommodating local Vietnamese culture and recognizing social customs. This is apparent, for instance, in Ernest Hébard's efforts as a part of the Town Planning and Architecture Service towards merging Beaux-Arts plans and structures with traditional roof forms and decorative programs. The so-called Indochine Style that emerged in buildings like the Lycée Petrus Ky of 1928 bear this out, even though in more contemporary terms they are seen as controversial for alleged superficiality and inclusion in a projection of grandeur. Throughout the 1930s, under the influence of Art Deco and Modernist idioms, eclecticism continued (Wright, 1991; and Schenck, 2020). Luang Prabang, once the Laotian capital, became the host of numerous French colonial houses and civic buildings well into the 1950s (Vongvilay, Shin, Kang et al., 2015). Within the British colonial tradition of Myanmar, by the 1920s local adaptions and building modifications began to become prevalent. For example, the Kayah Gayhar guesthouse was constructed to house visiting state dignitaries as a conscious blend of vernacular elements with the previous style of colonial Victorian architecture. In particular, copious use was made of breezeways, high ceilings, elevated floors, open wooden grille work along verandahs in this spacious three-floor building (Inglis, 1998, p. 97f.). In the Philippines, however, adaption was even more abrupt and necessary, provoked by destructive earthquakes. There, beginning as early as the late 16th century, church proportions became lower and wider, side walls were made thicker and were heavily buttressed for stability during shaking. Just as conspicuously, bell towers were usually lower and shorter in comparison to those in less seismically active parts of the world. Several were even detached from the body of the church to avoid cross-damage due to earthquake destruction, such as at Saint Augustine of Paoay of 1694 (Esparza, 2019). The Manila Cathedral, first built in 1581, was destroyed several times, including having its bell tower toppled by an earthquake in 1880 (Cerbo, 2021).

As time wore on, as suggested above, Art Deco architecture emerged among the Western colonial possessions of the region. Originally it was a style of architecture, visual arts and design that first appeared in France just before World War I. The term is a contraction of *Arts Décoratifs*

Lycée Petrus Ky, Saigon, 1928

Art Deco Villa, Luang Prabang, Laos

Kayah Gayhar Guesthouse, Rangoon, 1920

Saint Augustine, Paoay, the Philippines, 1694

and later derived from the Exposition Internationale des Arts Décoratifs et Industriels Modernes held in Paris on a 23-hectare site along the Seine in 1925. Influenced by bold geometric forms from Cubism and the Vienna Secession, primarily in Europe, its dominance ended by the onset of World War II and subsequently the rise of International Style modernism. It featured new materials and technologies like reinforced concrete, plate glass and aluminum. An early example can be seen at the Théâtre des Champs-Elysées by Auguste Perret of 1910–1913. In Southeast Asia, it was imported during the Western colonial period, strongly in French Indochina as might be expected, but also in the Dutch East Indies and particularly to the city of Bandung in western Java, where it was extended to office buildings, civic functions, homes and even churches. Notable among these structures was the Gedung Sate, or Governor's Office, of 1920 by J. Gerber, which combined Art Deco with classical architectural elements. Then, more clearly Art Deco in style is the Kologdam Building of 1920 and the three-storied Merdeka Building of 1921, both by Wolff Schoemaker, a major proponent of the style, as well as his tall and upwardly pointed Saint Peter's Cathedral of 1922 and his later cylindrically inclined Villa Isola of 1933. This building is located in the northern area of Bandung, overlooking a valley. In fact, it is aligned on the north-south axis with Mount Tangkuban Petrahu to the north and Bandung to the south. Originally it was built for the Dutch media tycoon Dominique Willem Berretty, the founder of the Aneta press agency in the Dutch East Indies, in 1917. The building was transformed into a hotel after Berretty perished in an air crash in 1934, later becoming a headquarters for the Japanese occupation in 1942. Then in 1954, it became the main office of the Indonesia University of Education, with the surrounding area as its campus. To the north, the villa was situated at the end of a long formal garden with a rectangular pond and statue at its center. To the south, the lower reaches of the villa spread into a wide semi-circular terrace stepping down into the valley. Several works by Albert Aalbers followed, though in the Streamline Moderne style with the DENIS Bank of 1935–1936 and the curvilinear Savoy Homann Hotel of 1939. Though born in Rotterdam, Aalbers moved to the Indies in 1928. In addition, Medan in Sumatra also became a haven for Art Deco in the Dutch East Indies (Hartono, 1989; Akihary, 1990; and Davis, 2017).

Gedung Merdeka, Bandung, Indonesia, 1921

Villa Isola, Bandung, 1933

Savoy Homann Hotel, Bandung, 1939

Housing Indigenous Migrations

As noted in the introduction, the Chinese migrations south into Southeast Asia in large numbers were mainly confined to the European period, though in point of fact beginning earlier among traders in the area of the South China Sea (*Nanyang*) and even earlier through campaigns of conquest. None other than Kublai Khan invaded the northern coast of Java, for instance, in 1293, though driven back by the reigning Majapahit. Still earlier, around 990 CE, and later, trade into today's Taiwan took place during the Northern Song Dynasty. Then during the epic voyages of Admiral Zheng He from the Ming Dynasty in the 15th century, contact with China was increased though intermittently before a further hiatus roughly from 1450 to 1520. Then with subsequent legalization of private trade by China in 1567, distinct communities began to rise quickly in Southeast Asia and particularly in what is now the Indonesian archipelago and parts of Malaysia like Malacca. Indeed, the Strait of Malacca supported favorable sailing from *Nanyang* as it coincided geographically with the ends of the monsoons that regularly swept the region and, therefore, the necessary calm as the prevailing winds changed allowing swift sailing to the west and then to the north. This enabled Gujarati mariners from India, for instance, favorable access for trade. In addition, traders from China's southern provinces who came to Malacca were an established class by about 1400. In effect, with the Northeast Monsoon, traders left China at the end of the year and sailed back with the Southwest Monsoon in the middle of the year. This duration allowed for about five months in the north and south, respectively, and the setting up of homes in Malacca as well as in China, where local wives were typically Malay as the Chinese did not bring women on hazardous journeys. This also resulted in the formation of merchant communities of what became known as Straits Chinese, Baba Chinese and Peranakan, as noted earlier. Exotic trade in spices extended into the 1820s and beyond, as well as in agricultural products more generally. With the arrival of Stamford Raffles and the British East India Company to what is now Singapore in 1819, free trade was initiated and proved to be very attractive to Chinese migration. In fact, by 1826 there were more Chinese there than Malays. Much of this was due to the intrinsic 'pushes' and 'pulls' in the broader region, where abject poverty and the lack of available land for local populations in dynastic China was counterbalanced by 'pulls' of migrant-friendly policies in pursuit of needed labor and economic opportunity. In the diaspora that ensued in Singapore, for example, which by the late 19th century had become the capital of the colonial Straits Settlements, the Baba aligned themselves with the British and became the local leaders politically. Elsewhere, China trade and immigration also abounded, though with more mixed results. In the Dutch East Indies, after first encouraging Chinese workers the VOC violently discriminated against them, massacring several thousand, for example, in Batavia in 1740. With the coming of Dutch colonial rule in 1815, legislation against Chinese interests also arose (Siang, 1993; Ee, 1996; Selya, 1995, Wilkinson, 2012; and Wong, 2020).

Almost without exception the architectural contributions of this diaspora have been mainly shophouses and terrace houses, in addition to more colonial building typologies such as the *bahay na bato* (house of stone) of the Philippines. Generally, a shophouse is a building type that serves both as a residence and a commercial business. Typically, they open

Shophouses on Geylang Road, Singapore

Terrace Houses on Koon Seng Road, Singapore

onto the pavement through the commercial premises, usually in the form of a store, with the owner's residence located above, or behind in single-floor examples. In almost all circumstances shophouses lined up in terraces of buildings were also designed to fit narrow and deep lots, allowing many businesses to be accommodated along a street. In addition to the front area of business, rear areas were informal spaces for family members, toilets, bathrooms, kitchens, storage infrastructure and even open courtyards. According to regulations issued as early as 1822 in Singapore by Stamford Raffles, each shophouse had to provide a verandah of a certain depth, open at all times as a continuous passage on the side of the street. These became known as 'five foot ways' and a distinctive feature of the Straits Settlement style of shophouse (Buckley, 1902). Covered walkways could also be found in southern China, Taiwan and elsewhere, known as *qilou* and originating in Guangzhou. Again, they were mandated by government regulations at the end of the Qing Dynasty and in Taiwan under Japanese rule after 1895. Early examples of shophouses were most often unadorned buildings, with more ornate and elaborate examples developing later in line with the increasing wealth of merchant (Chinese) owners. Initial shophouses were one-floor-atop structures with businesses in the front. Terraced houses were the more purely residential counterpart of the shophouses, invariably also constructed in long rows, for wealthy merchant families. They were sometimes referred to as 'Palladian Chinese', again because of the adoption of this style of architecture in Singapore and because of the eclectic mix of Chinese, Malay and European classical elements. In the case of the Dutch East Indies and even Malacca, these buildings were a combination of Dutch (European) row houses with Chinese characteristics such as plaques identifying owners, roof styles and decorative motifs. In Malacca in particular there were two types. The first, constructed up until the mid-18th century, were two stories in height and equipped with secondary roofs between the upper and lower floors but with no continuous walkways. The later second examples were typically two and three floors tall with decorative plasterwork and with the upper floors overhanging lower floors, providing shade without the secondary roofs between floors. There was also the presence of 'Dutch doors' segmented into upper and lower leaves, allowing both ventilation and

'Five Foot Way' in Singapore

surveillance of the street outside with some degree of privacy. The most important rooms of terrace houses were usually ancestral halls toward the front, sitting rooms and open-air wells with bedrooms attached towards the rear. Usually, these wells, like the Chinese *heyan* style of house, had slightly sunken floors for drainage.

Beyond these general typological characteristics of both shophouses and terrace houses there were local variations. In Singapore, for instance, there were several outstanding examples. In Chinatown, shophouses were typically four stories tall, with the uppermost floor often for rental. At Blair Road, elaborate examples of terrace houses were found to be built up to the 1920s, two stories in height and using a mix of Chinese, Malay and European elements. Small open courts with decorative masonry on low fences provided entry on the street, with rich plasterwork and louvered windows on the facades. Emerald Hill, laid out in 1901, featured continuous front verandahs and a common elevational treatment, whereas at Geylang Road shophouses, built after World War I, had more ornate decoration to upper floors than lower ones. Even more elaborate was Koon Seng Road with red roof tiles, carved timber fascias, heavily decorated entablatures above second-floor windows, numerous bas-reliefs and an assortment of pastel colors. Art Deco facades made their appearance later from the 1930s onwards (Liu, 1984; and Lin, 1995). In Vietnam, the Hanoi shophouse, also known as the 'tube house' because of the groups of 'one-*gain*' buildings that shared sidewalls with next-door houses, arranged along very deep lots, with sidewalls usually jutting forward and along the building envelope. There, a *gain* referred to a module or a bay determined largely by the width of timber beams (Balderstone and Logan, 2003, pp. 140–145). In Thailand, the *Ban Thai* (Thai house) in its pre-modern incarnation was constructed from local materials, usually wood, with a skeletal form of structure clad with light exterior skins. There was also often the use of terraces and balconies for climatic purposes along with prominent gabled roofs and elevation above grade on piles. The 19th-century shophouse (*Hong Thaeo*) was a Chinese adaption of wooden or masonry structure as a combined workplace and residence used particularly by Sino-Thai traders in local towns. Often, they were long and narrow, two stories in height with the lower floor clad in masonry and the upper one in timber siding. A more prominent gable roof at the front and a verandah attachment signaled the business location (Askew, 2003, p. 273). Then the *bahay na bato* of the Philippines were something of a different typology. They were the urban residences during the Spanish occupation and made from stone, usually aligned side by side with pitched gabled roofs on two-storied structures. Rectangular and uniform in plan, they were often clad with upper-level balconies and equipped with sliding wooden shuttered windows. Their longevity of over 350 years is a testament to their inherent permanence (Villalon, 2003, pp. 212–213).

Tube Houses, Hanoi

Bahay na bato, the Philippines

Contemporary Projects

Contemporary projects span across three categories of considerations. They are, first, further adaptations and forms especially with regard to local environmental factors, programmatic and surrounding opportunities, as well as materials. Second are Art Deco conservation and refurbishments to existing structures of note, including renewal projects among both well-developed and less-developed countries. Third is continuation of original shophouse and terrace house traditions matched to contemporary circumstances. Again, an attempt is made to be reasonably representative of contemporary architectural preoccupations.

Further Adaptations and Forms

The School of Design and Environment 4 at the National University of Singapore of 2019 by Serie Architects, Multiple Architects and Surbana Jurong arose from a competition launched in 2013 for additional facilities in the existing Design and Environment precinct of the university. What resulted was the first new build, net-zero-energy structure in Singapore that has also proved to be of significant demonstrable

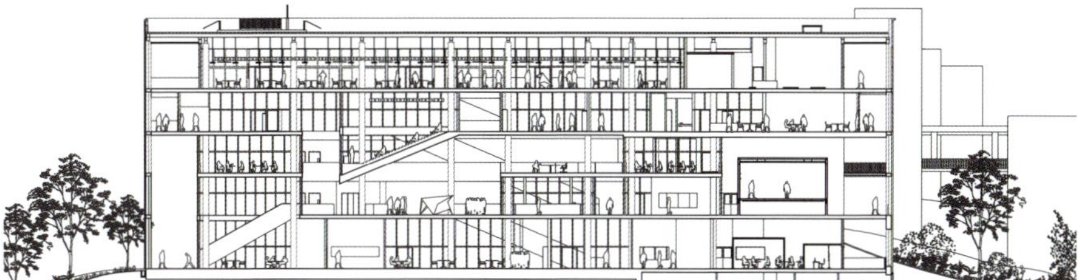

School of Design and Environment 4, Singapore, 2019

usefulness to the academic programs it houses. In broad outline, the school is a six-storied, multi-disciplinary space totaling some 85,000 square meters of space. This is further comprised of 1,500 square meters of design studio space, 500 square meters of open plaza, along with a variety of public and social spaces, workshops, research units, a new café and a library. Featuring flexible design and high efficiency, rooms were provided in a variety of sizes, thus allowing flexible rearrangement to accommodate exhibitions, school-specific installations and future changes in use. Architecturally, this has been envisioned in the form of a porous architecture with a juxtaposition of platforms and boxes as specific programmatic responses and at points in time. Built for an institution that actively promotes design, sustainability and education in Southeast Asia, the design concept challenges the idea that an energy-efficient building has to be opaque. More than 50 percent of the total built area is ventilated naturally, and most rooms can be opened to prevailing breezes on its hillock site. Spaces interspersed between cooled volumes benefit from cross-ventilation and act as thermal buffers and social spaces in the manner of more traditional verandahs of old. What unfolds is an architecture of alternating terraces, landscaped balconies and informal spaces, billed as a scaffolding for learning. A large over-sailing roof protrudes along the main facade, embedding a tropical patio built around existing trees. A southern garden also acts as a water purification system with over half the plants in the form of native species. Net-zero energy is achieved through a range of sustainable features like 1,200 solar photovoltaic panels and an innovative cooling system especially designed to supply rooms with 100 percent fresh pre-cooled air distributed by circulating fans (ArchDaily, 2019).

The City Center Tower in Manila of 2016 by Carlos Arnaiz Architects or CAZA, is a 27-floor, mixed-use building in Metro Manila, the Philippines. It is located adjacent to a park on the north-south Quezon roadway on the northern side of the Pasig River, which connects the Laguna de Bay to Manila Bay. Among its merits, one is the overall aim of defying the average core and shell design of the standard corporate office buildings that have burgeoned in Manila in recent years. There, modern steel and glass towers have sprung up in commercial

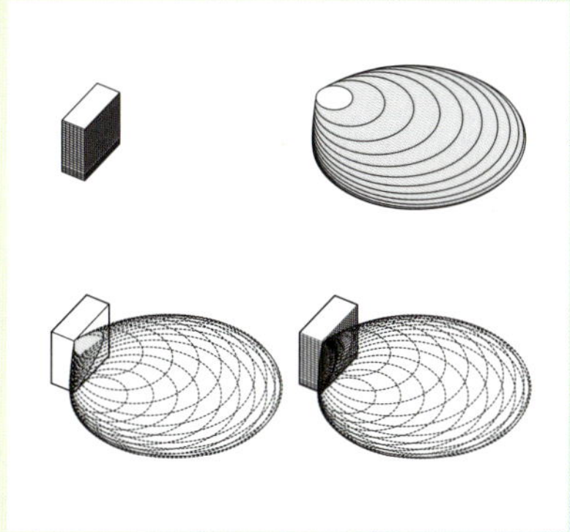

City Center Tower, Manila, 2016

areas like Makati, Fort Bonifacio, Pasay, among other upcoming business districts, largely on the heels of Business Process Outsourcing, or BPO, which in the Philippines accounts for an increasingly large share of the business especially for the English-speaking world, second only to India. Essentially, BPOs are third-party vendors who provide business support services, the main one of which is the call center for various international companies. These call centers, in turn, require commercial space, 24-hour use across international time zones and some proximity to a skilled workforce. In contradistinction to the standard commercial building, the City Center Tower caters directly to the 24-hour BPO office environment. In particular, there is the fifth-floor space, above the basement parking and retail floors, that is outfitted as a lofted restaurant area, overlooking the adjacent park and with an expansive balcony area featuring an urban beach and wading pool, together with hammocks and lounge spaces. Then in the tower that rises above, different geometries have been introduced into the floors to produce a new user experience. These include infusion of a series of concentric circles across the horizontal axes of each floor. The resulting exterior facade then marries the stacked shape of a cube with the free-form organic pattern of a wave. The outer curtain wall is inflected and twists into a row of balconies that run up and down the building facade. The outcome not only offers the building occupants unusual views of the surrounding landscape but establishes a clear, exceptional visual quality to the tower itself (ArchDaily, 2016; and Welch, 2016).

The MAIIAM Contemporary Art Museum in Chiang Mai, Thailand, of 2016 by All(Zone) is located in the San Kampheang District of this city in the northern part of the country. It is in an existing warehouse that was transformed to provide a versatile platform for art activities across some 3,300 square meters of space. The art museum houses an important private collection of regional and national contemporary art now made permanently accessible to the public. The renovated warehouse is an asymmetrical arrangement with a gable-roofed double-height space, the rear portion of which is divided into two floors of gallery space, while the larger front portion essentially encloses the large double-height volume with a terrace along its front edge. Two large light wells are introduced into the former warehouse in order to provide natural light to the exhibition spaces below. The building's front facade and narrow enclosure of support facilities is clad in numerous mirrored tiles that reflect the light, nearby trees and other visual qualities of the adjacent environment. In fact, this is a decorative technique found in traditional Thai temples and also produces a constantly changing pattern of shapes and colors synonymous with the reality of different movements in the contemporary art world. A low rectangular horizontal segment of this mirrored wall clearly reveals the café of the support program inside, much like a painting placed on a gallery wall. The industrial spirit of the warehouse interior has been maintained, further implying the non-permanent contemporaneity of the establishment (Stevens, 2016).

The Kontum Indochine Café in Kontum, Vietnam, of 2013 by Vo Trong Nghia (VTN) Architects is part of a hotel complex along the Dakbla River, which flows through this city in the Central Highlands close to the Cambodian border. The café serves as a dining area for hotel guests, as well as a semi-outdoor banquet hall for wedding ceremonies. Essentially, it is composed of two parts. The first is a rectangular area under an extensive roof of bamboo structure. The second is an adjacent kitchen area made of concrete frames infilled with stone. The main café building is surrounded by a shallow artificial lake allowing the flow of air across its surface to be cooled before entering the well-shaded semi-open space, obviating the need for air-conditioning in the tropical climate. The roof structure is comprised of 15 inverse cone-shaped units, tapered towards the bottom, made from bamboo and inspired by traditional Vietnamese fishing baskets. These units are aligned in the rectangular space to form a regular arrangement of five by three arched bays. The roof is made of fiber-reinforced plastic panels and thatch. Transparent synthetic panels are partly exposed in the ceiling to provide natural light into the deep central areas of the café space below. Traditional treatment was given to the bamboo structure, including low-tech joint details of rattan tying and bamboo nailing. Each column unit was prefabricated and then erected on site in order to achieve the quality and accuracy required. Patrons of the café can enjoy the panoramic view of the mountains and the Dakbla River, framed by the bamboo arches (ArchDaily, 2013).

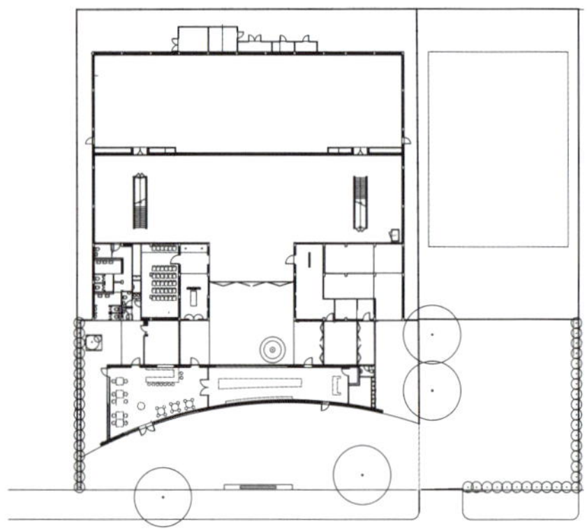

**MAIIAM Contemporary Art Museum,
Chiang Mai, Thailand, 2016**

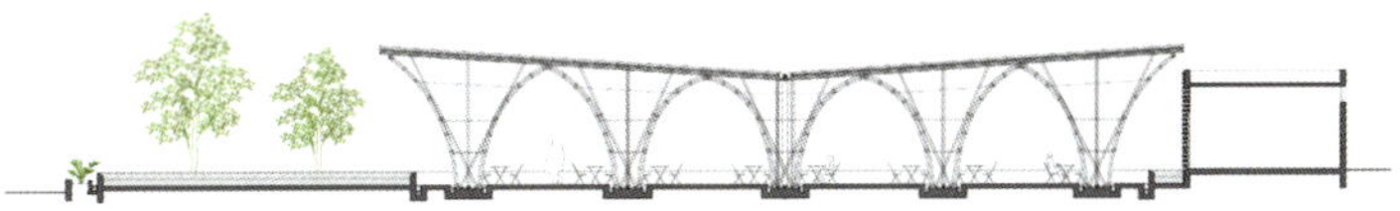

Kontum Indochine Café, Kontum, Vietnam, 2013

Bamboo Sports Hall for the Panyaden International School, Chiang Mai, Thailand, 2017

The Bamboo Sports Hall for the Panyaden International School in Chiang Mai, Thailand, of 2017 by Chiangmai Life Architects (CLA) combines 21st-century engineering and the natural material of bamboo to create a hall large enough to hold 300 students, though remaining well integrated into the larger school context of earthen and bamboo buildings and a naturally hilly landscape. Covering an area of 782 square meters in a single span, the exclusive use of bamboo maintains a low carbon footprint and adheres to the 'green school' mission of Panyaden. Shaped in the manner of a lotus flower, the mixed-use structure is also consistent with the school's infusion of Buddhist teachings into its academic program. The facility hosts futsal, basketball, volleyball and badminton, with special courts marked out on its timber floor. It can also host other kinds of performances on a stage that is raised automatically, with a backwall with storage behind and a front wall allowing projection and backdrops for film and dramatic performances. The long sides of the hall have balconies providing additional space for parents and visitors to spectate sports events and shows. The flowing shape and design of the layers of the tiled overhanging roof, together with the semi-open condition of the hall, provide for a naturally ventilated and comfortable space. The exposed bamboo structure was based on specially developed bamboo trusses, spanning some 17 meters without steel reinforcement or connections. A *tour de force* of engineering, this structure can withstand high-speed winds, earthquakes and other natural forces. With a zero-carbon footprint – due to the amount of carbon absorbed in the building material prior to construction being greater than that expended by the embodied energy of treatment, transport and construction – the life expectancy of the building is around 50 years (Zapartan, 2017).

Art Deco Revival and Conservation

As noted above, Art Deco was the last architectural style associated with modernization during the colonial period of many Southeast Asian nations. In the absence of significant enough capacities let alone aspirations to architecturally modernize according to contemporary trends elsewhere in the world, the Art Deco structures from the 1930s onwards became subject to adaption with conservation, and revival.

This was often particularly the case in pursuit of tourism in places as varied as Laos and Singapore. Moreover, there was also a commonality of approach to conservation and revitalization throughout the region, epitomized perhaps by Bandung in Indonesia, already described as a major site of Art Deco colonial construction. There, a conservation area was delineated and careful adaptive re-use was encouraged in building and urban transformation, especially to better accommodate tourist exigencies. In addition, pedestrian access throughout the conservation area was meticulously improved through the local government sidewalk program of 2016. Specific and targeted buildings were also carefully assessed with regard to cultural significance, scarcity and the need for physical refurbishment. Construction and conservation were then carried out accordingly. The fate of Schoemaker's Villa Isola, discussed above, and now the Rectorate of the Indonesia University of Education, was a clear case in point. There, the function-form-meaning aspect of the change from residence to office was acknowledged from the standpoint of historical significance, alongside the place of the building for enjoying surrounding scenery or its social significance. Finally, the adaption of European modernity – Art Deco styling – to local conditions was undertaken from the standpoint of architectural and symbolic significance (Suryono, Sudikno and Salura, 2013; and Soewarno and Duhita, 2019).

The Tiong Bahru Estate in Singapore of 1936 and 2000 by Alfred G. Church and the Urban Redevelopment Authority of Singapore (URA) is one of the oldest housing estates in the island city-state, originally undertaken by the former Singapore Improvement Trust (SIT), the British forerunner of the contemporary Housing and Development Board (HDB) and the URA. The estate consists of 30 apartment blocks with a total of 900 dwelling units. The blocks are comprised of two- to five-storied flats, with the units arranged into three- to five-room apartments. A dominant aspect of the architectural style is Art Deco, with flats featuring rounded balconies, flat roof tops, outdoor semi-enclosed spiral staircases, light wells and underground storage and shelters. During the 1930s, it was regarded as a choice place to live for upper-income dwellers and a place where mistresses were kept, earning it the sobriquet of 'Mei Ren Wo' or 'Den of Beauties'. After World War II, occupancy increased and the estate gradually lost its exalted status. More recently, younger people have been moving in due to the relaxation of HDB rules prohibiting the buying of smaller flats near the city center. With this gentrification, the area has become 'hip' and fashionable again. The original site of 28.5 hectares was swampy and hilly and construction led to the displacement of some 2,000 squatters. The project architect was Alfred G. Church, who was appointed by the colonial government. Recently, the URA has undertaken a detailed conservation plan for the pre-war Tiong Bahru units. It provides guidance but also requires property owners to obtain renovation permits for any work affecting main facades. This applies inside a designated conservation area as at Bandung. It also specifies the main building facades to be conserved, acknowledging the presence and maintenance of Art Deco architectural features, including the abundance of Streamline Moderne shapes, recessed fair-faced brick balconies, window and vent details, alongside preclusion of awnings and external air-conditioners. Other significant features of the Tiong Bahru Estate, such as the large, verdant open courtyards and semi-enclosed spiral staircases, are not included in this facade plan but remain conserved. Other nearby amenities include the Tiong Bahru Market, dating from 1955 and renovated in 2006. Some studies show that the URA tends to focus its conservation activities on historical and physical aspects and also with an eye towards enhancement of tourism as elsewhere in the region. Since the late 2000s, the distinctive townscape has hastened a trend of older residents being replaced by an influx of younger residents – the gentrification remarked on earlier (To, Chong and Chong, 2014; and Conservation Department, 2019).

Villa Isola, Bandung, Indonesia, 1933 and 2016

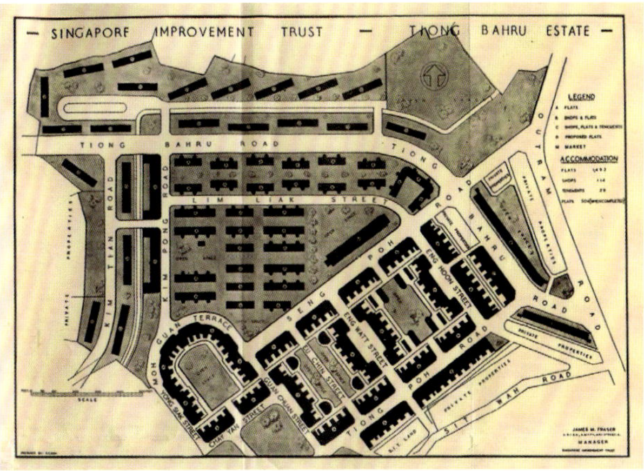

Tiong Bahru Estate, Singapore, 1936 and 2000

Central Market, Phnom Penh, Cambodia, 1937 and 2011

The Central Market of Phnom Penh, Cambodia, of 1937 by Jean Desbois and 2011 by Arte Charpentier for the French Development Agency, is an Art Deco architectural landmark in the city. It is dominated by a dome 26 meters high, with four tall arch-roofed wings branching out diagonally across its square site. The subject of a competition in 2005, the market was re-opened in compliance with the general compositional principle of *psar thmey*, the Cambodian term for 'central market'. Compositionally, this emphasizes halls infilling the space between the diagonal structure of the older refurbished market building and the square outline of the site. The halls also restore a new uniform facade of a succession of arcades overlooking sidewalks and allowing for continual animation on the outside of the market, with a curvilinear walkway becoming a trading area open to the city. From its inception, the Central Market has exerted influence on the shape and urban space of Phnom Penh and as a model of covered markets. Despite its age and low maintenance due to a lack of resources in the interim years, the structure has retained its functional qualities. Four ideas appear to have guided the design of the market restoration and extension. They were, first, to integrate the market into its urban environment of roadways and ad hoc, mainly low-lying buildings. This reconciliation also required reorganization of the surrounding area, particularly for better continuity in pedestrian access and traffic. Parking areas and drop-off areas are now clearly defined, with this work being supported by the City of Paris. The second aim was enhancement of the historic building and especially the central domed space and arched side aisles. The third aim was to provide spaces with a good level of comfort, hygiene and safety, as well as satisfying a fourth aim of maintaining all the merchants on site. At its opening in 1937, the market was the biggest in Asia and is still one of the most distinctive in Southeast Asia. Over the years, it was supposedly used as a horse stable during the Khmer Rouge regime, becoming a market again in 1979 before becoming private in 1989. The renovation project by Arte Charpentier commenced in 2009. Unlike many regular markets in Cambodia, the Central Market today is still very traditional and reflective of Cambodian culture and modern development for locals and overseas visitors alike (Lombolt, 2016; and Thim, 2020).

The Siang Savan Theater in Luang Prabang, Laos, of 1950 and 1975 by anonymous architects is an Art Deco building in the broad area of the town constituting Luang Prabang's UNESCO World Heritage site. This site was listed in 1995 for unique and well-preserved architectural, religious and cultural heritage in a blend of urban and rural developments over centuries, including French colonial influence during the 19th and 20th centuries. The theater was built in the late 1950s and was the first bricks-and-mortar theater in the former capital of northern Laos. It was partially nationalized after the 1975 takeover by the Pathet Lao, meaning that the film fare on display favored productions from Vietnam, Russia and non-aligned India. Unfortunately, the Siang Savan has been closed since the 1990s, though for a brief period it was rehabilitated as a restaurant. Meaning 'heavenly sound' in Lao, the theater faces squarely onto the street at a corner and was entered via steps up to a raised narrow plinth creating a widened sidewalk. The facade today is in disrepair but is symmetrically composed of some three stories in height with a raised central parapet. In Art Deco form, curved overhangs protrude above the ground floor and the next floor above. Vertical grilles on the flat wall segments to either side further reinforce the overall centralized composition. Ornate Art Deco plaster moldings adorn the front facade and some express Buddhist themes. On the right-hand side adjoining the theater is a one-story traditional structure that juts out into the street further emphasizing the theater's widened outdoor entry area. The cornice molding with the Siang Savan name emblazoned on it suggests the theater was built by someone of Sino-Laotian origins, judging from the Chinese characters. From the Luang Prabang UNESCO citation, the theater would seem to qualify for warranted restoration due to its representativeness of a colonial style of architecture, authenticity to a colonial lifestyle and in keeping with colonial houses and other civic buildings mentioned in the earlier commentary. According to UNESCO guidelines, responsibility would fall to the national and local heritage committees (Jablon, 2009).

Siang Savan Theater, Luang Prabang, Laos, 1950 and 1975

Finally, the Asia Insurance Building in Singapore of 1955 by Ng Keng Siang represents a jump up in scale as it was one of the city's earliest skyscrapers and designed in Art Deco style. Originally intended to be only seven stories, in compliance with a request by authorities for a 4.5-meter back lane, the building was then redesigned rising to a height of 18 stories. Designed by one of Singapore's pioneer architects for one of the first local insurance companies at a time under the British when Singapore was pushing into the modern commercial sector, the project suffered from a sequence of setbacks that seem to have stemmed from its novelty. Although plans were approved in 1948, the soil conditions of the site required testing in Britain, delaying construction until approval in 1950. Then the contractor's application to store steel nearby was rejected. This was followed in 1951 during piling operations by the discovery that subsoils were softer than expected, requiring further investigation and delay. The steel skeleton erected by 1953, the year of the coronation of Queen Elizabeth II, first had to be used as a giant decorative statue of commemoration, before the building finally opened in 1955 at over double the cost calculated in 1947. In 2006, the building was sold and became Ascot Raffles Place. Though one of the tallest buildings for a long time, it has been hemmed in and overshadowed by taller adjacent structures. Nevertheless, the building retains most if not all of its key features, including its L-shaped structure on its corner site and Art Deco facades. These include a corner circular tower element that is capped by a stainless steel crown. This narrow tower is flanked on its two sides by Travertine marble cladding across repetitive rows of windows, with horizontal ledges providing sun-shading to the windows in between. The five-foot way around the corner perimeter was paved with a rare type of black Italian marble with whitish and gold veins. During the restoration and conservation of the building in 2006, 146 serviced residential units were created to be opened in 2008. Many of the building's original features were retained including a mosaic staircase and timber railing, the existing window frames with brass handles, while a gym and rooftop swimming pool were added. The restoration was undertaken by RSP Architects Planners & Engineers, winning an Urban Redevelopment Authority award in 2009 for architectural heritage and sensitivity for present-day use (Renuka, Chuan and Ying, 2014).

Asia Insurance Building, Singapore, 1955 and 2007

Shophouses and Terrace Houses

The Lorong 24A Shophouse Series in Singapore of 2012 by seven assorted architectural firms was a collective project executed by Pocket Projects, a local development consultancy firm engaged by Figment, a shophouse studio provider. The aim was to restore and conserve the eight shophouse facades in the row on Lorong Street and then to integrate contemporary designs and creative functionality into the traditional archetype of the Southeast Asian shophouse. The row was originally built in the 1920s and is located on Lorong Street, running between Geylang Road and Guillemard Road in the Geylang District of Singapore. Very popular in the property market, many of the former shophouses are now mixed-use and mostly with sizeable extensions in the rear of the original row. Today they serve a variety of purposes from places to stay to event venues. Number 5 within the ensemble, or row, is by Atria Architects and is a conversion into a three-bedroom house, well skylit and with maid's quarters. Number 9 by Liu and Wo Architects features a major ground-floor space with a water body. Number 11 by Linghao Architects has a major extension that syncopates the floor arrangement in the original shophouse by way of half-levels, stressing the vertical connectivity that is possible within the basic type. Number 13 by HYLA Architects also has a substantial rear extension, and features a vertical steel trellised volume that is skylit from above. Number 15 by Ong Ker-Shing Architects provides for an extensive gallery space on the ground floor. Number 17 by the ZARCH Collaboratives also has an extensive public area at the ground level, united vertically with the remainder of the structure via a prominent spiral staircase. Number 19, also by HYLA Architects, has a somewhat more modest and lower rear extension but features a skylit shophouse interior with a ground-floor water body. Finally, Number 21, by KD Architects with FARM, provides for a relatively seamless connection horizontally from the shophouse to the extension, which, in turn, is large (Figment, 2012).

Lorong 24A Shophouse Series, Geylang, Singapore, 2012

Lorong 24A Shophouse Series, Geylang, Singapore, 2012

The Space Block of the 36th District in Hanoi, Vietnam, of 2003, by Kazuhiro Kojima and the Kojima Lab of Tokyo University in collaboration with Hanoi University was an experimental, replicable prototype for construction on narrow and 70- to 80-meter-long commonplace lots in the city derived from earlier agricultural use. A test of the prototype was constructed on the grounds of the Civil Engineering Department of Hanoi University, comprised of six dwelling units and a density of some 220 plus units per hectare or about 1,000 persons per hectare at typical living densities. In the process, a so-called 'Space Block Methodology' was developed and deployed. In essence, this involved cutting into a volume four floors in height stretched the length of the narrow lot, with patios intertwined three-dimensionally and openings that created well-ventilated spaces. With stacking determined by computer fluid dynamic analysis, it was an extraction process that took place until a 50 percent fill ratio was met. Each unit was then designed to accommodate home-office functions, together with family apartments and live-in private rooms for elderly residents. Unit sizes ranged from 39 to 45 square meters in area and the overall Floor Area Ratio was 1.72. The illustrations on p. 218 depict the distribution of the unit types and their sectional qualities within the extracted volume. One obvious outcome was expression of light and shade in a pleasing and environmentally sympathetic manner (Huynh, 2003).

The Terrace House Renovation in Sungal Buloh, Malaysia, of 2015 by O2 Design Atelier is an outward expansion of an existing building on a standard 153, or so, square meter lot in a gated community in the Sungai Buloh area of Selangor, about 16 kilometers from downtown Kuala Lumpur. In contrast to typical terrace houses in the area, the front of the house was converted into a lush green porch area in which cars can park, rather than the converse, an arid parking area devoid of greenery. The interior of the two-story house was conformed to an open plan arrangement, particularly with regard to living, dining and kitchen areas. A double-height space was created in the center of the house, also for greenery and to allow natural light to penetrate. This led towards the traditional concept of a courtyard house and involved removal of part of the upper-floor slab and ceiling, in addition to roof tiles being replaced by clear polycarbonate tiles to admit natural light

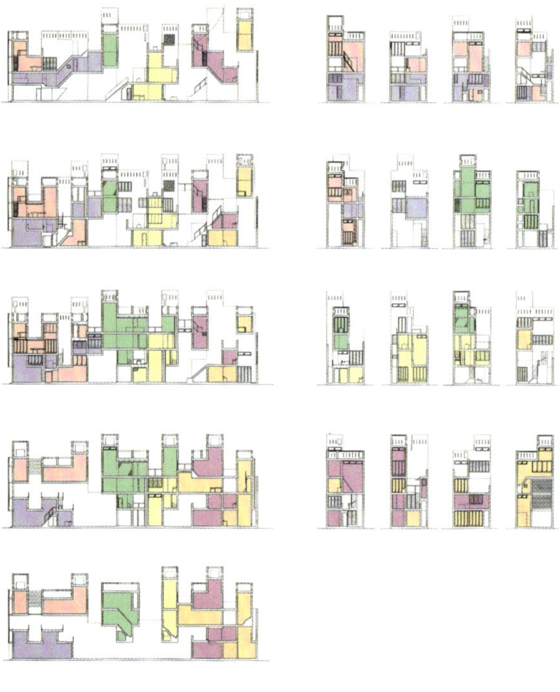

Space Block, 36th District, Hanoi, 2001

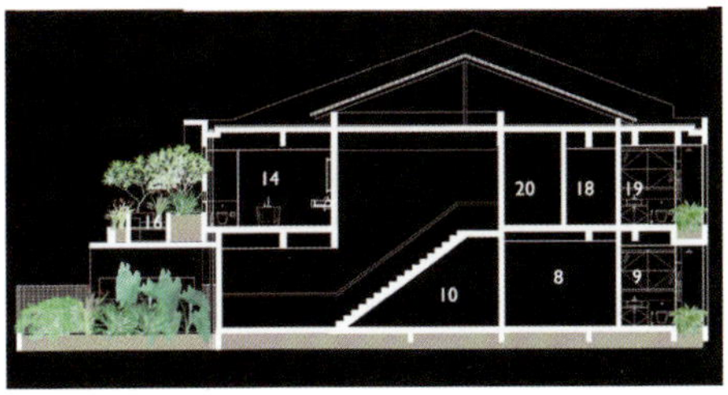

Terrace House Renovation, Sungai Buloh, Malaysia, 2015

into the space below. Several trees and shrubs were also planted within this central space. Additionally, natural ventilation was enhanced by replacing walls of the space at upper levels with full-length sliding windows. This also allowed for more substantial contact between upper and lower floors. In effect, the central area became 'the heart' of the house, so to speak. Upper-floor bedrooms also benefitted from immediate adjacency to green terraces, as did the stacked bathrooms at the rear. Almost at every turn on the by now crowded site, vegetated areas were introduced around a core ensemble of spaces that otherwise reflected the arrangement of a traditional terrace house (ArchDaily, 2016).

The Townhouse in District 7 of Ho Chi Minh City, Vietnam, of 2015 by MM++ Architects / MIMYA is a contemporary, narrow dwelling on a busy street, designed to reflect the traditional shophouse-terrace house typology. It has a modest built area of some 236 square meters and was constructed on a 4 by 17-meter lot, not untypical of its densely populated neighborhood. Rising a total of four stories, the ground floor also accommodates business activity during the day in the manner of a shophouse and with the owner's dwelling above, again like the typology. A notable feature of the front facade is a retractable shutter that when open provides shade to the ground-floor foyer of the house, while when closed still allows ventilation to occur. In fact, the operable and fixed shutters extend for two floors of the front facade. It is a relatively simple contrivance, typical of older Southeast Asian colonial architecture. The space of the house in the longitudinal direction is divided into three vertical segments, running from front to back, separated by the stairway riser and a full-length, skylit area also containing some vegetation at the ground level. This division follows the traditional pattern, with more public and main areas to the front of the house, more private and living areas in the central segment and bathrooms in the narrower rear segment. The fourth-floor rooftop at the front is a semi-enclosed terrace offering views over the neighborhood. The internal structure of exposed brick along one party wall is also noticeable, with the remainder of finishing in a commonplace contemporary palette of white plaster, metal and natural timber (Stevens, 2015).

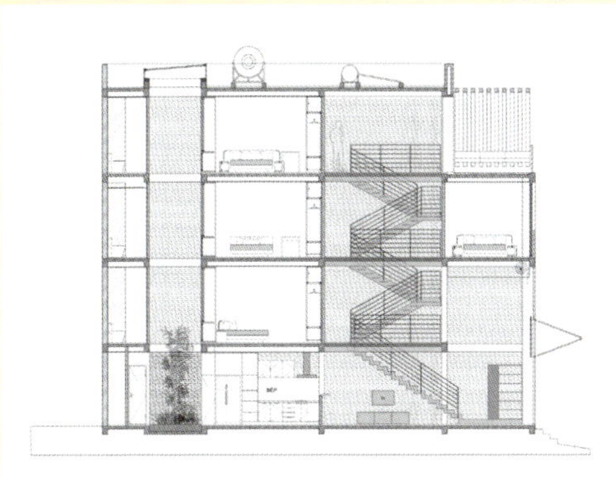

Townhouse, District 7, Ho Chi Minh City, 2015

Number 31 Boon Tat Street in Singapore of 2003 by Forum Architects is an unusual interpretation of the traditional shophouse and the first of its kind in a designated conservation area of the city-state. Although using contemporary materials of exposed concrete, broad glazed panels and metal screens, along with unusual angular geometries, the office, though now without a residence, conforms to a traditional shophouse in almost every other respect. Boon Tat Street is located in the downtown center of Singapore and was designated as a heritage site by the Urban Redevelopment Authority (URA). Indeed, it is one of the most centrally located hawker centers, allowing food vendors together with facilities for preparing and serving food in a hygienic surrounding, and aims to provide an 'authentic' tourist experience. Nevertheless, Number 31 is very much an office location, with almost half of its 720-odd square meters of built area being leased by the prominent firm of Collier International as a part of their recent consolidation of space in the downtown area. To this end, space within the building is divided into two sections. The first consists of the first and second floors, and the second consists of the third and fourth floors. These spaces are also largely devoid of partitions and the upper segment, in particular, is fluid and open. Voids in space carved out to convert inter-floor spaces serve as portals for natural light and to augment sight lines within the office. A top-lit stairway toward the front of the complex does depart from the original typology, although adapting it at the same time through the use of modern materials and methods of construction. The front facade along Boon Tat Street is probably the most unusual and uncharacteristic aspect of the building. It is made of vertical concrete fins that frame views of the outside while not corrupting interior layouts. This, together with the angular metal roof treatment and the five-foot way expressed as a series of *pilotis*, also affirms a contemporary interpretation of the traditional shophouse type (Wong, 2005, pp. 314–317; and Rowe and Kan, 2014, p. 148).

Number 31 Boon Tat Street, Singapore, 2003

Post-Coloniz-ations

Chapter 5

During the period of immediate and subsequent post-colonization in Southeast Asia, today's nation states were formed, though certainly not all at once nor necessarily with the same orientations or agendas, as sketched out in this book's introduction. Almost without exception though, modernization was embraced along with a sense of freedom and national pride. Social progress was anticipated along with emancipation and some other, although not necessarily all, features of modernity. Typically, many shared broad ambitions to make life's opportunities accessible to everyone, for instance, but the means by which this might be accomplished were subject to debate and, later, sometimes resulted in civil unrest and even sustained conflict. In addition, the commonly accepted idea that representation of the past was central to the symbolic constitution of a national consciousness was acknowledged but not completely. As has been described by others, we may be the historical objects in official narratives but that does not preclude us as subjects from contesting those narratives either in part or as a whole. Moreover, as times changed, different and even conflicting representations emerged. In the architecture produced during these post-colonial periods, as with other aspects of material and immaterial culture, the tensions, as well as the coming and going of dominant positions, were manifest in most places. In some situations, for instance, there was a strong officially backed assertion of a particular form of cultural modernism, adopted almost wholesale by a regime in power. In other cases, this adoption was a pointed reaction to what had gone on before, particularly during colonial eras, rather than a complete assertion of a new way forward. In addition, post-colonization of development allowed a more global modernism to be embraced, though rarely, if ever, without local inflection. In the Hegelian sense spoken of in the introduction, the 'present-future' was also looked at with regard to the 'present-past' (Hegel, 1966; Bhabha, 1995; Canclini, 1995; and Rowe, 2017).

Assertions of Cultural Modernism

Perhaps the strongest demonstration of the assertion of architectural modernism in Southeast Asia came on the heels of Ferdinand Marcos' ascension to power in the Philippines in 1965 and the end of the strongly U.S.-backed rule of the former colony. The major proponent was Leandro 'Lindy' Locsin, a local architect, although his brutalist style of modern architecture was prefaced by others, such as Roberto Novenario at his Villamor Hall at the University of the Philippines, Diliman Campus, of 1960. With its bold red brick-clad volumes intertwined with off-form concrete ones, the theater building made a sharp break from the sedate neo-classicism of earlier institutional and public buildings. As with other brutalist architecture, popular elsewhere in the 1950s through '70s, these volumes were associated with specific functional zones of the complex with the term 'brutalist' coming from the choice of '*béton brut*', or raw concrete, attributed to Le Corbusier,

Villamor Hall, University of the Philippines, Diliman Campus, 1960

Cultural Center Complex, Manila, 1969

as a dominant material. This, in turn, also coincided with the material's relative abundance and cheapness in the Philippines at the time. However, it was with Locsin's architecture from around 1967 onwards that the forward-looking brutalist style associated with the new regime became firmly instantiated. Of the numerous works he was to design during his illustrious career, arguably it is the Cultural Center Complex in Manila and particularly the National Theater (Tanghalang Pambansa) of 1969 that stands out most and epitomizes his sculptural concept of the 'floating volume'. The Complex was a 77-hectare arrangement of art and cultural buildings located in the newer area of Pasay City, Manila. The National Theater featured a huge plain rectilinear block covered in travertine, some 12 meters high and cantilevered on three sides atop a massive podium, looking for all the world as if it were floating in space. This appearance was further enhanced by the sweep of the vehicular ramp rising up to the raised lobby area beneath the 'floating volume' and inscribing a large pool of water within its bounds. Locsin then went on in a similar vein to design the Philippine International Convention Center in 1976 and the Integrated Bar of the Philippines in 1979. Other architects of this same brutalist persuasion, at least at the time, included Carlos Arguelles, Federico Ilustre, Pablo Antonio and Cresenciano de Castro. By 1986, however, democracy and a renewed architectural respect for traditional Filipino elements began to appear (Banham, 1966; Lico, 2010; and Girard, 2021).

National Theater, Manila, 1969

Philippine International Convention Center, 1976

Istiqlal Mosque, Jakarta, 1978

Although with a somewhat less exclusive purchase on a particular style, the architecture in Indonesia under President Sukarno was undeniably modernist and openly nationalistic in its projection of pride in the newfound independence. The Istiqlal Mosque in Jakarta is a case in point. Commissioned in 1955 as the result of a competition won by Friedrich Silaban, a Christian architect, and with the laying of a foundation stone by Sukarno in 1961, it was not completed until 1978. Located around the Merdeka Square in central Jakarta, opposite the Jakarta Cathedral, it was intended to symbolize the peaceful co-existence of religions in the newly independent nation. Notable also for its scale, the mosque is the largest in Southeast Asia and the sixth-largest in the world. Built in the manner of a modernist project in materials and construction techniques, it also conforms to a Middle Eastern style of a Friday mosque with requisite dome, courtyards, gardens and minaret. In other words, it looks the part, so to speak, in a generally expected sense, making clear to the world at large that Indonesia is a Muslim country, at least by majority suffrage. The mosque is imbued with symbolism, including the twelve stainless steel-clad pillars supporting the dome and representing the Prophet's birthday. Its five interior floors clearly represent the five pillars of Islam and the 45-meter diameter of the dome commemorates the original proclamation of independence in 1945. Further, the term *istiqlal* itself means independence and its seven entrances denote the 'seven heavens' of Islamic cosmology. The 9.5-hectare site of the complex is replete with surrounding gardens and water bodies on the former Wilhelmina Park, introducing a certain tranquility to such a central location. Capable of accommodating 200,000 worshippers, it functions as a communal space for society and as a witness of architectural development at that point in Indonesia's history (Purba, 2010; and Dhiracitta, 2020).

When Burma, now Myanmar, gained independence from Britain in 1948, architectural production in a variety of foreign and local hands began to radiate the modern attitude of the newly independent nation. In the span of time from 1948 to 1962, when a military coup brought an end to the early democracy, several striking modernist projects were completed in Rangoon, now Yangon, by American, Soviet and British architects, as well as locals. In the late 1950s, for instance, the Tripitaka Library by the American Benjamin Polk was completed. Commissioned by U Nu, the first post-independence prime minister, it was built primarily in concrete because of the scarcity of building materials in a poor country. So was the Inya Lake Hotel of 1962, with its nautical themes, by the Soviet pair of Viktor Andreyev and Kaleriya Kislova. Perhaps most prominent and expressively modernist was the University of Medicine or formerly the Engineering College of Rangoon University of 1956 by the British architect, Raglan Squire. Funded through the Colombo Plan, which was to convince countries in the Asia-Pacific region to remain politically non-aligned during the Cold War, the building was most notable for its sheer and pristine rectilinear slab form, clad in precast panels of small, coffin-shaped windows. These windows, in turn, formed outward-opening louvers for ventilation, with blue and green glazing that introduced a dappled effect inside, much like among jungle foliage. Backlit at night, the building glowed appealingly. Raised on *pilotis*, the front entrance was clearly delineated by an upward-turned canopy. Squire's Technical High School, also of 1956, by contrast, was a low-rise structure with an arched sequence of bays across its front facade and with two classroom wings raised on columns. In addition, as noted, local architects like U Tun Than and U Kyaw Min entered the fray, designing in a distinctly modernist style. Indeed, the former was among the first graduates from the university in 1958 and designed the multi-storied Yangon Children's Hospital with its novel shading devices on the facade. The latter was responsible for the simple but stately Thakin Kodaw Hmaing Mausoleum of 1966 (Oka, Bansai and Fox, 2016).

Tripitaka Library, Rangoon, 1950s

Inya Lake Hotel, Rangoon, 1962

University of Medicine (formerly the Engineering College), Rangoon University, 1956

Thakin Kodaw Hmaing Mausoleum, Rangoon, 1966

Other Imaginaries

During the post-independence years in Southeast Asia there were also pointed architectural reactions to what was and had been in place, but of a more radical kind than the assertion of modernism described above. Typically, they were rather more spasmodic and isolated, but nevertheless imagined other futures. Among these was the Jengki Style in Indonesia during the late 1950s and into the early 1960s, occurring at much the same time as the nationalistic modernism of the Sukarno regime. A corruption of 'Yankee Style', this Jengki architecture reflected the U.S. influence on architecture, especially in the tropical interpretation of American post-war suburban housing. Visceral in its geometric acrobatics, it was a palpable expression of a political spirit of freedom translated into an architecture that was starkly different from what the Dutch had done before. Among other places, it was manifested in Kebayoran Baru, a district of southern Jakarta that was developed as a satellite town in 1955 to house the middle-class staff of the Bataafsche Petroleum Maatschappij (BPM). There, houses were angular in configuration and made use of strongly sloped roofs, intersecting and almost colliding volumes, along with a playful use of color and very much the rejection of the stricter cubic forms of the Dutch. In fact, Jengki

Houses in the Jengki Style (Yankee Style), Southern Jakarta, 1955

or Yankee Style, as the names suggest, was derived from the Googie Style in the United States, which became popular from about 1945 to the early 1970s. The term was apparently coined by the architect John Lautner, who designed Googie's Coffee Shop on L.A.'s Sunset Boulevard in 1949. The style gave rise to extensions of Streamline Moderne into an architecture influenced by car culture, jets and the Space Age (Tjahjono and Miksic, 2003; and Hess, 2004).

The Grand Hotel in Taipei, Taiwan, of 1973 by Yang Cho-Cheng represents another sharp architectural reaction to a state of affairs that went in another direction, leapfrogging, as it were, over expected modernist leanings towards a lost but glorious past. Located on Yuanshan Mountain in the Zhongshan District of Taipei, the hotel was completed shortly after Taiwan and the Republic of China ceased to represent China as a member of the United Nations in 1971, who from then on recognized the People's Republic of China instead. For Chiang Kai-Shek this was a final break with mainland China and, when it came to building new representative architecture, an excuse to reach backwards in time to a well-established architectural past. After all, the architecture of the Nationalist period over which he presided conformed, where possible, to the soubriquet of 'glorifying China's past while building in a modern manner'. The hotel is one of the tallest of all Chinese classically styled buildings at 87 meters in height. With its vermillion color and prominent upturned gable roof, it is almost a caricature of the traditional Chinese hall typology. Further, the decor in each of the eight guest levels spread across a total of 490 rooms, represents a different Chinese Dynasty. Reputedly suggested by Madame Chiang, the hotel's ostensible purpose was to host foreign dignitaries to Taipei in a luxurious style befitting them in a new republic. Recent rediscovery of secret underground passages built to evacuate Chiang Kai-Shek in the event of an emergency only underlined the nagging weakness of claims to China. The eastern route led to the 823 Artillery Battery Memorial Park on the edge of the Keelung River, where a seaplane was moored to evacuate Chiang and his entourage, whereas the western route led to more the hospitable grounds of Jiantan Park. Apparently, kinks in these routes were intended to frustrate pursuing troops from trying to shoot an escaping Chiang (Harding, 2010).

**Googie-Style Coffee Shop,
Southern California, 1950s**

Grand Hotel, Taipei, 1973

Perhaps even more declarative in expressing national ambition, the Istana Nurul Iman in Brunei of 1984, by Leandro Locsin, is the world's largest living residence of a head of state. Construction of the palace coincided with Brunei's independence from Britain and symbolizes the absolute rule of the Sultan, who has insisted on the adoption of Shariah Law. The dimensions of the building also indicative of the sheer wealth of the small nation. Standing in a bucolic setting on the banks of the Brunei River, it is a huge complex of some 200,000 square meters of space, replete with a gold-domed mosque with four gold-topped minarets, the residence of the Sultan and his famous car collection, as well as the Prime Minister's Office and, essentially, the seat of Brunei's government. Locsin's design was an attempt to unify Brunei's Islamic and Malay architectural traditions. The mosque and other related elements clearly refer to the former, whereas the use of Austronesian-looking curvilinear pointed roofs functions as a referent to the latter. The overall structure comprises some 17 floors, including underground space, and rises above the surrounding trees. The interior, designed by Khuan Chew, is a mix of traditional elements with an ultra-luxurious modern decor (Saunders, 2002).

Finally, at the other end of an architectural spectrum, the work of Jimmy C. S. Lim in Malaysia is a consummate rejection of much of the region's modern architecture and a turn in the direction of low-energy tropical building, conservation and adaptive re-use, sustainable development and the use of recycled materials and traditional construction techniques. Though certainly an able modernist to begin with, after returning to Malaysia in 1972 and establishing CSL Associates, his own firm, in 1978, Lim began to experiment with and propose this sustainable architectural direction. One of the first instances came with his own house in Teluk Pulai in the southwest of Kuala Lumpur. Over time it went through as many as nine iterations, each aimed at improved environmental and material performance. Nowadays, this direction is epitomized by the Salinger House of 1992 by Lim while at CSL Associates. It was a home built as a weekend retreat in a rural district and for a client who wanted to embrace Malaysian heritage and their Muslim faith. Lifted on stilts, the house barely touches the ground, allowing the natural contours of the land to continue.

Istana Nurul Iman, Brunei, 1984

Salinger House, Kuala Lumpur, 1992

Oriented to capture the prevailing winds, it is entirely naturally ventilated. Given a client brief that emphasized the three activities of cooking, dining and living, they became integrated into the house plans and led to another trilogy of living, dining and a terrace. Expressed as two equilateral triangles abutting each other, private and public areas were separated by changes in floor levels. Within the arrangement, one of the walls faced Mecca, reflecting the orientation of the traditional Malay house and the client's Muslim faith. No metal connectors were used in the construction, with traditional materials and joinery techniques used instead (Malaysia Architecture, 2012).

Global Modernism with Local Inflections

Among the Southeast Asian nations, those in the former French Indochina are clear examples of a turn towards global modernism but with local architectural inflections either by way of literal atmosphere, past cultural influence or both. In Vietnam, for instance, architectural modernism appears to be related to a found freedom to live in the absence of colonial pressures and with the promise of social progress and a capacity to meet the modern age head-on, as it were. Nevertheless, there was also an acute awareness of the tropical environmental circumstances of the country and, to only a slightly lesser extent, some aspects of its past cultural heritage. Therefore, the modernist architecture, especially during the 1950s and '60s and before the American conflict, was both forthrightly modern and yet also locally inflected, though in a less obviously backward leaning way than in, say, nearby Thailand or Cambodia. The Independence Palace in South Vietnam of 1966, for example, was intended as an expression of national identity and of independence from colonial rule. Designed by Ngo Viet Thu as the result of a competition, it was placed on the foundations of the former Norodom Palace, which had been the Governor's residence and headquarters since the 19th century. It also took on the classical organization and symmetrical facade arrangement of the former palace,

Independence Palace, Saigon, 1966

but with a two-story brise-soleil made of precast concrete panels in an abstract tetrahedral pattern. In addition, Chinese ideographic characters informed the facade composition, and the bas-reliefs under the windows of the bays at both ends of the building were of local figures. Similarly, the General Sciences Library of 1971 by Nguyen Huu Thien had a screen facade in cast concrete, with an intricate decorative pattern of ideographic figures. It was a public library in District 1 of Saigon, now Ho Chi Minh City, providing local lending services and reference support. In addition to brise-soleils, double-wall configurations again for climatic reasons as noted in the earlier colonial period, were deployed, sometimes along with the sun-screen either forward or recessed on the facade's double face. The eight-story Vinatex office building also in District 1 of Saigon by Nguyen Quang Nhac, for example, featured a brise-soleil grid in front of the structural facade of the building (Schenck and Garel, 2020).

As alluded to, the situation in post-independence Cambodia was somewhat differently inclined though still modernist. The ruler, Prince Sihanouk, commissioned some 100 or so buildings after independence in 1953 and before he was overthrown by the military in 1970. He also did much of this in collaboration with the local architect Vann Molyvann, who had worked under Le Corbusier prior to returning to Cambodia around 1964 to take on the National Sports Complex on a 39-hectare site, comprised of a 60,000-seat stadium, an 8,000-seat indoor sports hall and an Olympic-sized swimming pool, among other facilities. In the general layout of the site though, Molyvann also incorporated *barays* in the manner of the reservoirs of Angkor during the Khmer Empire, together with raised walkways and walls. Much like the rectangular Srah Srang of the 10th century, measuring 700 by 350 meters, they are prominent in the National Sports Complex landscape. Subsequently at the Institute of Foreign Languages in Phnom Penh, Molyvann pursued a similar homage to Angkor with the entry passage along an elevated walkway. In yet another modern building, the Independence Monument, there was certainly emulation of the Arc de Triomphe in Paris but also striking resemblance to the central tower of Angkor Wat. In all these projects, the materiality, functional form and expression of the buildings was orthodoxly modernist.

General Sciences Library, Saigon, 1971

National Sports Complex, Phnom Penh, Cambodia, 1964

The outer edges of the National Stadium, for example, canted outwards, revealing the ribbed underside pattern of the supporting structure and the evenly spaced cast-concrete stairs leading into the stadium. Similarly, the stark contrast between seating, corner roof supports and glazed walls was very much an architectural essay in form following function and materiality following both in the sports hall. Laos enjoyed a similar effusive architectural moment once the socialist project that was set in motion in 1975 subsided after both the French and American wars. The National Assembly Building of 1990 by Hongkad Souvannavong was a modernist building materially and in the expression of horizontal bands of spatial volumes. However, the prominent pyramidal central portion of the facade closely mirrored the symmetrical and tall tower arrangement of the Buddhist Wat Chan in Vientiane constructed in 1565. The later Lao National Cultural Hall of 2000 also had a similar profile in its four-story structure, with soaring columns around the central entry (Pholsena, 2006; Brookes, 2007; and Balian, 2015).

Though also very much in the spirit of buildings asserting architectural modernism, at least of a brutalist kind, the People's Park Complex and the Golden Mile Complex, both of 1973 and both by DP Architects in Singapore, were simultaneously designed to capture the liveliness and mixed-use environment of traditional commercial environments, albeit in a vertical manner. Designed by the team of William Siew Wai Lim, together with Tay Kheng Soon and Koh Seow Chuan, the retail commercial environments, in particular, catered to small merchandizers as in times gone by and created an animated, bazaar-like atmosphere. They were both at the very forefront of Singapore's attempts at integrating multiple operations into mixed-use real-estate developments. The People's Park Complex, adjacent to Chinatown as its name suggests, has a large atrium space with a complex layering of floor planes and dramatic staircases. It provided an early prototype for Singapore's now fashionable 'all under one roof shopping'. It was capped by a slender 25-floor residential slab tower with a roof component of shared facilities like a creche and open-air play space, also much like its offshoots. The Golden Mile Complex is located on Beach Road in the Kallang District of Singapore. It is a linear building in the manner of Le Corbusier and Soria y Mata. It is renowned for its sloping slab form that slices through

Golden Mile Complex, Singapore, 1973

People's Park Complex, Singapore, 1973

Singapore Conference Hall and Malaysian Federation Office, 1970

State Mosque of Negeri Sembilan, Seremban, Malaysia, 1970

the structure and provides natural light and ventilation into the heart of the building. Its architecture bears some resemblances to the Japanese Metabolist Movement, which materialized in 1960. Lately, it has become an ethnic enclave of Thais and something of a slum. Both buildings are primarily built of concrete and are brutalist in style, as noted earlier. They also both occupy rectangular sites of much the same size, around a hectare (Powell, 2004; and Wong, 2005, pp. 158–169).

Prior to these buildings, William Lim left his position at James Ferrie and Partners and started the Malayan Architects Co-Partnership (MAC) together with Lim Chong Keat and Chen Voon Fee. Their breakthrough project came in winning a competition in 1961 for the Singapore Conference Hall and Trade Union House (Dewan Persidangan Singapura) prior to both Singapore's and the Malaysian Federation's independence. Other projects followed and MAC opened an office in Kuala Lumpur before disbanding in 1967, with William Lim going off to join DP Architects. The Singapore Conference Hall was completed in 1965 and inaugurated by Prime Minister Lee Kuan Yew a couple of months after Singapore gained independence. It was a five-story building in two parts, with the trade union accommodated on one side and the conference hall on the other and both accessed separately. It was expressly designed for the local tropical conditions, particularly through the use of a cantilevered roof and terraces providing for shade and natural ventilation. In keeping with MAC's precepts, it also reflected Malayan characteristics in these regards, but was clearly modernist, with its expansive butterfly roof and compact, projecting spatial volumes. A little later on, in 1963, MAC won another competition, namely to design the State Mosque of Negeri Sembilan, located in Seremban, a city south of the Malaysian capital Kuala Lumpur. Again, their proposal encapsulated traditional architectural values and was modern and innovative in construction and material application. Built between 1967 and 1970, the formal crux of the scheme was a prominent roof made up of a series of nine concrete conoids referencing the gable roofs of traditional Minangkabau architecture of the region. Also, the choice of nine was a clear reference to the name of the location, meaning 'nine states' in Malay. Overall, there was a conscious association with both international style and indigenous vernacular architecture (Edwards and Keys, 1996; and Rasdi and Hussain, 2006).

Contemporary Projects

Several broad trends emerged among the post-independence architecture built across Southeast Asia. The first was explicit recognition and sustainable responsiveness to the tropical climate of the region. The second was the adoption of a more or less global architectural modernism as a liberating expression of independence. The third involved almost the opposite, namely an expression that referenced indigenous vernacular of one kind or another. Also during this period, urbanization accelerated in most places, resulting in high-rise development, as elsewhere in the world. Several iconic examples of high-rise architecture occurred in Southeast Asia. During the 1950s, the urbanized proportion of populations among nations in the region was low. All, with the exception of Singapore which, anyway, was still part of Malaya, were still below 30 percent urban. By the 1970s, when post-colonization was well underway everywhere, all but Singapore, Brunei and parts of Polynesia were still below 50 percent urban, rising by 2010 to include Singapore, Brunei, Indonesia, Malaysia, Thailand, Taiwan and Polynesia. Among these nations, Indonesia, Thailand and Taiwan saw a doubling or more from 1975, as shown in the graph opposite.

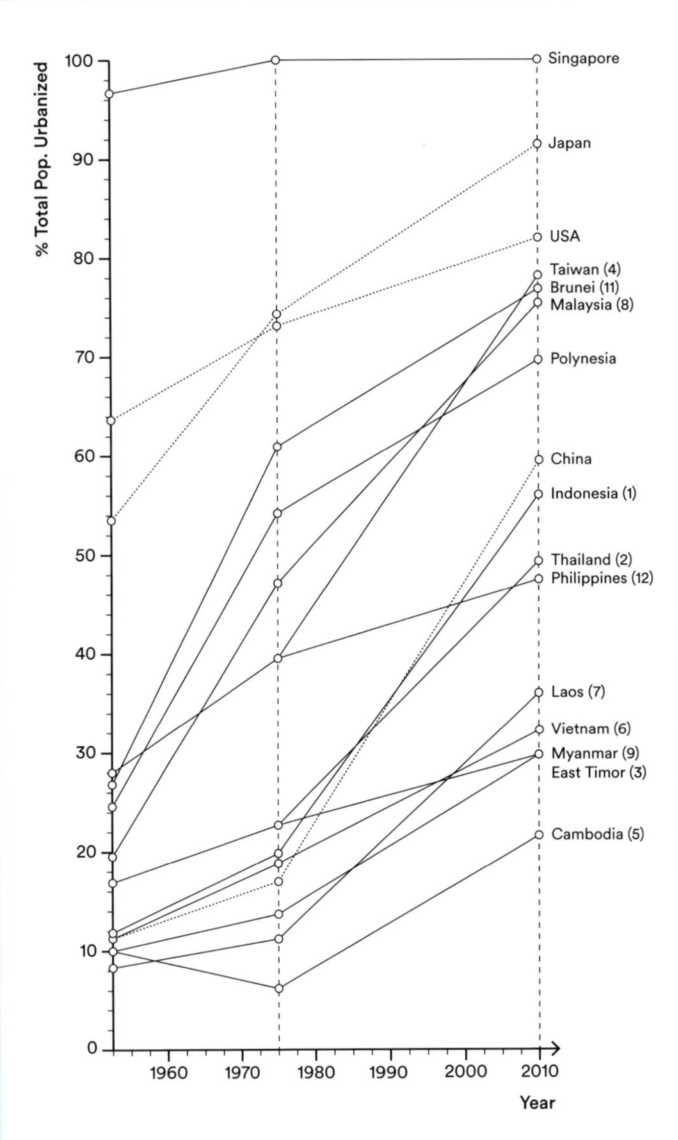

Proportion of Total Population Urbanized by Nation, 1950–2010

Nevertheless, for nations in the mainland areas of the region, like Cambodia, Vietnam, Laos and Myanmar, population-based proportions of urbanization were still low and below 50 percent. Shifting to major cities in the region, several like Jakarta and Bangkok are very populous with over 10 million inhabitants each, although not necessarily very dense compared to, say, Manila and Yangon, which both have above 40,000 people per square kilometer. Clearly, high-rise development all over the world is influenced by a number of factors such as property scarcity, prevailing urban density, relatively high rates of urbanization and, of course, local economic capacities and aspirations associated with the making of iconic buildings. Therefore, in places like Singapore and Kuala Lumpur in Malaysia and, perhaps less so, Jakarta in Indonesia, tall and potentially iconic high-rise commercial or residential towers might be expected as circumstances in each place match, sufficiently, influential factors. To a lesser extent, Taipei in Taiwan and Bangkok in Thailand would also seem to be rife for high-rise buildings, although overall urban densities are not conspicuously high. Extremely dense cities like Manila and Yagon, by contrast, already have stocks of high-rise buildings but have relatively lower rates of urbanization as well as available economic capacities (United Nations, 2018).

Beyond Brutalism

The 100 Walls Church in Cebu City, the Philippines, of 2013 by Carlos Arnaiz Architects (CAZA) is located on the southern fringe of the city and can accommodate some 1,100 worshippers. The overall space of the church is around 8,900 square meters, though set into a landscaped site of 14 garden components. The area occupied by the church proper was also raised 3.5 meters to avoid adverse effects of local flooding. The plan of the church is spatially defined more or less symmetrically around a central axis, as are many churches. The central area of rows and pews is rectangular in plan and elongated along the central axis in the east-west direction. The dominant elements, however, are the numerous concrete walls that define the spaces of the church and also imbue it with its very particular character and expression, away from the earlier brutalist architecture of the Philippines, even while using the same basic material. Each wall is different though facing in the same direction. When viewed from an east-west direction, for instance, the image of the church from the outside is opaque, whereas in the north-south direction it is far more transparent. The choice of different concrete walls was motivated by the relative cheapness and abundance of the material, given that the structure was built on a very tight budget, and because the singularity of each wall via differences in width and height, but with the same thickness, could also be achieved and even reinforced by slight differences, if any, in craftsmanship. The positioning of the walls was according to an underlying grid related to the rectangular array of rows and pews at the building's center. Rather than being surrounded by walls on all four sides, 'rooms' were defined as interconnected voids in the overall arrangement. The obvious maze-like character served the purpose of expressing religion through the mysteries and stories of individuals and without the immediate legibility of the appearance of a church. Just as Jesus Christ wandered through the Garden of Gethsemane, so worshippers make their own journey across the site, through the garden and the church. The homogeneity of white walls and the multitude of doors is there to remind worshippers that there are many paths to being drawn into the faith. Further, each wall's difference is a manifestation of both the diversity of life and the fact that humans belong to a family and a singular species (Fraser, 2015).

The Cherry Orchard Cemetery in Yilan County, Taiwan, of 2005 to 2014 by Huang Sheng-Yuan and Fieldoffice Architects is a remarkable synthesis of building and topographic landscape that gives '*béton brut*' or 'raw concrete' new meaning. Yilan County covers a plain in northern Taiwan on its eastern side. Although only 40 kilometers, or so, east of Taipei, it is separated by the central mountain spine down the center of the island and is a rural world apart from the dense urbanity to the west. It is where architect Huang settled in 1994. The Cherry Orchard Cemetery was situated some way up the 750-meter-high Hunglodei, also known as Nanshijiao Mountain, and overlooks the Langyang plain below. The cemetery consists of four parts. The first is the Jin-Mei pedestrian bridge that links to the project site and provides access. It is in the form of what has been termed a 'parasite bridge' by being suspended over the side of an existing road bridge across the divide. The second component is a support building and

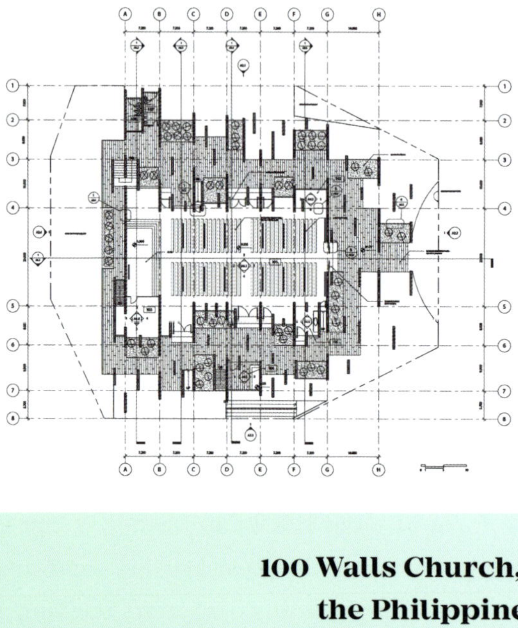

100 Walls Church, Cebu City, the Philippines, 2013

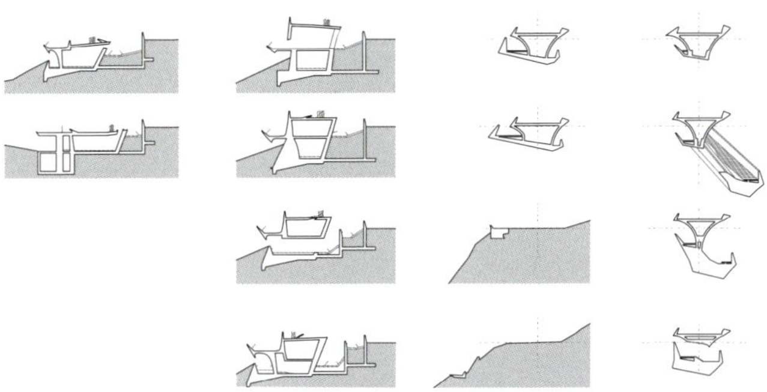

Cherry Orchard Cemetery, Yilan County, Taiwan, 2008

visitor center that follows the hillside topography, with spaces unfolding across the terraced slopes. The third component is the interment part itself, expressed in two different forms. One, designed by Atelier Zo with Takano Landscape Planning, is precise in layout in an orderly manner across the landscape. A second by Huang incorporates seven monoliths that step down and across the landscape and shape it at the same time. A series of U-shaped columbaria make up these shapes with outer edges made of slate. The cemetery is not zoned by religion nor family areas and is organized where the terrain is gently managed with retaining walls following natural contours and with the placement of vegetation including trees optimizing *feng shui* conditions of the site. Death is not spoken of for fear that it would occur. Consequently, Cherry Orchard Cemetery neither celebrates nor ignores it by skillfully integrating its architecture into the landscape. The fourth component is the Chiang Wei-Shui Memorial for the anti-colonist activist and public figure who fought the Japanese and promoted Taiwanese culture and well-being. Throughout, the concrete on site predominantly uses rough shuttering with broad sweeps and organic curves (Goodwin, 2016).

The AM Residence in Jakarta, Indonesia, of 2012 by Andra Matin as his own home, is located on a trapezoidal site in the Bintaro area in the south of the city. The corner site adjoins a small nearby community park and is also vegetated. Taking advantage of this, the house is designed as an element in the landscape. A baobab tree, for instance, is in the narrow courtyard at the center of the house and the pool and other exterior elements differ from the existing landscape. Overall, the house is compact and follows a clean modern architectural approach with a concrete structure that is manifested in many of the interior and exterior finishes, as well as a painted local brick cladding in places, which produced a dappled pattern across otherwise expansive flat facade surfaces. Throughout, distinctions between indoors and outdoors are blurred, particularly in the openness of the floor plans. Programmatically, the configuration of spaces within the residence is defined in layers of ascending privacy, beginning with the service and semi-public functions of the ground level. Shared family activities are then located above, including a first-floor wooden deck serving the living and dining area. Next, the private realm of bedrooms follows

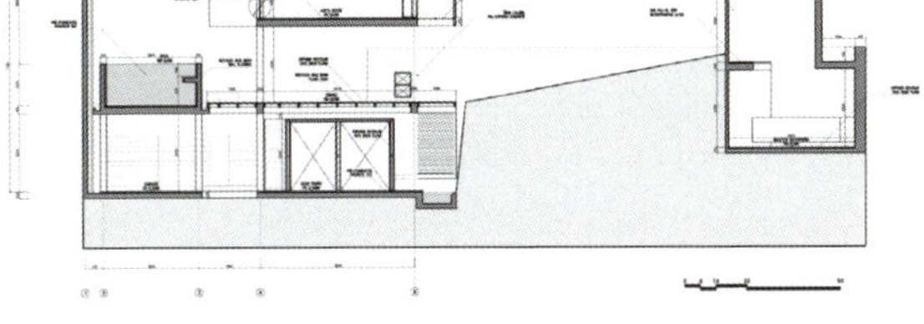

AM Residence, Jakarta, 2012

and with relatively compact spaces in order to minimize the use of air-conditioning support required. Finally, a grass-covered flat roof provides for family outdoor space. All these layers are then connected to form a veritable *promenade architecturale* through the residence. Indeed, this house and the remainder of Andra Matin's work present a contemporary interpretation of traditional values, including living with landscapes, inhabiting tropical circumstances and making use of readily available and local materials (Sopandi and Hartanto, 2015).

The Satay by the Bay Food Court in Singapore of 2012 by KUU and Linghao Architects is comprised of two clusters of street food-style stalls, close-by seating areas in a quiet corner of Gardens by the Bay, adjacent to the Marina Bay Channel in the center of the city. A joint venture largely between the architects Kok-Meng Tan and Satoko Saeki, these concrete-roofed structures successfully re-create a partial home for the small family-run businesses, street hawkers and outdoor living environments like those found in Singapore's traditional Little India, Chinatown and Arab Street. The food court is a low-rise and lush building ensemble covered in curvaceous concrete. The shelters are ergonomic and undulating on slim cylindrical columns, ventilated by sea breezes and large ceiling fans. Other ordinary local materials have also been brought to bear, including cement, plywood and recycled bamboo. The built area covers some 2,000 square meters, with the plant-covered concrete roofs mimicking the surrounding canopy of the Gardens by the Bay site. More locally, a landscape of ferns and creepers is navigated by pathways between plant-filled eco-ponds. The roofs of the shelters were then used to direct rainwater to these ponds in order to maintain them in a natural, sustainable condition. Open on all sides, the roof of the food court is also punctuated by organically shaped openings, further providing natural light and ventilation to those below the curvilinear concrete roof (San, 2013; and Hall and Koren, 2021).

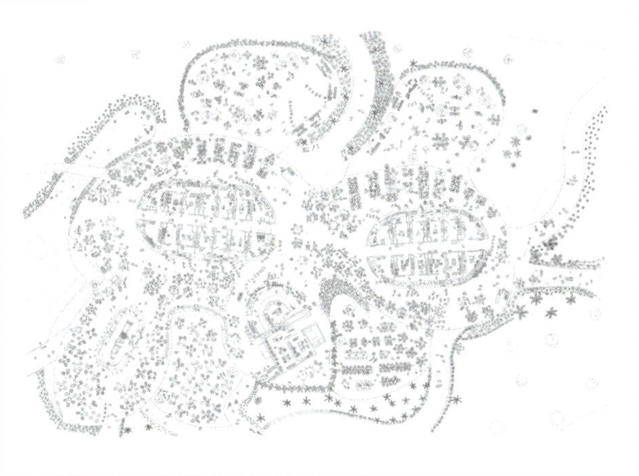

Satay by the Bay Food Court, Singapore, 2012

Morodok Techo National Stadium,
Phnom Penh, Cambodia, 2021

The Morodok Techo National Stadium in Cambodia of 2021 by China IPPR International Engineering is scheduled to be used to host the 2023 Southeast Asia Games. It is the main facility in a new 94-hectare sports complex being built about 18 kilometers north of central Phnom Penh. The complex site area covers a single urban block and is rectangular in plan layout, with the stadium in a prominent, almost central location surrounded by other sports facilities and with adjacent tower buildings for housing athletes and for administrative and related offices. Among the other facilities beside the stadium are a badminton and table tennis venue, a gymnastics hall, a multi-purpose sports facility, a sports hall and a gymnasium. The overall attendance capacity of the complex is of the order of 100,000 spectators. The stadium was designed by the Chinese and Cambodian technical team to resemble a sailing ship and to commemorate Cambodia-China relations in ancient times, including Admiral Zheng He's historic voyages to Cambodia and the rest of Southeast Asia. It has a seating capacity of 75,000 and was funded by a donation from the People's Republic of China. The stadium stands are about 40 meters tall, with seating divided into three levels, crowned by a lightweight translucent roof of petal-shaped panels, after the *rumduol* or national flower of Cambodia. Located on a 16-hectare site, the stadium's elliptical plan is punctuated at either end by prow-shaped, upturning towers some 99 meters tall, alluding to the Cambodian greeting gesture, *sampeah,* of clasped hands, similar to the Thai *wai* gesture and more generally to gestures of Indian origin. Other symbolic references are also made in the complex site. The stadium is ringed by a moat of Angkor-style water bodies, for instance, echoing the older stadium of 1963 by Vann Molyvann described earlier in the book, and of course the layout of Angkor Wat. The stadium is accessed by two prominent walkways, perpendicular to each other, again as at Angkor. Far from being brutalist in architectural style, the stadium has graceful, light-flowing lines to its largely concrete structure (Vorajee, 2019).

Climatic Turns

The Mesiniaga Tower in Petaling Jaya of 1992 by Ken Yeang is the IBM headquarters building near Kuala Lumpur and is one of the first contemporary medium-to-tall buildings in Southeast Asia and beyond to incorporate modern bioclimatic principles in its design. In fact, it culminated architect Ken Yeang's ten-year research into the topic, which was becoming influential throughout the world at the same time. The structure of the 15-story circular tower is supported by eight columns outside the building envelope, allowing maximum flexibility for interior layout and design. A naturally ventilated elevator and stairway core is located on the eastern side of the building, effectively blocking intense morning sun. Vegetation has been introduced into the project at the base and through a series of landscaped 'sky courts' conspicuously open on the cylindrical facade. Apart from facilitating natural ventilation, these 'courts' also connect building occupants with nature and provide deep shading of adjacent interior spaces. In addition, aluminum louvers on the facade, placed in accordance with the position of the particular portion of the facade on the equatorial solar path, further prevent solar heat gain. The western aspect of the building is then shielded by broad bands to block out harsh afternoon sun. The crown of tubular steel at the top of the building supports photovoltaic panels, supplementing electrical needs within the building, while also shading a rooftop recreation area and swimming pool. The placement of open-plan office landscapes next to the windows also maximizes the use of natural light illuminating the inside of the building (Yeang, 1996; and Douglass-Jaimes, 2015).

The hotel complex PARKROYAL on Pickering in Singapore of 2013 by WOHA was one of several works by this pioneering local office to advocate for a 'green city' in terms of the sheer amount of vegetation on a given site. Located on Pickering on a narrow rectangular site on the edge of Singapore's central business district, this 'hotel as garden' more than doubled the site's potential area of greenery. With a total close to 30,000 square meters of space, the profile of the building is divided into relatively distinct components in its vertical rise. The first five floors are composed of the public functions of verandah and restaurant,

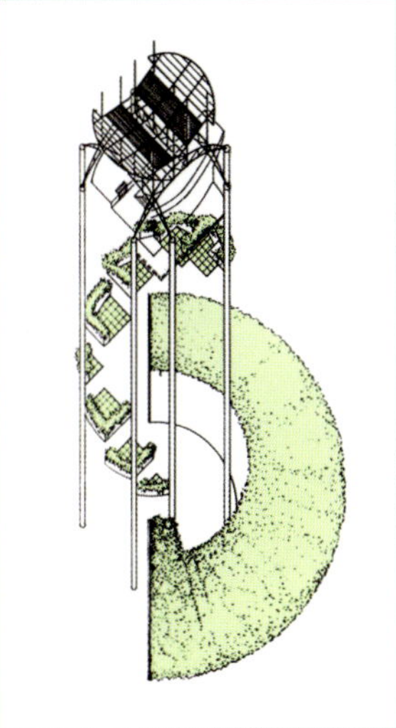

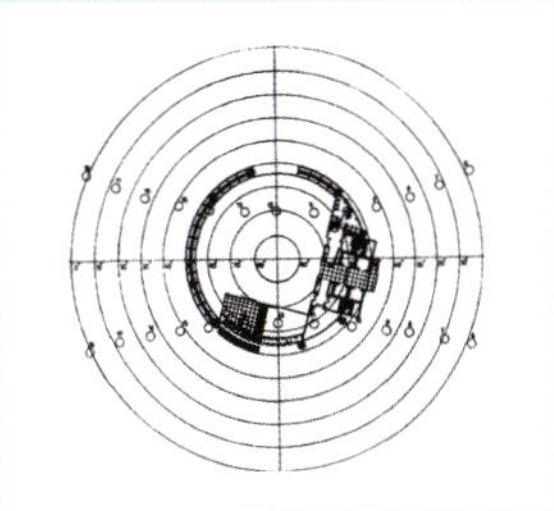

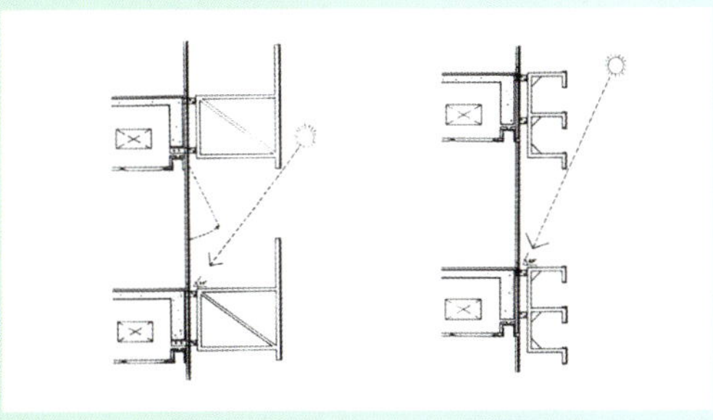

Mesiniaga Tower, Petaling Jaya, Malaysia, 1992

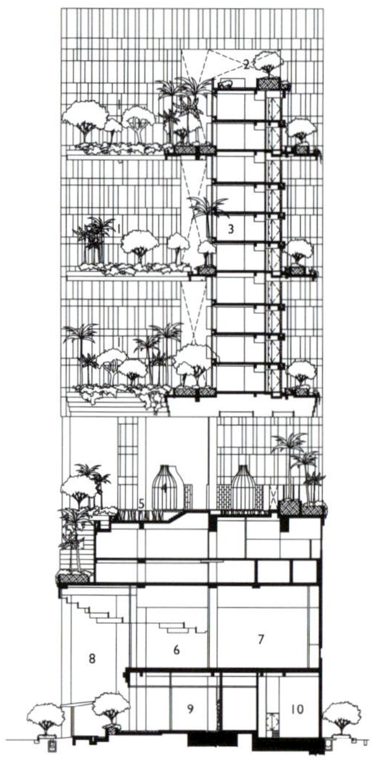

PARKROYAL on Pickering, Singapore, 2013

function rooms and conference room, plus the recreation areas of swimming pool and cabanas. The top section is made up of twelve floors of guest quarters, housing 367 rooms and suites. The building plan is a flat E-shaped figure facing onto the adjacent park on Pickering. Massive curvaceous sky-gardens occur at every four floors of the guest quarters, draped with tropical plants. The ground-floor verandah on Pickering is a monumental embellishment of the public realm as is the general porosity of the scheme towards adjacent pedestrian areas. The guise of the hotel is distinctly towards a progressive tropical urban image versus a more usual generic attitude. Its architecture is both organic and fluid in geometry, supporting the copious vegetated and natural agenda. In fact, as early as 2009 and 2011, Singapore took steps to officially promote green living walls and roofs, via its Landscape Replacement Policy. According to this, a landscape equivalent of a developed site must be provided in the form of landscape at ground level, on sky terraces, mid-levels and on rooftop gardens. This was supported further by the National Parks Board's commitment to cover 50 percent of the installation costs. It also quickly found its way into the Housing and Development Board public housing in projects such as SkyVille@Dawson and the Punggol Waterway Terraces. By 2017, Singapore had 100 hectares of vegetated roofscape, with much more to come (Design Chronicle, 2014; Rowe and Hee, 2019, pp. 107–108; and Schröpfer, 2020, pp. 82–85).

The Oasia Hotel Downtown in Singapore of 2016 by WOHA continued their greening efforts, although mainly through green building facades rather than terraces. As the name suggests, the hotel is located in downtown Singapore and amid other tall towers. It has a gross floor area of approximately 19,400 square meters and is comprised principally of 100 office units and 314 guest rooms. Like the PARKROYAL on Pickering, the architecture consists of a series of strata or layers in its vertical rise. This begins with the drop-off, reception and restaurant, followed above by parking, five floors of offices, eight floors of hotel guest rooms, a recreation area and then a roof garden partially enclosed by a porous inward-turning crown. More importantly for this discussion, these vertical layers of program are broken by sky-gardens and open spaces at levels 6, 12, 21 and 27. The vertical circulation

Oasia Hotel Downtown, Singapore, 2016

cores are placed at the corners, with an interconnecting central corridor through the programmed blocks concentrated on two sides and effectively framing the sky-gardens and views over the city. Billed as a 'living tower', fully 98 percent of the abundant greenery is located above grade and primarily on the building facades, replacing the site area and accounting for some 18.2 square meters of green area per building inhabitant. In addition to compensating for the lack of landscape space on the site, the greened facades also function as vertical catchments for stormwater that, in turn, help regulate surface runoff into the city drainage system. When it is not raining, an auto-irrigation system helps maintain the green facades. From a performance perspective, the greened facades are an effective strategy for helping to cool and regulate the temperature of the building. At no time does its surface exceed 45°C and the greened surface assists in the protection of the facade from solar radiation. Though not all native species, the biodiversity of plant materials is quite high with around 56 distinct species. Bird counts are comparatively low, however, primarily due to the surrounding and nearby habitat (ArchDaily, 2016; and Schröpfer, 2020, pp. 134–151, 168–191).

The Stacking Green residence in Ho Chi Minh City, Vietnam, of 2011 by Vo Trong Nghia Architects is a typical 'tube house' like so many in the nation's major cities. Usually, they were constructed on lots arrayed along urban streets of around 4 meters wide and 20 meters deep. During the early 20th century, if not before, they were typically two stories tall and often had one or two light wells in their depth for natural light and ventilation. Over time, commercialization of the ground floor at the front of the house occurred and the dwelling rose in height to from three to five stories, effectively becoming shophouses of the kind described earlier. Still others, like Stacking Green, remained as dwellings, in this case housing an extended family in about 250 square meters of floor space across four stories. Over time, Ho Chi Minh City's population expanded, to now nearly 9 million inhabitants and with a residential density that is the nation's highest and even exceeds Shanghai's density. With the dominance of the 'tube house' typology, vegetated urban green space is scarce, and the design of Stacking Green attempted to address this scarcity on two fronts. The first was to make vegetation more visible within the urban neighborhood. The second was to enhance the experience of vegetation close by from inside the house. Consequently, both the back and front facades are entirely composed of layered horizontal planters around twelve in number, cantilevered from the residence's side walls. The spacing between these layers across the house's four stories varies according to the height of the plants in each planter. Roof gardens are additionally provided above the third and fourth levels. An open staircase is located in the rear along with a garden space between the building envelope and the stacked screen of vegetation. Bioclimatic principles of traditional Vietnamese courtyard housing were also applied, including a light well at the center of the house. Inside the reinforced concrete frame, few partitions are provided, ensuring a fluent and well-ventilated interior space. A car park is included at the front, setting the house back somewhat on its narrow lot. Nevertheless, the stacked rows of planting are both highly visible and distinctive (Chalcraft, 2012).

The Binh Tanh House also in Ho Chi Minh City, Vietnam, of 2014 by Nishizawa Architects, manifests another architectural approach and version of the 'tube house', in which various programmatic volumes, across the building's five stories above grade, vary backward and forward in order to create gardens and vegetated spaces. Shunri Nishizawa, the architect and homeowner, lives on the top two floors with his family and placed his architectural office in the basement. The first through third floors in between, are rented by another Vietnamese family. The various floor levels then alternate between being open and closed depending upon use. Across the front facade at the third and fifth floor levels are concrete sun diversion screens, based on hollow concrete blocks though with larger openings. By combining them with the grided layout of open and closed skylit openings on the top floor terrace, a remarkable dappled pattern of light and shade was introduced into the space, both mystifying and amplifying perception of the garden in the space. The alternating extension and subtraction of floors in the longitudinal section of the building, as shown in the diagram on p. 276, also provided shading to the floors below and for convenient balconies for plants at the second and fourth levels. A hefty cast-in-place concrete spiral staircase, rising up through the garden at

Stacking Green, Ho Chi Minh City, 2011

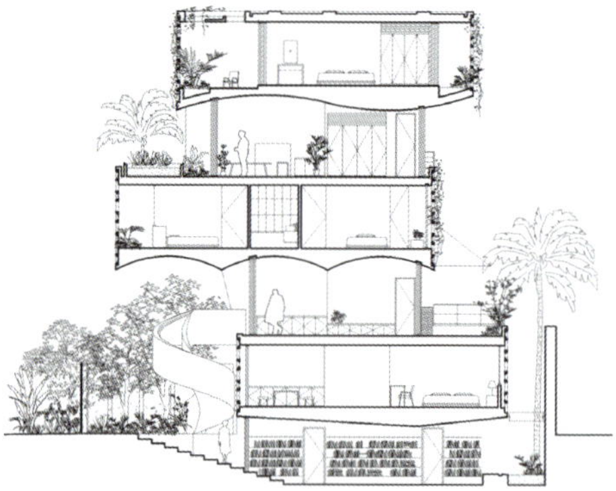

Binh Thanh House, Ho Chi Minh City, 2013

ground level, provides access from the first to the second floor levels of the house. Again, as in other contemporary 'tube house' versions, like those of VTN Architects mentioned earlier and the Dong Anh House also by Vo Trong Nghia, among others, architectural effort was directed towards imbuing houses and neighborhoods with greenery and engaging in bioclimatic design towards natural light and ventilation like that in traditional Vietnamese housing (Suthlapa, 2017).

Contemporary High-Rise Buildings

The Petronas Towers in Kuala Lumpur of 1998 by César Pelli are twin skyscrapers that were the tallest buildings in the world from 1996 to 2004 at 88 stories high, and remain the tallest twin towers in the world, topping out at 452 meters. With about 395,000 square meters of floor area, they are the home of Malaysia's national petroleum company and were inspired by Prime Minister Tun Mahathir bin Mohamad's vision of his country as a global player. Although unusual at that height, twin towers as an architectural form are not uncommon, particularly if one thinks of Gothic cathedrals and their spires. Tests of the initially chosen site, which was located on the grounds of the Selangor Turf Club's horse racing track, showed that half of the proposed building site was over decayed limestone and soft, whereas the other half was over rock. This necessitated moving the building some 60 meters or so in order to place it more evenly over the rock foundation. This then required construction of the world's deepest foundation, with the pouring of 104 concrete piles from 60 to 114 meters deep and finally capping it with a 4.6-meter-thick concrete raft foundation. The two towers were then constructed by two building consortiums. One was Japanese and led by Hazama Corporation and the other was South Korean and led by Samsung C&T Corporation, with the latter group completing the job first. The structural system used was a tube-in-tube design invented by noted engineer Fazlur Khan. Due to the high cost of steel, the towers were fabricated from cheaper super-high-strength reinforced concrete, which effectively reduced the amount of sway but was far heavier on the foundations. Essentially the towers are supported by 23 by 23-meter concrete cores and an outer ring of wide-spaced super columns. The towers taper towards the top antennas and on the way up accommodate copious amounts of column-free office space. The facade and profile of the building designed by Pelli were based on motifs found in Islamic art, as Malaysia is a predominantly Muslim country. Specifically, the cross-section of each tower was based on the *Rub el Hizb,* or Islamic Star, of two overlapping squares producing the outline of an octagon. The other motif for the tower aspect was based on the *Qutub Minar,* a very tall minaret in Delhi, India. In addition to the twin towers, at their base there is a shopping mall of 140,000 square meters, alongside the Petronas Philharmonic Hall. A 54-meter-long sky bridge was located between the 41st and 42nd floors that moves in and out of the towers to accommodate half a meter or so of sway without breaking. It also serves as an evacuation route in case of emergency. Vertical circulation was located at the center of each tower and the entire complex sits in the KLCC Park, a 6.9-hectare area replete with jogging paths, fountains, wading pools and a children's playground (Lee, 1997; and Kroll, 2011). In other parts of the region and in the same era, distinctive high-rise towers also arose, such as Wisma 46 in Jakarta, Indonesia, of 1996 by the Canadian Zeidler Partnership Architects with DP Architects of Singapore in the post-modern shape of a 46-story, 262-meter-high 'fountain pen', wrapped in a sheath of concrete walls. In 2019, there were in Southeast Asia and the Pacific region some 127 or so high-rise towers of 150+ meters tall, though few very tall towers, illustrating again the issue of spread in the city's overall urban form (Hahijary, 2016).

Taipei 101 in Taipei, Taiwan, of 2003 by Chu-Yuan Lee and Chung-Ping Wang is also an extremely tall skyscraper, classified as the world's tallest between 2004 and 2009 at 508 meters in height and with 101 floors. Like much of Lee and Wang's work, the tower evokes numerous Chinese symbolic aspects. Although American educated, Lee views architecture as a 'language' and does not shy away from quotational sensibilities in his architecture. His early Hung Kuo Building, for example, also an office block in Taiwan, takes its curved upward shape by reference to a lotus plant. Dragon symbolism was embodied in Lee's Beijing Pangu Plaza Hotel and the Buddhist gestural bringing of hands together inspired his large Sarira Pagoda of Famen Temple in China's Shaanxi Province. With Taipei 101 the rhythms of a pagoda linking earth to sky are recalled, as is the avowed resemblance of the building profile to a bamboo stalk, otherwise also an icon for learning and growth. There the green-tinted glass and eight-floor segments reinforce the bamboo reference but also reflect Chinese numerology and the association of eight with abundance, prosperity and good fortune. Constant use of the *ruyi* figure recalls a talisman of ancient origin associated with heavenly clouds and *feng shui* is brought into play with the fountain in front of the tower, redirecting flows of *ch'i* into appropriate directions. Even '101' was viewed as being one more than 100 and the traditional ascending number for perfection, as well as referencing the binary system 1,0,1 at the center of the digital economy. Located in the Xinyi District of Taipei, formerly occupied by military facilities, Taipei 101 is also known as the Taipei World Financial Center after its client, the Taipei Financial Center Corporation, who is a major sponsor of the district's re-use as a commercial realm of international significance. Designed to withstand typhoon winds and earthquake tremors, the tower is both flexible and structurally resistant. High-performance steel construction was used and a 36-column tube-in-tube format was designed, with an interior core and an exterior linked every eight floors by outrigger trusses. A foundation comprised of 380 pillars reaches down 80 meters with 30 of those meters into bedrock. Between the 87th and 92nd floors a 660-metric ton steel pendulum serves as a tuned mass damper, swinging to offset movements caused by strong wind gusts. The specially trussed facade system resists seismic lateral displacement and also acts as a damper. Its green double glazing provides heat and ultraviolet light protection, blocking external heat by around 50 percent and water recycled from the facade and roofs accounts for 20 to 30 percent of total water needs. Overall, Taipei 101 is certified as the world's tallest green building with LEED standards. The site also accommodates observation decks, restaurants, sky lobbies, a mall, parking and a metro station (Binder, 2008, p. 20f.; and Cheng and Shih, 2008).

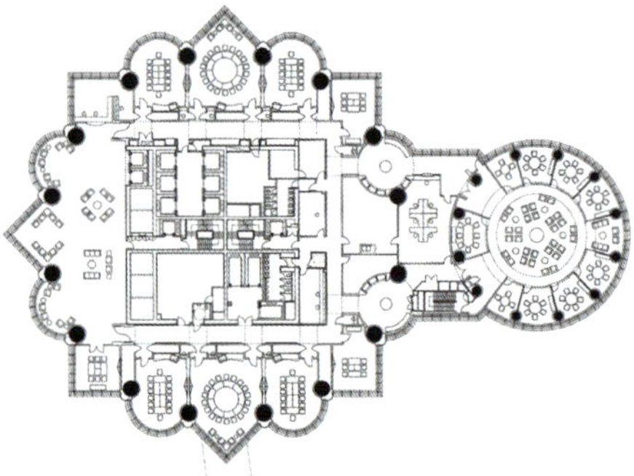

Petronas Towers, Kuala Lumpur, 1998

Taipei 101, Taipei, 2003

The MahaNakhon Tower in Bangkok, Thailand, of 2018 by Ole Scheeren of OMA is located in the Silom-Sathorn central business area of the city and has been recognized as the tallest building in Thailand at a height of some 314 meters and 77 stories. With about 150,000 square meters of space, the program of uses was primarily residential with related functions. More specifically, it was comprised of MahaNakhon Square at its base, a public plaza providing access to a railway station. Beside this plaza are the MahaNakhon Terraces, made up of 10,000 square meters of luxury retail space with gardens and terraces spread over seven floors of building full of restaurants, cafés and a 24-hour marketplace. The Ritz-Carlton Residences Bangkok follow in the upward sweep of the building, with 200 customized single- and double-level homes, each offering the atmosphere of a luxury apartment and managed according to Ritz-Carlton five-star standards of service. This was joined by the Bangkok Edition in the guise of a boutique hotel with some 150 guest rooms, capped by a multi-level rooftop sky bar and restaurant. The apartment-homes range in size from 125 to 830 square meters. Architecturally, the tower building has been carved out, so to speak, to introduce a three-dimensional ribbon of 'pixels' of more complete building forms that extend upward and encircle the building's full height. The overall design concept departed appreciably from the typical podium and tower ensemble by beginning at the ground and plaza level with the seven-story base of retail and dining as shifting protrusions of a terraced landscape. The form then dissolves upwards into the body of the tower with the 'pixelation' of protrusions and excavations continuing to the top. These forms were also designed and located, in turn, to maximize the panoramas of the city available to residents. Also incorporated were bifold balcony windows to be used as secondary ventilation panels (Welch, 2019).

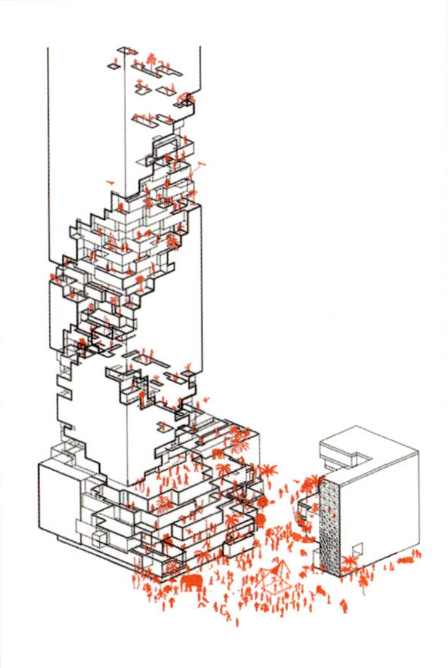

MahaNakhon Tower, Bangkok, 2018

Marina Bay Sands, Singapore, 2010

Marina Bay Sands in Singapore of 2010 by Safdie Architects is a large complex with three hotel towers, a sky-park and an adjacent array of a casino, shopping, a convention center, a museum and several theaters. The three hotel towers, rising some 220 meters above ground and with 50 floors, house some 2,600 luxury accommodations and form upwardly sloping pedestals for the sky-park above, with inclines of 26 degrees to vertical as 2 + 6 = 8, the most propitious number in Chinese numerology for 'prosperity'. The plan underlying the three towers is also curved and the presence of these fluid shapes marks something of a transition by Safdie from Euclidean to curved Riemannian Forms, while there is a continued interest in mathematical geometries. The sky-park is extensive at over 1.0 hectares in surface area and 220 meters in length, cantilevering 50 meters outwards on the northern side. With the capacity to host about 3,900 people, it is comprised of a row of trees on its eastern side and then jogging paths, gardens, spas and a 150-meter-long 'infinity pool' on its western side affording unprecedented and magnificent views of the city across Marina Bay. The Waterfront Promenade that runs continuously around this bay forms something of a seamless lobby for the hotel on one side and the rest of the complex on the other side. This is made up of a multi-level retail arcade and three shell-like structures, combining civic spaces and both indoor and outdoor public areas. Within this ensemble is housed an atrium-style casino, luxury shopping and restaurants, a convention center of around 45,000 square meters in area, and two 2,000-seat theaters. Finally, the ArtScience Museum is located at the northern tip of the complex before the double-helix bridge crossing of the channel. It has ten fingers of space at its base that curve upwards to form a lily flower-like configuration. Efforts have been made throughout to maximize environmental performance. Rainwater capture and recycling are prominent features of this strategy, as is the use of energy-efficient elevators, where the kinetic energy generated is converted into electricity for internal use, along with various specialized waste management techniques. The incorporation of the casino, with government backing, was a departure from Singapore's official straitlaced attitude. However, recognition of the regressive social aspects was outweighed by the need to keep Singapore competitive (Rowe, 2011; and ArchDaily, 2010).

The Pinnacle@Duxton also in Singapore of 2009 was a collaboration between Lim Khim Guan, Louis Tan, Khoo Peng Beng, Belinda Huang, RSP Architects Planners and Engineers, ARC Studio Architecture + Urbanism and Sandy Ng, or, more simply by ARC Studio Architecture + Urbanism and RSP Architects Planners and Engineers. It is a 50-story residential development next to the central business district and Chinatown. Comprised of seven towers, it is the world's tallest public housing complex and features two large sky-gardens, each 500 meters in length. It was the subject of a competition conducted by the Urban Redevelopment Authority (URA) of Singapore for the Ministry of National Development in 2001. The building complex was constructed in response to the scarcity of property available for housing and as the first in a series of high-rise public housing developments, departing from the earlier Housing and Development Board (HDB) practice of lower-rise buildings in the public housing estates. The site was the former location of the first two-story HDB blocks, which were among the oldest in the country. In addition to housing, several other components were included. These were accommodation of a community club, landscaping strategies that incorporated neighboring Duxton Plain Park into the sky-gardens, and retention of other mature trees around the property boundary. Two special types of residences were proposed, allowing for some 35 different unit variations, with dissimilar combinations of extended bays, balconies, bay windows and planter areas. In fact, the initial residents in each unit were able to select these combinations. The overall effect was to vary the facades considerably within the seven connected vertical slab blocks. Pre-cast methods were used involving transportation of molded components to the site, followed by hoisting them into place on the building structure. The sky-gardens at the 26th and 50th floors incorporate jogging tracks, playgrounds and viewing areas. Also incorporated within the scheme are a food center, basketball court, day care center, other recreational facilities and an underground car park. All the internal walls were made of lightweight concrete and could be removed and reconfigured by unit owners (Tham, 2010; and Lee, 2011).

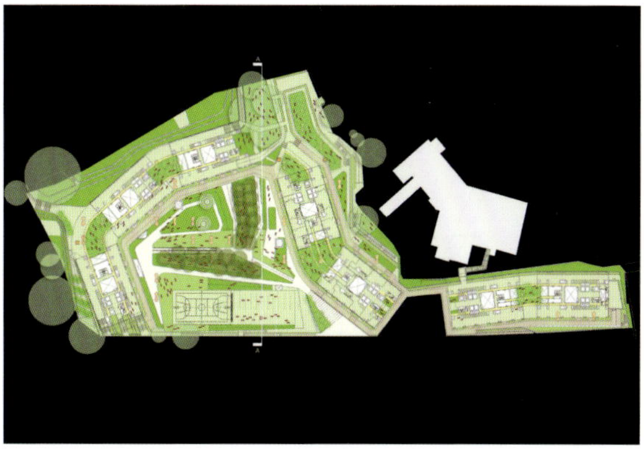

Pinnacle@Duxton, Singapore, 2010

Observations and Conclusions

Chapter 6

Looking across this material, several broad observations can be made about the architecture of Southeast Asia. As much as if not more than in many other regions of the world, natural environmental conditions, as both constraints and opportunities, have constantly influenced building and the making of architecture. Prevailing and often varied mixes of climatic forces and hazardous factors, for instance, have strongly shaped where and what was constructed, as well as the material manner in which this construction took place. Among contemporary projects, this is very evident and particularly with regard to working towards minimal environmental footprints. So-called green building takes place in virtually all the projects in some manner. Then too, development within the region also reflects the uneven rise of nation states. A few are well-developed by any measure, whereas most are not. Moreover, when combined with the mixed national circumstances of tractable levels of technology and related capacities, not unexpectedly, architectural production varies. In all, it appears that at least five specific observations can be offered, collectively characterizing the architecture of Southeast Asia.

Practical Reckoning with Need

One immediate observation about an underlying identity to Southeast Asian architecture is often the strong inheritance of a practical reckoning with need and a leaning back in the direction of tradition in order to move forward, as it were. After all, 'tradition' comes from the Latin *traditum* or *traditio* meaning essentially 'to pass on to others' or 'to bring across', implying, of course, something worth doing at the present time. The practical reckoning is immediately apparent in the early Austronesian building practices that resulted from both elemental needs to provide shelter and habitation, as well as to nurture the intimate relationship to society and to the environment. In the latter case, this involved invariably reflection of indigenous cosmological beliefs and reliance on the use of locally available materials and, in a parsimonious manner, dealing with a prevailing environmental circumstance such as tropical climate. As a consequence, and as shown in chapter 2, many buildings in the region had simple yet distinctive framed skeletal structures crowned by prominent roofs, often with local thatch, and were raised on stilts to avoid flooding and to afford ventilation. The upper segments of the interior of the tall roofs were also used for storing valuable relics. These tendencies, in turn, led to a vernacular, often synecdochic with traditional, derived from being indigenous, native, commonplace and domestic in character and value. As Modernism in architecture moved from the heady experimental inter-war years of 'orthodoxy' into the post-World War II period of the International Style, returns to vernacular have gained notoriety along with other reactions like Critical Regionalism. Both are largely negative reactions to the deculturalization of the International Style through its apparent ignorance of environmental contexts, disinterest in climatic conditions and lack of cultural references. In Southeast Asia, this was conspicuous in many contemporary projects discussed here and in the theoretical stances taken by architects like William S. W. Lim in contradistinction to his earlier work with DP Architects on Singapore's brutalist modern-style structures described in chapter 5. Outside the region, Kenneth Frampton took up the cause more generally with a pastiche of post-modernism (Frampton, 1983; and Lim and Beng, 1998).

This brings us then to 'contemporary vernacular' and, at times anyway, a set of seemingly self-contradictory terms of timelessness and temporality. Nevertheless, when viewed in a dynamic or less static perspective, as others have pointed out, modernizing tradition and/or vernacular need not be so contradictory and can, instead, be a process of bringing forward culturally accepted values and ways of doing things into a contemporary context and then making adjustments accordingly. Literary modernists like T. S. Eliot and James Joyce around the early 20th century are also instructive in this regard. In his famous essay titled "Tradition and the Individual Talent", of 1919, Eliot argued that tradition in literature at any one time is a completed whole out of which an author creates a new work. Tradition is, therefore, a continuum. Moreover, composition is an impersonal process engaging creative and critical faculties but nothing else by way of authorship. In addition, 'moderns' could then improve on the work of their ancient forebears. Through this argumentation by way of separation, Eliot instantiated an idea of tradition not being static and one in which it should be regarded as a living cultural force. Similarly, Joyce in the publication of his novel *Ulysses* in 1922 and through his deployment of stream-of-consciousness techniques, raised the specter of counterparts from the past by way of his direct references to Homer's epic poem, as well as using his acute focus on the temporal setting of each of the 18 episodes set in a 24-hour period, to convey the concreteness of the 'here and now' of an episode as instrumental in giving meaning to life and re-affirming the value of timelessness and temporality. Indeed, it is through the processes of hybridization at work in much contemporary Southeast Asian architecture that this twofold condition is satisfied, primarily in the manner of eclecticism and amalgamation directed towards the two-way adaptation of 'integration' or the adoption of the traits of one scheme onto another or 'transculturation'. A relatively frequent instance of integration can be seen in the formal and figural arrangements of space and surface, especially in places of worship, as described in chapter 3, that are time-honored but also materially and expressively contemporary. Moments of transculturation can often be observed again with the relatively constant deployment in otherwise contemporary modern buildings of older time-tested aspects of passive climatic control (Eliot, 1919; Canclini, 1995; and Bulson, 2006).

Syncretic Search for Outcomes

The second observation about Southeast Asian architectural identity involves the somewhat equal immediacy of all but the most recent past and a simultaneous syncretic form of engagement of subscribing to different orientations at once within the region. When responding to the colonial period, for example, the architecture reached back, as it were, to the deep Austronesian history and to the more recent Indian and Sinic dynastic periods and even early colonialism with equal readiness. When faced with incoming regimes of power during dynastic times, as described in chapter 3 and during the colonial period, as seen in chapter 4, architecture responded but only really as seemed to be required by the kinds of facilities being built and by whom and little more. Reactions that occurred were typically of a broad socio-political or cultural kind, like availing a community of some perceived liberating aspect of a contemporary work or, by contrast, conforming closer to religious or nationalist dicta. Moreover, such vacillations were not an issue of authenticity or the lack of it. They were genuine and valid and more likely representations of 'both-and' kinds of conditions. One example was the nationalism of Indonesian 'official' architecture during the Sukarno period and the freedom-seeking liberation of the Jengki style, in places, at much the same time. The various and numerous incarnations of Hindu and Buddhist stupas is another case of simultaneous architectural acceptability. Additionally, building types and programs were not tied to a specific period when they were introduced. Also, in some cases like shophouses and townhouses a basic typology persisted formally even as its figuration may have changed with time. With regard to authenticity here, someone like Lionel Trilling can be instructive by drawing attention to sincerity and authenticity. In his classic work on the subject, he regards authenticity as being largely a matter of staying true to oneself as distinct from being a sincere person. The difference hinges on the observation that sincerity in this context is subject to mutations and, therefore, is capable of being revised over time in tune with changing habits of mind, codes and community attitudes as occurred in the past towards modern secular subjective attitudes. Definitionally, for him, sincerity is a state of congruence between avowed (i.e. externally influenced) and actual (i.e. internal) feeling. Also, as we know from experience, it is quite possible for someone to be insincere and out of step with prevailing norms but authentic at the same time by simply being who they are. So too in these cases of Southeast Asian architecture, by giving the appearance of authenticity, other conditions of dissonance and inappropriateness at a point in time could be avoided (Trilling, 1972).

Object Qualities and Arrange-ments

A third observation is that the object quality of Southeast Asian architecture is pronounced. Buildings are conceived as objects that may be arranged, moved and combined more or less as needed. The nipa hut in the Philippines, for instance, was a stand-in, so to speak, for the national indigenous appearance of the Tanghalang Maria Makiling Theater by Locsin and on a much grander scale and with different material. The sheer physical movement of the Petronas Towers to accommodate better foundation conditions is also an example of this literal object portability, as is the adornment of Taipei 101 with *riyu* to suit local superstitions about prosperity. Perhaps more profoundly, though, this object quality is promoted by the perpetual village-like quality of urban settlement. As described in chapter 5, proportions of national urbanization remain relatively low across the region. Nevertheless, several cities are very populous, such as Jakarta at 10.9 million inhabitants, Bangkok at 10.7 million and Kuala Lumpur at 8.2 million. Within these large populations, however, scales of settlement and spatial transformations have occurred that tend to reinforce object qualities of buildings and their immediate settings compared to more conventional, lumpier monocentric and polycentric models. In Southeast Asia in most if not all cases *desakota* regions have formed, adding to the normal gradients of urban core, suburbs, peripheral developments and so on of Western models of urban regions. Moreover, within the spreading form, a mosaic-like quality has occurred, especially when population gradients are high but transformation of economic activities into higher-rise and distinctive tertiary forms of development are relatively low. This phenomenon is apparent, for example, in Ho Chi Minh City, Hanoi, Manila, Yangon and Jakarta. Bangkok appears to be slightly different, with more stable and conventional polycentric development asserting itself. One distinctive and prevalent architectural result is developer-driven commercial and mixed-use parks, usually with some prominent buildings within them, sometimes in the form of local cores. An exception is Singapore, where master plans and highly regulated consolidations of development have occurred for many years. Nevertheless, even there the object quality of many recent buildings has been pronounced (Ginsburg, Koppel and McGee, 1991; and Simmonds and Hack, 2000).

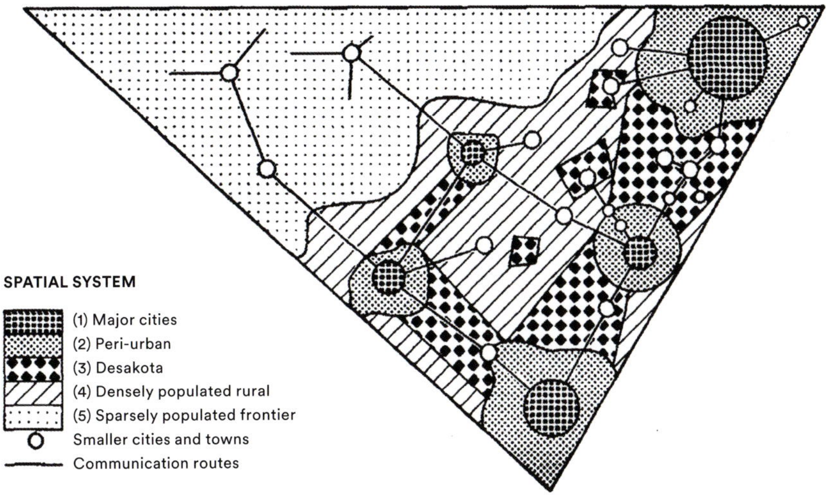

Desakota and Other Spatial Territories

Awareness of Local Environments

A fourth observation is the increasingly profound awareness that the regional natural environmental characteristics of Southeast Asia require careful consideration in all respects, including hazard mitigation, low energy use and diminished environmental footprints. Many Southeast Asian nations and cities are intimately shaped by their relationship with water for trade, culture and other historical reasons as described in chapter 1 and elsewhere in this volume. Today, climate change, demands of urbanization pushing up levels of land surface subsidence and other negative externalities of development, have also spawned a range of design and planning responses in many of these riverine-deltaic city environments, as described by the contemporary projects presented in this book. As pointed out, the region's geography and natural environments are very active. By many accounts, it is a hazardous and dangerous place. The Indian Ocean Tsunami of 2004, for instance, was caused by a magnitude 9 earthquake some 50 kilometers off the northwest coast of Sumatra, Indonesia. The unprotected coastline was immediately flooded, with wave heights of up to 30 meters. The town of Banda Aceh was partially destroyed and around

250,000 people perished. The region is traversed by several major river systems as outlined in chapter 1, like the Irrawaddy, Salween, Red River and Mekong, and numerous smaller systems. At their mouths, parts of these river delta networks have been dismantled and wetlands have been drained over the past 200 or so years to make way for rice granaries, alongside burgeoning urban development. Monsoons, which favored navigation and trade in earlier times, persist but so do tropical cyclones and storms. Very active tectonic plates, again as described in chapter 1, produce persistent earthquake and volcanic activity. Mount Pinatubo in the Philippines, for instance, erupted in 1991, covering large areas with volcanic ash and polluting the atmosphere. Indeed, volcanic hazards are concentrated in the Philippines and along the maritime strip of islands stretching from Sumatra, through Java and towards Timor in Indonesia. Landslides are also not uncommon, particularly due to soil erosion and urban expansion to hillside slopes in many areas. Water balance in the face of urbanization has become challenging along with low levels of adequate sewerage in many urban areas. Air and water pollution has mounted as has the inadequate management of waste disposal. In short, the region is substantially challenged environmentally and outright dangerous in places (Gupta, 2008).

Against this background, Southeast Asia confronts a number of issues. First, climate change is resulting in declining biodiversity, already noted in chapter 1, due largely to anthropocentric actions. In fact, between 2001 and 2016 there was a further overall loss of 14.5 percent. Second, there has been an increase in damaging climate change-related phenomena such as heat waves, flooding, drought, and the frequency of tropical storms and cyclones. In fact, it has been estimated that this has occasioned about an 11 percent loss in combined GDP across agriculture, tourism, energy demand, labor productivity, catastrophe risk, health and natural system impacts. By contrast, main areas of economic returns and gains from 'green spending' appear to be associated in the region with employment gains in clean energy transition, circular economy models, sustainable urban development, more productive and regenerated agriculture, and the making of healthy and productive oceans. Third, regarding oceans, the dumping of plastic waste is conspicuous in the region, accounting for something like 30 percent of the worldwide total. Partly this is due to the extensive amount of coastline in Southeast Asia, although it is also a matter of poor management practices. Indeed, waste management in general is poor in the region. Even in wealthy Singapore, recycling is not very effective and composting and incineration are practiced in a limited manner. Clearly, shifts to 'waste-to-energy' cycles are needed along with moves away from the prevalence of landfills and open dumps. On this score, Southeast Asia's active participation in global waste trade requires revision, particularly in the area of e-waste and toxic wastes, even though self-produced food and organic wastes are in considerably higher amounts. Fourth, the widespread if not ubiquitous use of concrete as the most available and cheapest building material, as noted several times in this text, requires reconsideration. Worldwide production amounts to fully 8 percent of greenhouse gas emissions, compared to only 9 percent for all of agriculture and far less for airline travel. Some shifts in the direction of less-polluting LC3 (limestone calcined clay cement) could be made, but fuller conversion to renewable natural building materials should also be encouraged. However, in the face of current economic circumstances these last classes of environmental impact may remain 'hard-to-abate' sectors (Gupta, 2008; Jambeck, Geyer, Wilcox et al., 2015; and Lim, Ng and Zara, 2021).

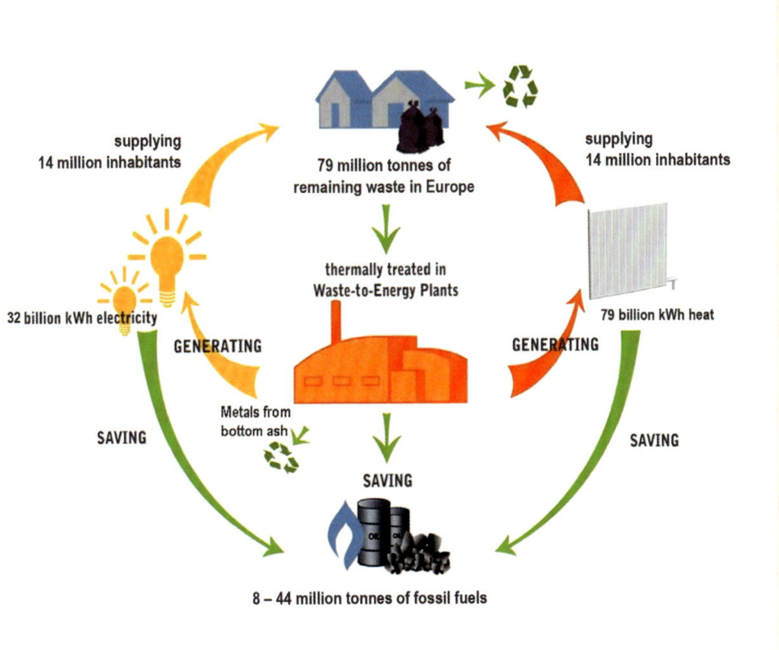

General Waste-To-Energy Cycle

Cost of Living Index and % of Population Urban

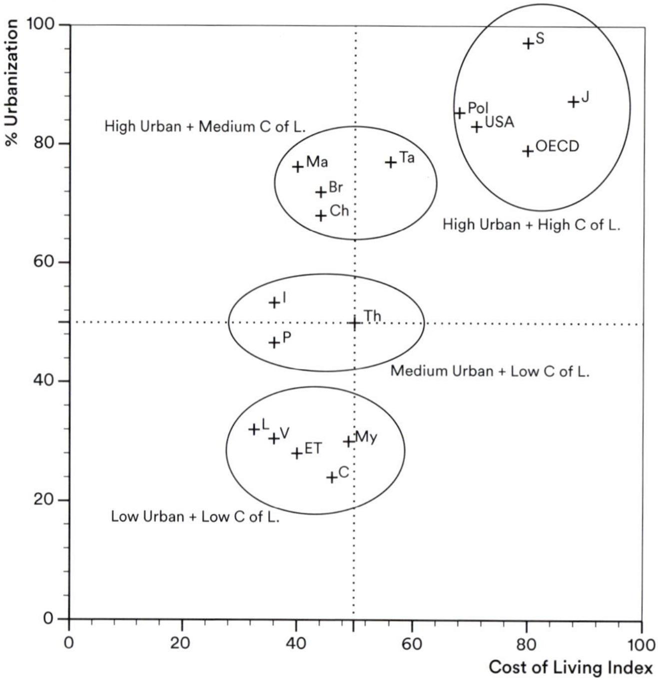

Cost of Living Index and % of Population Urban		
Country	% Urbanization	C of L. Index
Vietnam	33	38
Cambodia	22	48
Laos	36	36
Myanmar	30	48
Thailand	50	50
Malaysia	77	39
Singapore	100	80
Indonesia	57	37
Brunei	44	77
East Timor	30	42
Philippines	48	37
Taiwan	79	59
Polynesia	83	78
USA	83	71
OECD	80	80
Japan	92	88
China	64	43

Southeast Asian Nations by Levels of Development

Responses to Levels of Development

A fifth and final observation is that all but a few nations are relatively poor and unurbanized, as well as seriously constrained with regard to infrastructure development and management capabilities in the face of increasing urbanization and economic growth. Therefore, the material and technological availability and sophistication is similarly constrained relative to more fully developed circumstances and becomes reflected in building architecture and environmental adaptation and efficiency, as well as programmatic adaptation and expansion. The relative positions of the Southeast Asian nations under discussion here are plotted on the graph opposite. There, two recognized proxies for level of development are the proportion of national population urbanization and its rated cost of living index as a measure of relative wealth. The graph is also crisscrossed with the world urbanization and cost of living indices, hovering around 50 in both cases. These plots reveal four groups of nations and correspond, more or less, with the cliometric data presented in chapter 1 and in the book's appendix. Among the groups, the lowest with respect to proportions of urbanization and below the cost of living median are Laos, Vietnam, East Timor, Cambodia and

Myanmar, or most of the land-based as distinct from maritime countries of the region. This group is followed by Indonesia, Thailand and the Philippines, with the former two accelerating in the proportion of urbanization since 1975. With the exception of Singapore and parts of Polynesia, the remaining nations of Malaysia, Brunei and Taiwan have urbanization rates comparable to many well-developed nations and, indeed, higher than the People's Republic of China, although still relatively not very wealthy with regard to the cost of living index, with the exception of Taiwan. The final group of nations are both highly urbanized and wealthy. For comparison purposes, the relative positions of Japan, the USA and the OECD nations are also plotted. Rather than implying sharp breaks, these relative levels, seen in relation to the architecture discussed in this volume, probably point in the direction of further upward trends and tendencies among less well-off and under-urbanized nations towards lower-tech building practices, passive climatic and environmental approaches and adaptive re-uses (United Nations, 2018; and Numbeo, 2021).

SE Asia Nations GDP / Capita		
Singapore	USD	63,363
Brunei	USD	34,137
Taiwan	USD	26,104
Malaysia	USD	12,601
Thailand	USD	7,470
Indonesia	USD	4,260
Philippines	USD	3,290
Laos	USD	2,798
Vietnam	USD	2,747
East Timor	USD	2,342
Average	USD	**13,508**
Median	USD	**3,290**

Ranking of Southeast Asian Nations by GDP/Capita

Concluding Trends

From this survey, the essential character and identity of Southeast Asian architecture may be summarized as a confection of the following three observations. First, recognition of local natural environmental conditions and what that means for making lasting, useful and comfortable places for living, work and recreation has persisted and will continue to persist both because of the dangers and benign circumstances involved. Moreover, celebration and expression of 'being green', as it were, will remain. Often, surrounding scenic values and living possibilities add naturally to the aura of a place. The complimentary manner of building with this aura is also often a characteristic of the region's architecture and beyond simply environmental performance. On this latter score, use of local materials, passive climatic responses, reduced environmental footprints, and so on, are and will continue to be well-honed. In these last regards, many of the contemporary townhouse and shophouse projects in Vietnam offer useful insights. In particular, these would include VTN's 'House for Trees' projects in Ho Chi Minh City and Ho Khue Architects' Green Peace Village, along with the Space Block projects by the Kazuhiro Kojima Lab of Tokyo University of Science. Clearly also, all the contemporary post-colonial projects presented here under the category of 'Climatic Turns' qualify from both a performance and an expressive perspective.

Second, acknowledgment and working within appropriate levels of technology afforded by local levels of development is a defining feature of Southeast Asian architecture. As can be seen from the contemporary projects, this does not necessarily mean low technology, especially amid categories like modern high-rise buildings. Nor is it necessarily about low or entirely and overt 'green' technologies, such as the Bamboo Sports Hall in Chiang Mai, Thailand, or the Kontum Indochine Café in Vietnam. Rather it implies use of a mix of technologies depending on programmatic, aspirational and economic circumstances. Nevertheless, often and in many places within the region this mixture is oriented, if anywhere, towards ready-made, lower-tech niches, with some exceptions, like the tall towers, that prove the rule, as it were. In other words, as elsewhere, if there is a will there will be a way and some projects like the Tjibaou Cultural Center in New Caledonia by Piano, for instance, are certainly not technically unsophisticated but appear to conform to a time-honored and traditional appearance. The same may be said about the Multimedia Nusantara University Building by DCM, where the simplicity of the reference to an indigenous vernacular was established through the presence of a prominent and angular roof but also by involving considerable technical panache. Again, the level of technology, like the environmental awareness, was mixed with and subordinated to a deeper cultural sense of building form.

Third, approaches to both the timeless and more immediate temporal aspects of Southeast Asian architecture are deeply ingrained and persistent. Moreover, this immediately brings into play on the timeless side the question of what the real roots of the region's architecture are. As the structure of this text suggests, they are, indeed, varied and present to a lesser or greater extent in contemporary projects. They are not, however, limitless in number, nor untied from the earlier two characteristics of the regional architecture. The Austronesian origins of ocean peoples are architecturally manifest in low-rise contemporary arrangements of 'huts and longhouses', the organic arrangements of works like the Learning Hub and Gardens by the Bay in Singapore, as well as with the Tainan Art Museum in Taiwan. Also, as noted earlier, the village-like quality of many urban areas has been sustained and not become more modern in its patterns. With their strong and lasting religious connotations, the Hindu, Buddhist and Muslim influences that flowed into the region during dynastic periods remain influential, though often transformed in a contemporary modern key as in the Zaya Thakedi Monastery in Myanmar, various mosques in Indonesia and even the Termitary House in Da Nang, Vietnam. In each case traditional rules and spatial topologies remain identifiably in place, even as the figuration and materiality changed and were updated. Here, hybrids and amalgamations appear to have been dominant design strategies. Even in otherwise almost completely contemporary projects like the Morodok Techo National Stadium in Phnom Penh, Cambodia, transparent references to the grid-like planning and *baray* lakes of Khmer Angkor are present. Then too, the Western colonial period and post-colonial reactions to it, suffused the region with an architecture that was both mainstream modern and invariably locally inflected, as many of the contemporary projects show. On the more immediately temporal side of things, the multi-temporality tended to be tipped towards reinvigorating, reinterpreting and even extending tradition, but along the lines of continued reckoning with local environmental needs and available technologies and practices.

Cliometric Data Analyses

As stated in the introduction, the cliometric analysis of the region is based on graphical plots of the relative intensities of selected socio-economic and other characteristics pertinent to architectural production. These plots are summarized by the following time-dependent data profiles and supporting data from 1950 by nation state. Also included is a listing of nations in Southeast Asia by relative wealth measured by gross domestic product per capita (GDP per capita).

Coincidence of Hegemonic Eras

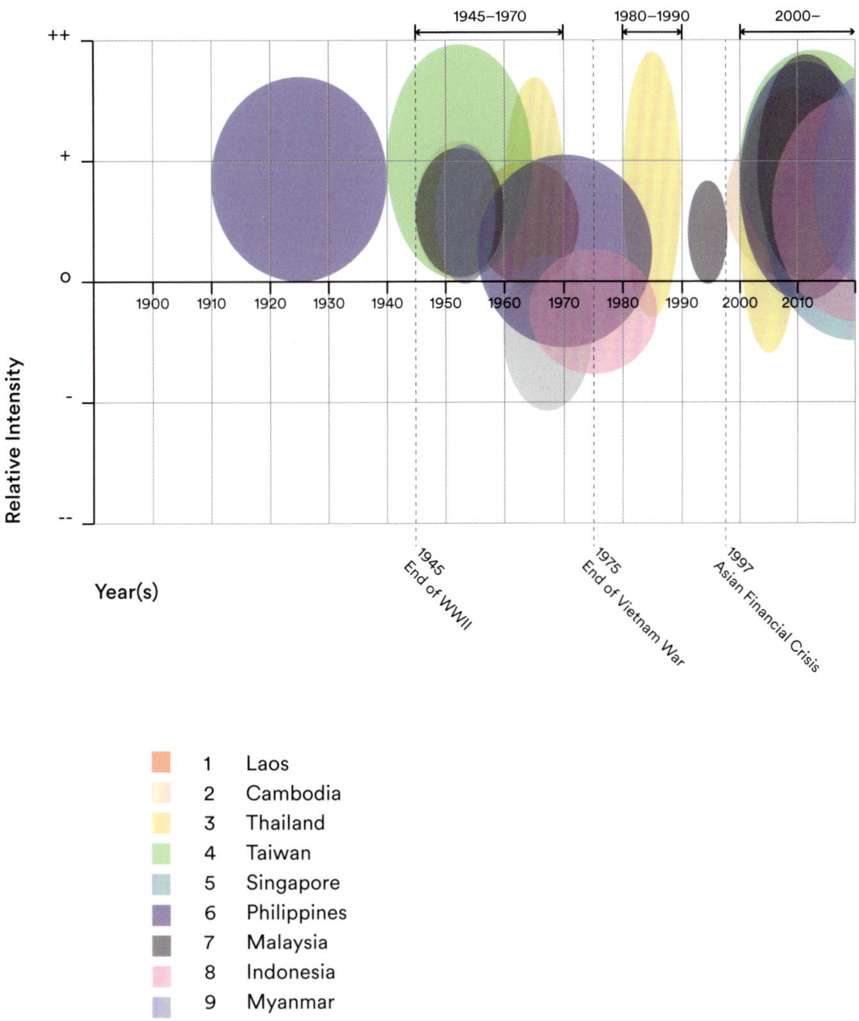

Cambodia – Intensity / Time

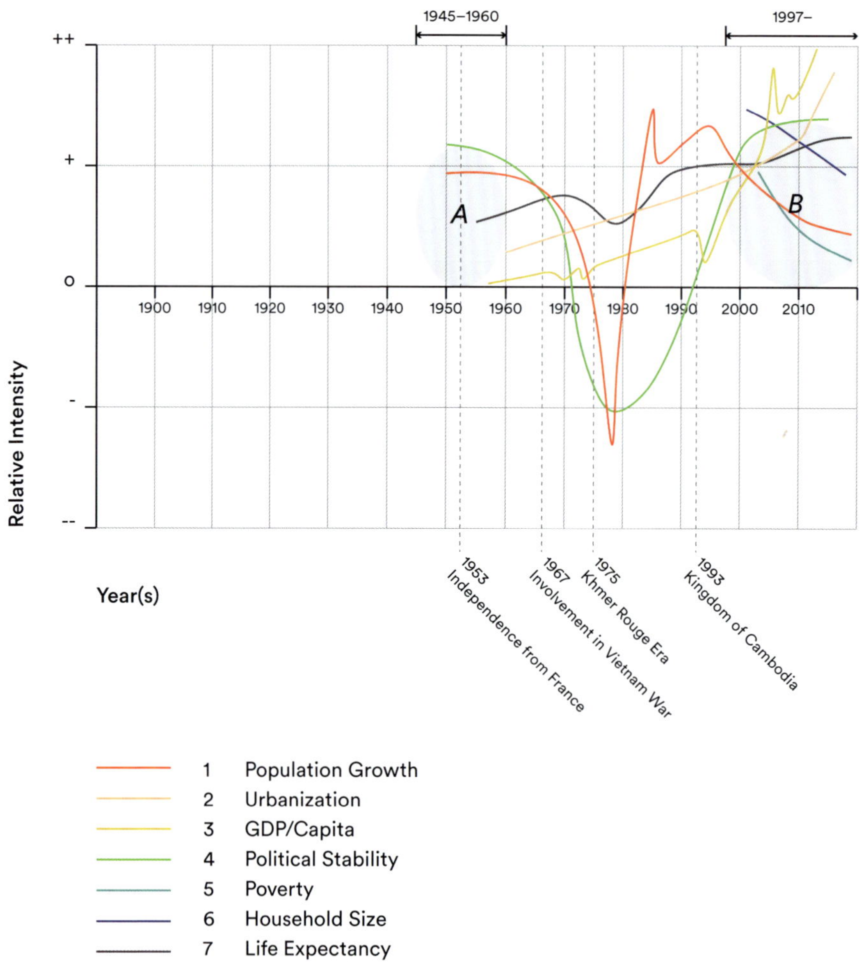

Indonesia – Intensity / Time

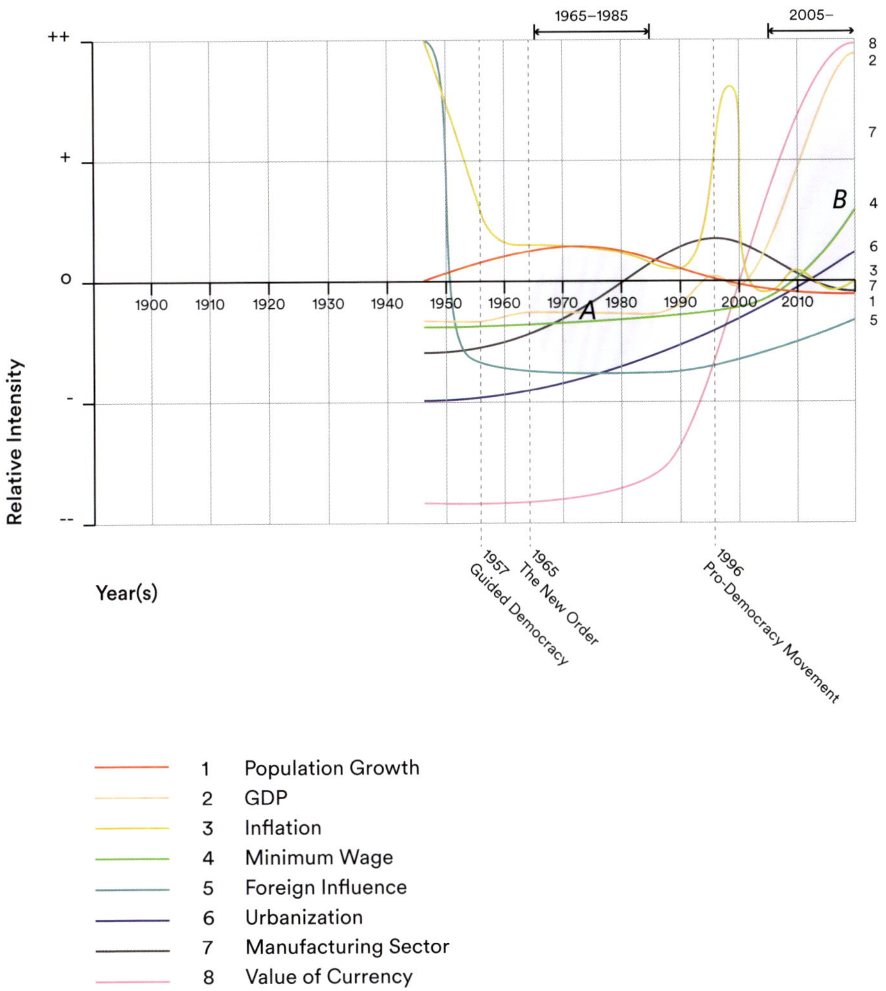

Laos – Intensity / Time

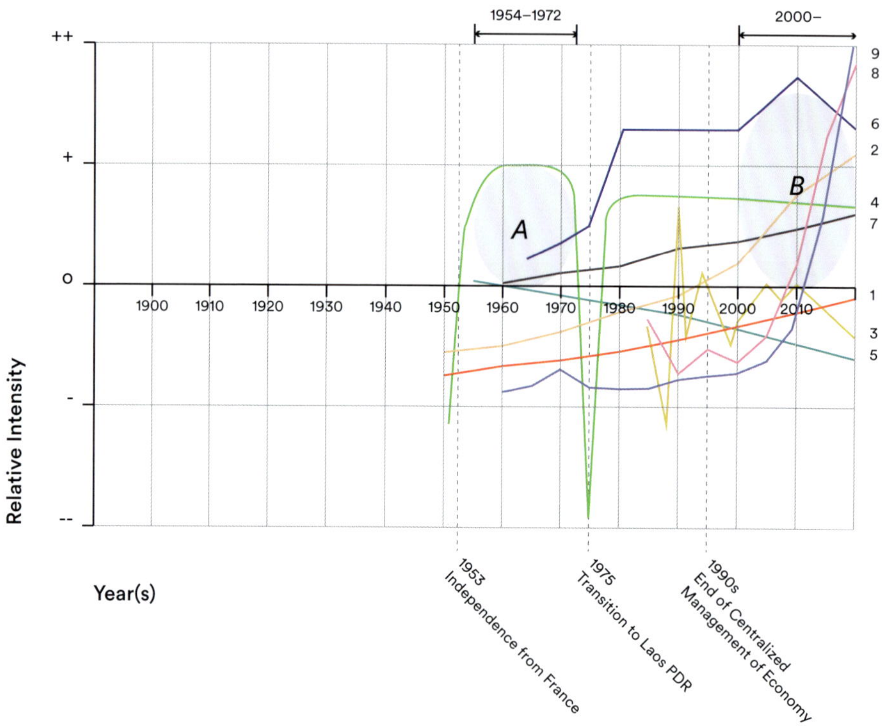

1 Population Growth
2 Urbanization
3 GDP
4 Independence
5 Agriculture Sector
6 School Environment
7 Life Expectancy
8 Gini Index
9 Carbon Emissions

Malaysia – Intensity / Time

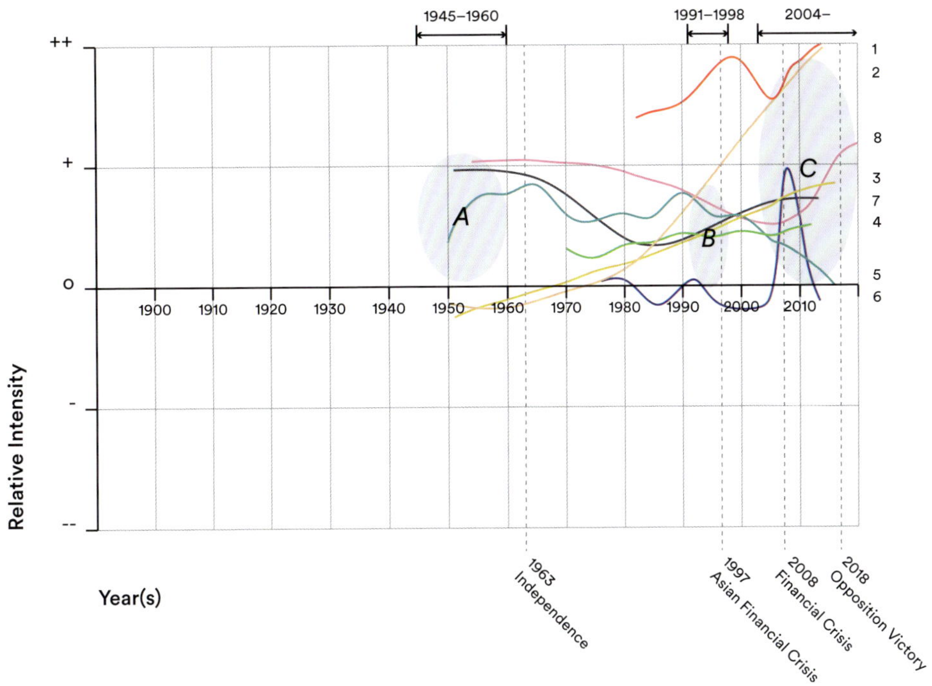

	1	Service Sector
	2	GDP/Capita
	3	Urbanization
	4	Gini Index
	5	Population Growth
	6	Housing Supply/Demand
	7	Environmental Concerns
	8	Political Stability/Strength

Myanmar – Intensity / Time

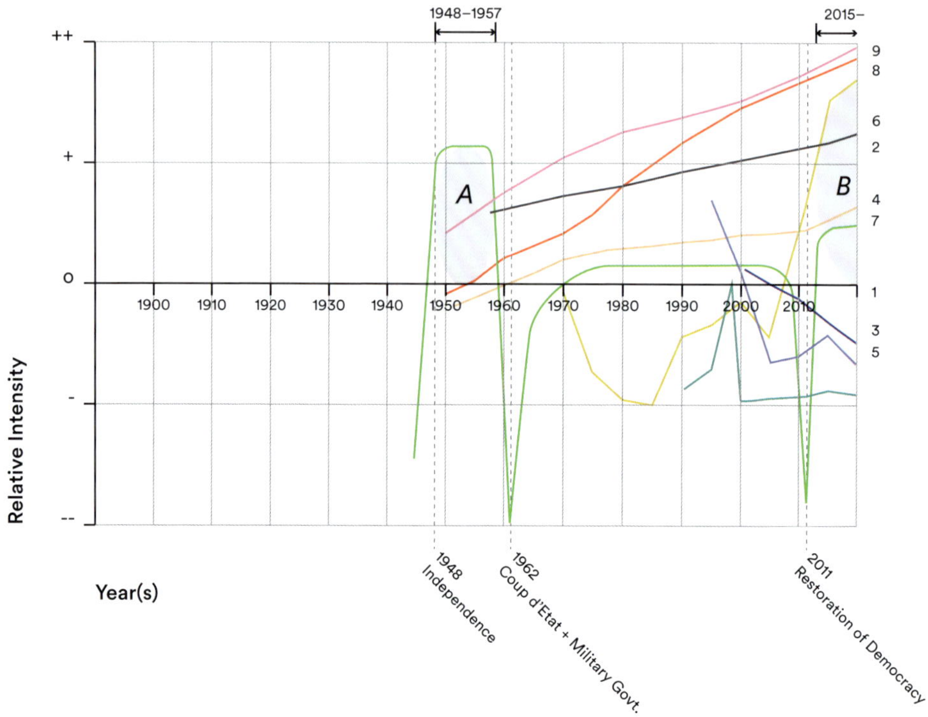

1 Population Growth
2 Urbanization
3 GDP/Capita
4 Independence
5 Inflation
6 Poverty
7 School Enrollment
8 Life Expectancy
9 Opium Cultivation

The Philippines – Intensity / Time

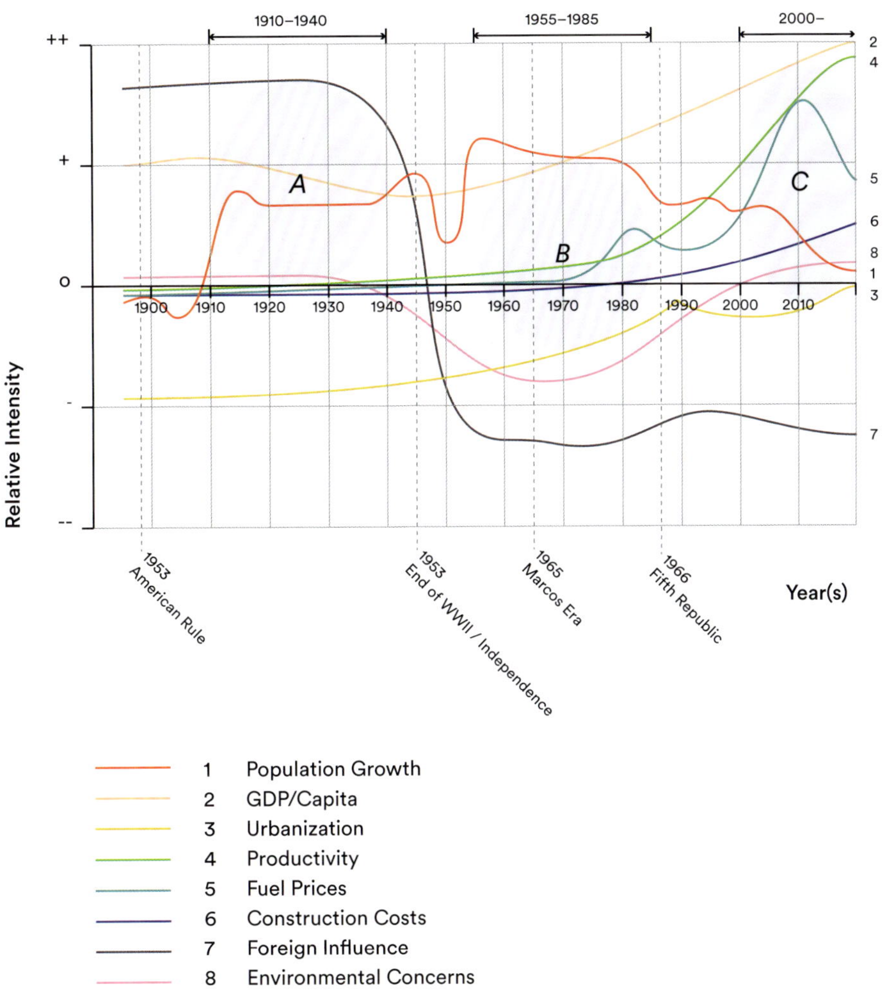

Singapore – Intensity / Time

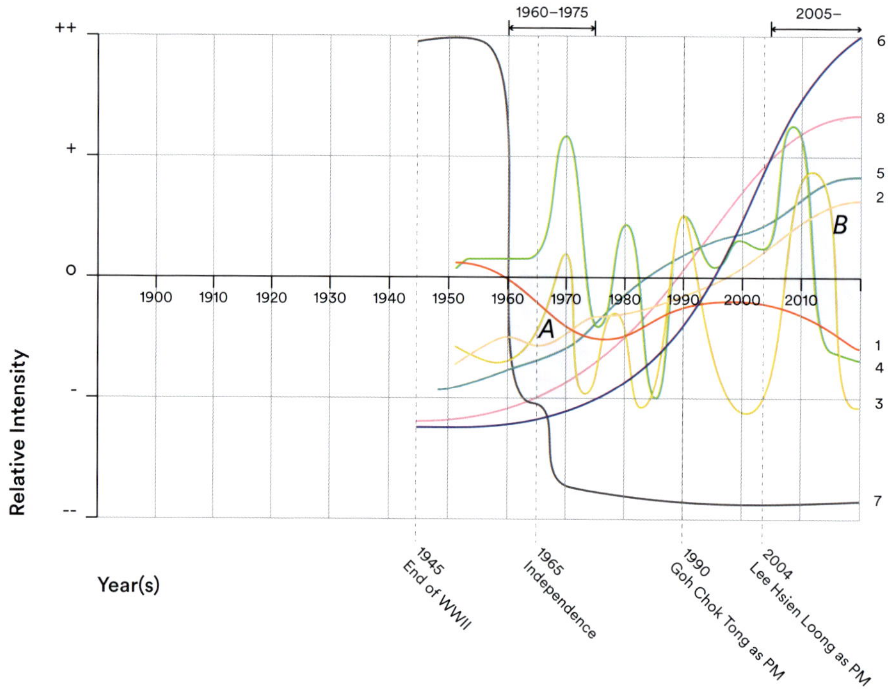

1 Population Growth
2 Population Density
3 Inflation
4 GDP/Capita
5 Consumer Price Index
6 Environmental Concerns
7 Foreign Influence
8 Housing Density

Taiwan – Intensity / Time

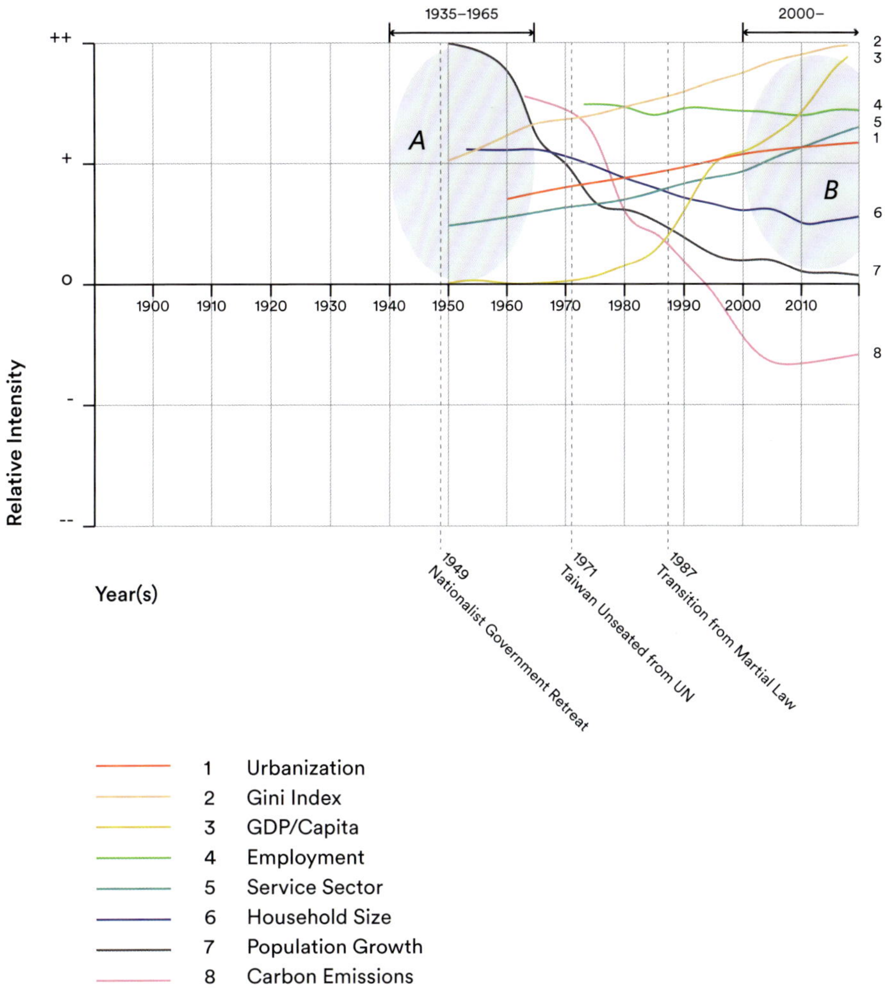

Thailand – Intensity / Time

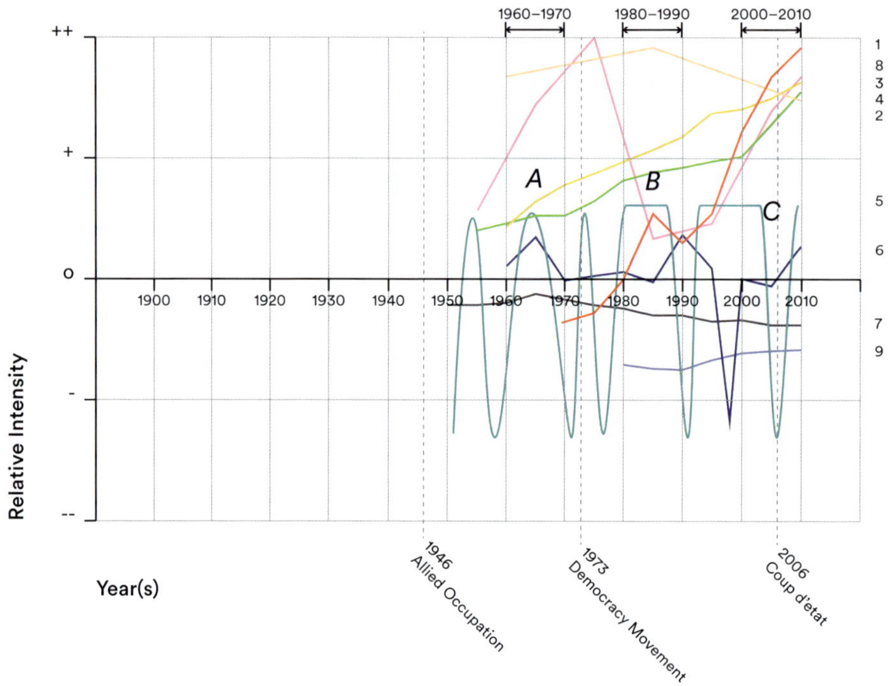

1 Tertiary Education
2 Service Sector
3 Industrialization
4 Urbanization
5 Political Stability
6 GDP/Capita
7 Population Growth
8 Change in Urban Area
9 Gini Index

Vietnam – Intensity / Time

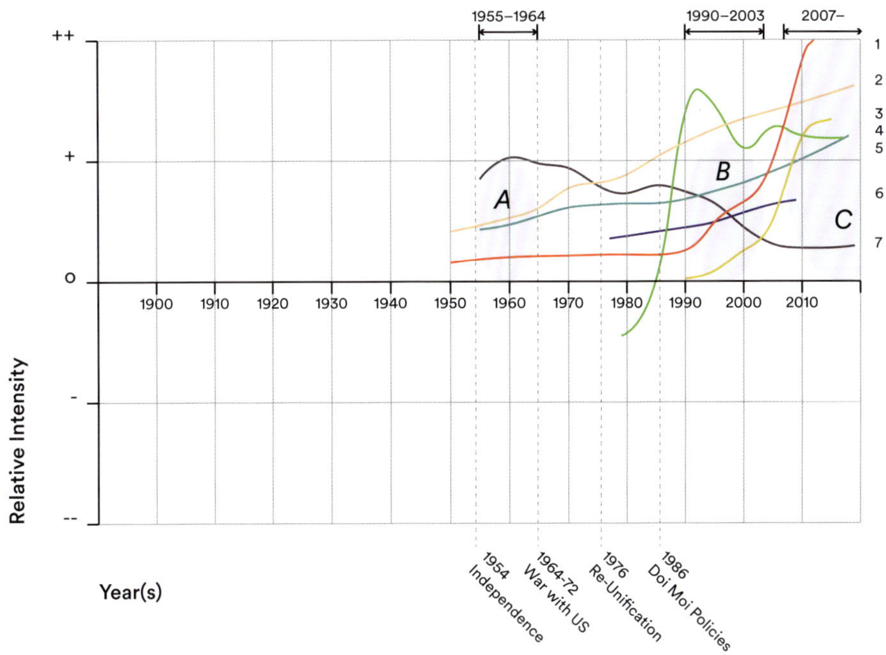

1 Population Growth
2 GDP
3 Inflation
4 Minimum Wage
5 Foreign Influence
6 Urbanization
7 Manufacturing Sector
8 Value of Currency

References

CHAPTER 1

Agoncillo, T. A. 1990. *History of the Filipino People,* 8th edition. Quezon City: R. P. Garcia and Garotech.

Andaya, B. W. and L. Y. Andaya. 2015. *A History of Early Modern Southeast Asia, 1400–1830.* Cambridge: Cambridge University Press.

Arnason, J. P. 1997. *Social Theory and Japanese Experience: The Dual Civilization.* London: Kegan Paul.

Ashton, P. 2014. *On the Forests of Tropical Asia: Lest the Memory Fades.* Richmond: Royal Botanic Gardens, Kew.

Aung-Thwin, M. 2005. *The Mists of Ramanna: The Legend That Was Lower Burma.* Honolulu: University of Hawaii Press.

Beck, U. 1992. *Risk Society: Towards a New Modernity.* London: Sage.

Bellwood, P. 1979. *Man's Conquest of the Pacific: The Prehistory of Southeast Asia and Oceania.* New York: Oxford University Press.

Blench, R. 2009. "Remapping the Austronesian Expansion". In *Discovering History through Language: Papers in Honour of Malcolm Ross*, edited by B. Evans. Canberra: Pacific Linguistics.

Blust, R. A. 2013. *The Austronesian Languages.* Canberra: Australian National University Press.

Blust, R. A. 2016. *History of the Austronesian Languages.* Honolulu: University of Hawaii Press.

Bowen, H. V.; M. Lincoln and N. Rigby, eds. 2003. *The Worlds of the East India Company.* Rochester: Brewer.

Brocheux, P. and D. Hémery. 2010. *Indochina: An Ambiguous Colonization, 1858–1954.* Berkeley, CA: University of California Press.

Brown, S. R. 2009. *Merchant Kings: When Companies Ruled the World, 1600–1900.* New York: St. Martin's Press.

Canclini, N. G. 1995. *Hybrid Cultures: Strategies for Entering and Leaving Modernity.* Minneapolis: University of Minnesota Press.

Chandler, D. 2008. *A History of Cambodia.* Boulder, CO: Westview Press.

Chew, E. C. T. and E. Lee, eds. 1991. *The History of Singapore.* New York: Oxford University Press.

Cœdès, G. 1968. *The Indianized States of Southeast Asia*, edited by W. F. Vella, translated by S. B. Cowing. Honolulu: University of Hawaii Press.

Dalrymple, W. 2019. *The Anarchy: The East India Company, Corporate Violence and the Pillage of an Empire.* New York: Bloomsbury Publishing.

De Bruyn, M; B. Stelbrink; R. J. Morley et al. 2014. "Borneo and Indochina are Major Evolutionary Hotspots for Southeast Asian Biodiversity". *Systematic Biology*, vol. 63, no. 6, pp. 879–901.

Deleuze, G. and F. Guattari. 1987. *A Thousand Plateaus: Capitalism and Schizophrenia.* Minneapolis: University of Minnesota Press.

Dick, N. 2002. *The Emergence of a National Economy: An Economic History of Indonesia, 1800–2000.* Honolulu: University of Hawaii Press.

Dolan, R. E., ed. 1991. *Early History of the Philippines: A Country Study.* Washington, D.C.: Government Printing Office.

Dower, J. W. 1999. *Embracing Defeat: Japan in the Wake of World War II.* New York: W. W. Norton & Co./ New Press.

Dutton, G. E. 2012. *Sources of Vietnamese Tradition.* New York: Columbia University Press.

Eisenstadt, S. N., ed. 2005. *Multiple Modernities.* New Brunswick, NJ: Rutgers University Press.

Evans, M., ed. 2004. *Empire and Culture: The French Empire 1830–1940.* Basingstoke, UK: Macmillan.

Ferguson, N. 2005. *Empire: The Rise and Demise of the British World Order and the Lessons for Global Power.* New York: Basic Books.

Fortunel, F. 2013. "Cross-border Rubber Production in Mainland Southeast Asia". *L'Espace Géographique*, vol. 42, no. 2, pp. 165–178.

Fourie, E. 2012. "A Future for the Theory of Multiple Modernities: Insights from the New Modernization Theory". *Social Science Information*, vol. 51, no. 1, pp. 52–69.

Gaonkar, D., ed. 2001. *Alternative Modernities.* Durham, NC: Duke University Press.

Gupta, A. 2005. *The Physical Geography of Southeast Asia.* New York: Oxford University Press.

Habermas, J. 1996. "Modernity: An Unfinished Project". In *Habermas and the Unfinished Project of Modernity: Critical Essays on the Philosophical Discourse of Modernity*, edited by M. P. d'Entrèves and S. Benhabib. Cambridge, MA: MIT Press, pp. 38–55.

Hall, D. G. E. 1960. *Burma.* London: Hutchinson's University Library.

Hammond, A. 2000. "Imperialism in Southeast Asia: Western Powers Rule Southeast Asia". *Adobe Spark,* pp. 796–799.

Harper, T. 2021. *Underground Asia: Global Revolutionaries and the Assault on Empire.* Cambridge, MA: Harvard University Press.

Harvey, G. 1992. *British Rule in Burma, 1824–1942.* New York: AMS Press.

Khoo, J. E. 1998. *The Straits Chinese: A Cultural History.* Kuala Lumpur: The Pepin Press.

Kiernan, B. and C. Hughes, eds. 2002. *Conflict and Change in Cambodia.* New York: Routledge

Kuhn, P. A. 2008. *Chinese Among Others: Emigration in Modern Times.* New York: Rowman & Littlefield.

Latadmin. 2020. "Introduction to Southeast Asia". *Latitudes: Your Gateway to Southeast Asia* website, 3 March. https://latitudes.nu/introduction-to-southeast-asia-11-countries-593-million-people/.

Lawson, P. 1993. *The East India Company: A History.* London: Longman.

Levin, M.; S. Forgan; M. Hessler et al. 2011. *Urban Modernity: Cultural Innovation in the Second Industrial Revolution.* Cambridge, MA: MIT Press.

Lintner, B. 2005. "How World War II Shaped Burma's Future". *The Irrawaddy,* vol. 13, no. 8, August. https://www2.irrawaddy.com/article.php?art_id=4911.

Mackerras, C., ed. 1995. *East and Southeast Asia: A Multidisciplinary Survey.* Boulder, CO: Lynne Rienner.

Middleton, C. and V. Lamb. 2019. *Knowing the Salween River.* Berlin: Springer Open.

Murphey, R. 1992. *A History of Asia.* New York: Harper Collins.

Myint-U, T. 2006. *The River of Lost Footsteps–A Personal History of Burma.* London: Farrar, Straus and Giroux.

Nee, S. 2014. "Professor John Maynard Smith, 1920–2004". *Trends in Ecology and Evolution,* vol. 19, no. 9, pp. 345–346.

Newitt, M. D. D. 2005. *A History of Portuguese Overseas Expansion, 1400–1668.* New York: Routledge.

Ngo, V. D. 2002. *Champa Ancient Towers: Reality and Legend.* Hanoi: The Gioi.

Nguyen, V. T. 2021. *The Committed.* New York: Grove Press.

Parsons, T., ed. 1968. *Knowledge and Society: American Sociology.* New York: Basic Books.

Pholsena, V. 2006. *Postwar Laos: The Politics of Culture, History and Identity.* Ithaca, NY: Cornell University Press.

Rashid, R. 1993. *A Malaysian Journey.* Selangor: Academe Art and Publishing Services.

Ricklefs, M. C. 1991. *A History of Modern Indonesia since c. 1300.* Basingstoke: Macmillan.

Ross, C. 2014. "The Tin Frontier: Mining, Empire and Environment in Southeast Asia, 1870s–1930s". *Environmental History,* vol. 19, no. 3, pp. 454–479.

Rowe, P. G. and H. Y. Kan. 2014. "Macau and its Borders". In *Macau: Cross-border City,* edited by C. Lee. Cambridge, MA: Harvard Graduate School of Design, pp. 50–65.

Rowe, P. G. and L. Hee. 2019. *A City in Blue and Green: The Singapore Story.* Singapore: Springer Open.

Solheim, W. G. 1985. "The Nusantao Hypothesis: The Origin and Spread of Austronesian Speakers". *Asian Perspectives,* vol. 26, no. 1, pp. 77–88.

Stibig, H.-J.; Beuchle, R. and Janvier, P. 2002. Publications of the European Communities, EUR 20129 EN, European Commission, Luxembourg.

Stoly, J. 2011. "Introduction to the Rainforests of Southeast Asia". *The Tropical Rainforests of Southeast Asia* blog, 24 November. http://rainforestsasia.blogspot.com/?m=0.

Taylor, C. 2001. "Two Theories of Modernity". In *Alternative Modernities,* edited by D. Gaonkar. Durham, NC: Duke University Press, pp. 172–196.

Turnbull, C. M. 1972. *The Straits Settlements, 1826–1867: Indian Presidency to Crown Colony.* London: Athlone Press.

Twitchett, D. C. and J. K. Fairbank, eds. 1979. *Sui and Tang China: 589–906 AD.* Cambridge, UK: Cambridge University Press.

Van Dongen, E. and H. Liu. 2018. *The Changing Meanings of Diaspora: The Chinese in Southeast Asia.* New York: Routledge.

Wallace, A. R. 1869. *The Malay Archipelago.* New York: Harper and Brothers.

Wellington, D. C. 2006. *French East India Companies: A Historical Account and Record of Trade.* New York: Hamilton Books.

World Bank. 2020. *World Population Review.* Washington, DC: The World Bank Group.

World Wildlife Fund. 1999. "WWF Report Highlights Sepik River's Extraordinary Richness". *Pacific Islands Report,* 11 August.

Wright, L. R. 1988. *The Origins of British Borneo.* Hong Kong: Hong Kong University Press.

Yellen, J. A. 2019. *The Greater East Asia Co-Prosperity Sphere: When Total Empire Met Total War.* Ithaca, NY: Cornell University Press.

Young, L. 1999. *Japan's Total Empire: Manchuria and the Culture of Wartime Imperialism.* Berkeley, CA: University of California Press.

CHAPTER 2

Archilovers. 2014. "Secondary School, Roong Village". *Archilovers* website. https://www.archilovers.com/projects/160058/secondary-school-roong-village.html.

ArchDaily. 2012. "Te Wharewaka / architecture +". *ArchDaily* website. https://www.archdaily.com/249112/te-wharewaka-architecture.

ArchDaily. 2014. "High School Thazin / a+r ARCHITEKTEN". *ArchDaily* website. https://www.archdaily.com/534728/high-school-thazin-ackermann-raff.

ArchDaily. 2019. "Bann Huay San Yaw Post Disaster School / Vin Varavarn Architects". *ArchDaily* website. https://www.archdaily.com/776325/bann-huay-san-yaw-post-disaster-school-vin-varavarn-architects.

Architect. 2017. "Taitung Aboriginal Gallery / Bio-architecture

Formosana". *Architect* website, 28 April. https://www.architect-magazine.com/project-gallery/taitung-aboriginal-gallery_o.

Astbury, J. 2019. "Zigzag Thatched Bamboo Roofs Shade Classrooms of School in Indonesia". *Dezeen* website, 28 August. https://www.dezeen.com/2019/08/28/alfa-omega-school-raw-architecture-tangerang-city-indonesia/.

Benedict, P. 1975. *Austro-Thai Language and Culture.* New Haven, CT: Human Relations Area Files Press.

Biggs, B. G. 1957. "The Story of Kupe. As Written Down by Himiona Koamira". *Journal of the Polynesian Society*, vol. 66, pp. 232–248.

Blaser, W. 2001. *Renzo Piano – Centre Kanak: Cultural Centre of Kanak People.* Basel: Birkhäuser.

Chiang, T. S. 2007. "Canopy idea ranked first in Art Gallery designs". *The Straits Times,* 31 August, p. 83.

Crook, L. 2020. "Photos Reveal Shigeru Ban's Tainan Art Museum Building in Taiwan". *Dezeen* website, 30 January. https://www.dezeen.com/2020/01/30/photos-shigeru-bans-tainan-art-museum-building-architecture/.

Dawson, B. and G. Gillow. 1994. *The Traditional Architecture of Indonesia.* London: Thames and Hudson.

Domenig, G. 1980. *Tektonik im primitiven Dachbau (Tectonics of Primitive Roof construction).* Zurich: ETH Zurich.

Doran, E. 1981. *Wangka: Austronesian Canoe Origins.* College Station, TX: Texas A&M University Press.

Fox, J. J. 1993a. "Memories of Ridge-Poles and Cross Beams: The Categorical Foundation of a Rotinese Culture Design". In *Inside Austronesian Houses*, edited by J. J. Fox. Canberra: Australian National University, pp. 141–177.

Fox, J. J. ed. 1993b. *Inside Austronesian Houses.* Canberra: Australian National University.

Girard, J.-C. 2021. *Leandro V. Locsin Architect.* Basel: Birkhäuser.

Herrmann, R. 2016. "Vn-A Hiong Thi Vu, Tuan Dung Nguyen New Church of Kadon Parish". *Divisare* website, 25 August. https://divisare.com/projects/324594-vn-a-huong-thi-vu-tuan-dung-nguyen-robert-herrmann-new-church-of-kadon-parish.

Hudson, D. 2012. "TYIN tegnestue architects: cassia coop training centre". *Designboom* website, 11 October. https://www.designboom.com/architecture/tyin-tegnestue-architects-cassia-coop-training-centre/.

Johnston, P., ed. 2007. *Intervention Architecture: Building for Change.* London: I. B. Tauris and Co, Ltd.

Mark, L. 2015. "Heatherwick's Singapore Uni Learning Hub Opens". *Architects' Journal* website, 10 March. https://www.architectsjournal.co.uk/news/heatherwicks-singapore-uni-learning-hub-opens.

Merrillees, S. 2015. *Jakarta: Portraits of a Capital, 1950–1980.* Jakarta: Equinox Publishing.

Metge, J. 1976. *Rautahi: The Maoris of New Zealand.* London: Routledge & Kegan Paul.

Murphy, B. 2002. "Centre Culturel Tjibaou: A Museum and Arts Center Redefining New Caledonia's Cultural Future". *Humanities Review*, vol. 9, no. 1, pp. 77–90.

Phillipps, W. J. 1952. *Maori Houses and Food Stores.* New York: R. E. Owen, Government Printer.

Rapaport, A. 1969. *House Form and Culture.* New York: Pearson.

Rowe, P. G. and L. Hee. 2019. *A City in Blue and Green: The Singapore Story.* Singapore: Springer.

Rudofsky, B. 1964. *Architecture Without Architecture: A Short Introduction to Non-pedigreed Architecture.* Albuquerque, NM: University of New Mexico Press.

Salmond, A. 1975. *Hui: A Study of Maori Ceremonial Gatherings.* Wellington: Reed.

Sather, C. 1993. "Posts, Hearths and Thresholds: The Iban Longhouse as a Ritual Structure". In *Inside Austronesian Houses*, edited by J. J. Fox. Canberra: Australian National University, pp. 64–115.

Scott, W. H. 1966. *On the Cordillera: A Look at the Peoples and Culture of the Mountain Province.* Manila: MCS Enterprises.

Siregar, A. R. O. 2015a. "Stella Maris Pluit Catholic Church". *Archinesia*, vol. 3, pp. 114–123.

Siregar, A. R. O. 2015b. "Multimedia Nusantara University". *Archinesia*, vol. 3, pp. 136–145.

Shim, B. 2011. "Reconstruction of Ngibikan Village, Yogyakarta, Indonesia". In *Implicate and Explicate*, edited by M. Mostafavi. Baden, Switzerland: Lars Müller Publishing.

Stevens, P. 2014. "Vo Trong Nghia Architects stacks houses for trees in Vietnam". *Designboom* website, 19 June. https://www.designboom.com/architecture/vo-trong-nghia-architects-house-for-trees-vietnam-06-19-2014/.

Studio TonTon. 2016. "Studio TonTon, Tangerang, Indonesia". *Divisare* website, 14 March. https://divisare.com/projects/312757-studio-tonton-studio-tonton-tangerang-indonesia.

Van Meijl, T. 1993. "Maori Meeting Houses in and Over Time". In *Inside Austronesian Houses*, edited by J. J. Fox. Canberra: Australian National University, pp. 195–216.

Vroklage, B. A. G. 1936. "Das Schiff in den Megalithkulturen Südostasiens und der Südsee (The Ship in the Megalithic Cultures of Southeast Asia and the South Seas)". *Anthropos,* vol. 31, pp. 712–757.

Walden, P. 1987. *Voices of Silence: New Zealand's Chapel of Futuna.* Wellington: Victoria University Press.

Waterson, R. 1990. *The Living House: An Anthropology of Architecture in South-East Asia.* New York: Oxford University Press.

CHAPTER 3

Aasen, C. 1998. *Architecture of Siam: A Cultural History and Interpretation.* Oxford: Oxford University Press.

Acharya, A. 2021. "Journey to the East: The Hindu-Buddhist Making of Southeast Asia". *The Diplomat* website, 15 February. https://thediplomat.com/2021/02/journey-to-the-east-the-hindu-buddhist-making-of-southeast-asia/.

Aga Khan Award for Architecture, 2007. "Assyafaah Mosque, Singapore". *Archnet* website. https://www.archnet.org/publications/1578.

Albanese, M. 2006. *The Treasures of Angkor.* Novara, Italy: White Star Publishers.

ArchDaily. 2010. "Al-Irsyad Mosque / Urbane". *ArchDaily* website, 10 November. https://www.archdaily.com/87587/al-irsyad-mosque-urbane.

ArchDaily. 2014. "Wat Ananda Metyarama Thai Buddhist Temple / Czarl Architects". *ArchDaily* website, 15 September. https://www.archdaily.com/547649/wat-ananda-metyarama-thai-buddhist-temple-czarl-architects.

ArchDaily. 2015a. "Regeneration of Taoyuan International Airport Terminal 1 / Norihiko Dan and Associates". *ArchDaily* website, 2 August. https://www.archdaily.com/771071/regeneration-of-taoyuan-international-airport-terminal-1-norihiko-dan-and-associates.

ArchDaily. 2015b. "Layerscape / Kien Truc O". *Arch Daily* website, 9 June. https://www.archdaily.com/639758/layer-scape-kien-truc-o.

ArchDaily. 2019. "Termitary House/Tropical Space". *ArchDaily* website, 13 November. https://www.archdaily.com/594339/termitary-house-tropical-space.

ArchDaily. 2020. "The Binh House / VTN Architects". *ArchDaily* website, 24 March. https://www.archdaily.com/868963/binh-house-vo-trong-nhia-architects.

Archilovers. 2016. "VAS Office Building, Da Nang, Vietnam". *Archilovers* website, 2 February. https://www.archilovers.com/projects/174601/vas-office-building.html.

Baird, G. 2001. *The Architectural Expression of Environmental Control Systems.* London: Spon Press.

Bairoch, P. 1976. "Europe's Gross National Product, 1800–1975", *Journal of European Economic History*, vol. 5, pp. 273–340.

Bronson, B. and J. Wisseman. 1975. "Palembang as Srivijaya: The Lateness of Early Cities in Southern Southeast Asia". *Asian Perspectives*, vol. 19, no. 2, pp. 220–239.

Brown, P. 2010. *Indian Architecture: Islamic Period.* New York: CBS Publishers.

Chang, T. 1976. "The Rice Cultures". *Philosophical Transactions of the Royal Society in London*, vol. 275, Series B, pp. 143–155.

Cœdès, G. 1968. *The Indianized States of Southeast Asia*, edited by W. F. Vella, translated by S. B. Cowing. Honolulu: University of Hawaii Press.

Congrong, H. 2021. "Architecture of Xia, Shang, Zhou Dynasties and Spring and Autumn Period". *Essential Architecture* website, October. http://www.essential-architecture.com/STYLE/STY-119.htm.

Davidson, J. 2003, *Balinese Architecture.* Singapore: Tuttle Publishing.

Desai, Z. A. 1970. *Indo-Islamic Architecture.* New Delhi: Publications Division, Ministry of Information and Broadcasting.

Dreyer, E. L. 2007. *Zheng He: China and the Oceans in the Early Ming Dynasty.* New York: Pearson Longman.

Federico, G. 2002. "The World Economy, 0–2000 AD". *Journal of European Economic History*, vol. 6, no. 1, pp. 111–120.

Gómez, L. O. and H. W. Woodward, Jr. 1981. *Barabudur: History and Significance of a Buddhist Monument.* Berkeley, CA: University of California Press.

Higham, C. F. W. 2014. *Early Cultures of Mainland Southeast Asia.* Bangkok: River Books.

Inglis, K., ed. 1998. *Myanmar Style: Art, Architecture and Design of Burma.* Hong Kong: Periplus.

Kelley, L. 2020. "Srivijaya 00: Un-Imagining 'Srivijaya' – A Series". *Le Minh Khai's SEAsian History Blog,* 30 October. https://leminhkhai.blog/imagining-srivijaya-a-series/.

Khue, H. 2019. "Ho Khue Architects Bring Jungle Life into a Terraced Apartment Building in Da Nang City, Vietnam". *Vietnam Architectural News*, vol. 3, no. 2.

Knapp, R. G. ed. 2003. *Asia's Old Dwellings, Resistance and Change.* New York: Oxford University Press.

Ma, B. 1999. *The Architecture of the Quadrangle in Beijing.* Tianjin: Tianjin University Press.

Maire, 2018. *Temples + Treehouses.com.* https://templesandtreehouses.com/.

Michell, G. 1988. *The Hindu Temple: An Introduction to Its Meaning and Forms.* Chicago: University of Chicago Press.

Michell, G. 1995. *Architecture and Art of Southern India: Vijayanagara and Successor States, 1350–1750.* New York: Cambridge University Press.

Miksic, J. 1997. "Sukuh and Ceto". In *Java*, edited by E. Oey. Singapore: Periplus, pp. 223–225.

Miksic, J. and G. Tjahjono, eds. 1998. *Indonesian Heritage. Vol. 6: Architecture.* Singapore: Archipelago Press.

Mills, J. V. G. 1970. *Ma Huan: Ying-Yang Sheng-Lan: "The Overall Survey of Ocean's Shores".* Cambridge: Cambridge University Press.

Murthy, K. K. 1966. "Dharma – Its Etymology". *The Tibet Journal*, vol. 21, no. 1, Spring, pp. 84–87.

Necipoglu, G. and A. Payne. 2016. *Histories of Ornament: From Global to Local.* Princeton, NJ: Princeton University Press.

Picon, A. 2020. *The Materiality of Architecture.* Minneapolis: University of Minnesota Press.

Rowe, P. G. 2019. "Three on Display at Shanghai's Expo 'Better City, Better Life'". In K. Provoost, *Beautified China: The Architectural Revolution.* Tielt, Belgium: Lannoo Publishers, pp. 12–14.

Rowe, P. G. and S. Kuan, 2002. *Architectural Encounters with Essence and Form.* Cambridge, MA: MIT Press.

Sasiwongsaroj, K.; S. Pornsiripongse; Y. Burasith et al. 2012. "Buddhist Temple: The Well-being Space for the Aged in Thailand". *Journal of Population and Social Studies*, vol. 20, no. 2, pp. 2–19.

Soekmono, R.; J. G. de Casparis and J. Dumarçay, 1990. *Borobudur: A Prayer in Stone.* Singapore: Archipelago Press.

SPINE Architects, 2021. *Zaya Thakedi Amata Zawdi Tharyar Aye Meditation Center: Master Plan and Program.* Yangon: SPINE Architects.

Tjokrosaputro, T. 2011. *100 Masjid Terindah Indonesia (100 Beautiful Mosques in Indonesia).* Jakarta: PT Andalan Media.

Wang, G. 1958. "The Nanhai Trade: A study of the early history of Chinese trade in the South China Sea". *Journal of the Malaysian Branch of the Royal Asiatic Society*, vol. 31, no. 2, pp. 1–135.

Welch, A. 2010 "Hanoi Museum Vietnam: Architecture". *E-Architect* website, 8 October. https://www.e-architect.com/vietnam/hanoi-museum.

Wheatley, P. 1983. *Nagara and Commandery: Origins of the Southeast Asian Urban Traditions.* Chicago: University of Chicago Press.

Wilkinson, E. 2012. *Chinese History: A New Manual.* Cambridge, MA: Harvard University Press.

Willson, A. 1999. *Places of Worship: Buddhist Temples.* Portsmouth, NH: Heinemann Educational.

Wilson, V. 2019. "A Modern Incarnation of the Ancient Spirit of Chiang Mai". *Habitusliving* website, 12 November. https://www.habitusliving.com/architecture/foothill-house-ssar.

Wu, L. 1999. *Rehabilitating the Old City of Beijing.* Vancouver: University of British Columbia Press.

Wu, M. 2015. "SPINE – Architects of Myanmar's Contemporary Design Movement". *Myanmore Magazine* website, 23 July. https://www.myanmore.com/2015/07/spine-architects-of-myanmars-contemporary-design-movement/.

CHAPTER 4

Akihary, H. 1990. *Architectuur & stedebouw in Indonesie, 1870–1970 (Architecture and Building in Indonesia, 1870–1970).* Zutphen, Netherlands: De Walburg Pers.

Alcazaren, P. 2005. "Juan M. de Guzman Arellano: Renaissance Man". *The Philippine Star*, 12 November.

Alacon, N. 2008. *The Imperial Tapestry: American Colonial Architecture and Urbanism in the Philippines.* Manila: University of Santo Tomas Publishing House.

ArchDaily. 2013. "Kontum Café / Vo Trong Nghia Architects". *ArchDaily* website, 27 June. https://www.archdaily.com/392710/kontum-indochine-cafe-vo-trong-nghia-architects.

ArchDaily. 2016a. "City Center Tower / CAZA". *ArchDaily* website, 23 December. https://www.archdaily.com/801549/city-center-tower-caza.

ArchDaily. 2016b. "Terrace House Renovation / O2 Design Atelier". *ArchDaily* website, 18 March. https://www.archdaily.com/783163/terrace-house-renovation-o2-design-atelier.

ArchDaily. 2019. "NUS School of Design and Environment / Serie Architects + Multiply Architects + Surbana Jurong". *ArchDaily* website, 25 February. https://www.archdaily.com/912021/nus-school-of-design-and-environment-serie-architects-plus-multiply-architects-plus-surbana-jurong.

Askew, M. 2003. "'Ban Thai': House and Culture in a Transforming Culture". In *Asia's Old Dwellings: Tradition, Resilience, and Change*, edited by R. G. Knapp. New York: Oxford University Press, pp. 259–281.

Balderstone, A. and W. Logan. 2003. "Vietnamese Dwellings: Tradition, Resilience, and Change". In *Asia's Old Dwellings: Tradition, Resilience, and Change*, edited by R. G. Knapp. New York: Oxford University Press, pp. 135–157.

Buckley, C. B. 1902. *An Anecdotal History of Old Times in Singapore.* Singapore: Fraser and Neave.

Cerbo, N. 2021. "Manila Cathedral Survives Earthquakes, Typhoons and Bombs!". *Philippines Travel Guide* website. http://www.philippines-travel-guide.com/manila-cathedral.html.

Conservation Department. 2019. *Tiong Bahru: Do It Right, A Quick Guide on Works to Conserve Tiong Bahru Pre-War Units.* Singapore: Urban Redevelopment Authority.

Coté, J. and H. O'Neill. 2017. *The Life and Work of Thomas Karsten.* Amsterdam: Architectura & Natura.

Davis, K. 2017. "Art Deco in Indonesia". *Indonesia Expat*, vol. 201, 8–21 November, p. 14.

Ee, K. J. 1996. *The Straits Chinese: A Cultural History.* Kuala Lumpur: The Pepin Press.

Esparza, D. 2019. "The Church of Saint Agustin of Paoay in the Philippines, A Great Example of 'Earthquake Baroque' Architecture". *Aleteia* website, 26 October. https://aleteia.org/2019/10/26/the-church-of-saint-agustin-of-paoay-in-the-philippines-a-great-example-of-earthquake-baroque-architecture/.

Figment. 2012. *Architectural Project Page: The Lorong 24A Shophouse Series.* Singapore: Figment.

Hartono, D. 1989. "Decorative Art in Architecture as a Part of Bandung History". *Bandung Society for Heritage Conservation* website. https://www.iis.u-tokyo.ac.jp/~fujimori/heritage/heritage.html.

Huynh, N. 2003. "Housing cat space block, Hanoi, 1999–2003". *Academia* website. https://www.academia.edu/22757992/Housing_cat_space_block_hanoi.

Inglis, K., ed. 1998. *Myanmar Style: Art, Architecture and Design of Burma.* Hong Kong: Periplus.

Jablon, P. 2009. "The Siang Savan Theater, Luang Prabang, Laos". *The Southeast Asia Movie Theater Project* blog, 5 July. http://seatheater.blogspot.com/2009/07/siang-savan-theater-luang-prabang-laos.html.

Lico, G. 2008. *Arkitekturang Filipino: A Study of Architecture and Urbanism in the Philippines.* Quezon City: University of the Philippines Press.

Lim, J. S. H. 1993. "The 'Shophouse Rafflesia': An Outline of Its Malaysian Pedigree and Its Subsequent Diffusion in Asia". *Journal of the Malaysian Branch of the Royal Asiatic Society*, vol. 66, no. 1, pp. 47–66.

Lin, L. K. 1995. *The Singapore House: 1819–1942.* Singapore: Times Editions.

Liu, G. 1984. *Pastel Portraits: Singapore's Architectural Heritage.* Singapore: Singapore Coordinating Committee.

Lombolt, I. 2016. "Phnom Penh Central Market in Cambodia". *E-Architect* website, 14 July. https://www.e-architect.com/cambodia/phnom-penh-central-market-in-cambodia.

Milone, P. D. 1967. "*Indische* Culture, and Its Relationship to Urban Life". *Comparative Studies I Society and History*, vol. 9, no. 4, pp. 407–426.

Moore, C. 1968. *Daniel H. Burnham: Architect, Planner of Cities, vol. 2.* New York: DaCapo Press.

Nas, P. J. M., ed. 2006. *The Past in the Present: Architecture in Indonesia.* Rotterdam: NIA Publishers.

Norindr, P. 1996. *Phantasmatic Indochina: French Colonial Ideology in Architecture, Film and Literature.* Durham, NC: Duke University Press.

Passchier, C. 2006. "Colonial Architecture in Indonesia: References and Developments". In *The Past and the Present: Architecture in Indonesia*, edited by P. J. M. Nas. Rotterdam: NIA Publishers, pp. 97–112.

Reed, H. H. and J. C. Farber. 1980. *Palladio's Architecture and Its Influences.* New York: Dover Publications.

Renuka, M.; O. E. Chuan and L. P. Ying. 2014. "Former Asia Insurance Building (Ascot Raffles Place)". *Singapore Infopedia* website, 16 October. https://eresources.nlb.gov.sg/infopedia/articles/SIP_592_2005-01-17.html.

Rowe, P. G. and H. Y. Kan, 2014. *Urban Intensities: Contemporary Housing Types and Territories.* Basel: Birkhäuser.

Schenck, M. 2020. *Southern Vietnamese Modernist Architecture: Mid-Century Vernacular Architecture.* Helena, MO: Melvin J. Schenck Publishers.

Selya, R. M. 1995. *Taipei.* New York: John Wiley.

SgArch, 2020. *Compradoric Architecture: Everyday Architecture in the Early Colonial Period Featuring the Shophouse and Godown.* Singapore: Singapore Architecture and Urban Planning.

SgArch. 2021. *Neo-Palladian Architecture: European Styles of Building in Early Colonial Singapore.* Singapore: Singapore Architecture and Urban Planning.

Siang, S. O. 1993. *One Hundred Years' History of the Chinese in Singapore.* Singapore: Singapore Chamber of Commerce.

Soewarno, N. and D. Duhita. 2019. "The Transformation of Heritage: Building as Tourist Attraction, Adaptive Re-use of Colonial Buildings at a Bandung Conservation Area". *Advances in Engineering Research*, vol. 156, pp. 131–140.

Stevens, P. 2015. "Narrow townhouse in Vietnam by MM++ features a retractable shutter screen". *Designboom* website, 17 November. https://www.designboom.com/architecture/mm-architects-townhouse-with-a-folding-up-shutter-ho-chi-minh-city-vietnam-11-16-2015/.

Stevens, P. 2016. "All (Zone) Clads Thailand's MAIIAM Art Museum with Thousands of Mirrored Tiles". *Designboom* website, 26 September. https://www.designboom.com/architecture/allzone-thailand-maiiam-contemporary-art-museum-mirrored-tiles-chiang-mai-09-26-2016/.

Summerson, J. 1980. *The Classical Language of Architecture.* London: Thames and Hudson.

Suryono, A.; A. Sudikno and P. Salura. 2013. "Conservation of Dutch Colonial Architectural Heritage on the Rectorate Building of the Education University of Indonesia in Bandung". *Journal of Basic and Applied Scientific Research*, vol. 3, no. 8, pp. 418–422.

Thim, R. 2020. "Explore the Central Market, Phnom Penh of Cambodia". *Tripily* website, 14 July. https://tripily.co/central-market-of-phnom-penh/.

To, K.; Z. W. Chong and K. H. Chong. 2014. *Identity of a Conserved Housing Estate in Transition: The Case of Tiong Bahru.* Singapore: Singapore University of Technology and Design.

Tyers, R. K. 2018. *Singapore Then and Now.* Singapore: Landmark Books.

Villalon, A. 2003. "The Evolution of the Philippine Traditional House". In *Asia's Old Dwellings: Tradition, Resilience, and Change*, edited by R. G. Knapp. New York: Oxford University Press, pp. 203–219.

Vongvilay, X.; J.-E. Shin; Y.-H. Kang et al. 2015. "The Influence of French Colonial Rule on Lao Architecture with a Focus on Residential Buildings". *Journal of Asian Architecture and Building Engineering*, vol. 14, no. 2, pp. 279–286.

Welch, A. 2016. "City Center Tower, Manila in the Philippines". *E-Architect* website, 14 December. https://www.e-architect.com/philippines/city-center-tower-manila-in-the-philippines.

Widodo, J. 2006. "Modern Indonesian Architecture: Transplantation, Adaptation, Accommodation and Hybridization". In *The Past in the Present: Architecture in Indonesia*, edited by P. J. M. Nas. Rotterdam: NIA Publishers, pp. 17–24.

Wilkinson, E. 2012. *Chinese History: A New Manual.* Cambridge, MA: Harvard University Press.

Wong, T.-C. 2020. "The Truth About the Chinese Migration to Malaya". *Malaysia Today* website, 16 January. https://www.malaysia-today.net/2020/01/16/the-truth-about-the-chinese-migration-to-malaya/.

Wong, Y. C. and S. T. Lee. 2005. *Singapore 1:1 – City.* Singapore: Urban Redevelopment Authority.

Wright, G. 1991. *The Politics of Design in French Colonial Urbanism.* Chicago: University of Chicago Press.

Zapartan, T. 2017. "Bamboo Sports Hall Combines a Modern Organic Design with 21st Century Engineering and a Natural Material". *Inspirationist,* Architecture, website, 29 August. http://inspirationist.net/bamboo-sports-hall-combines-a-modern-organic-design-with-21st-century-engineering-and-a-natural-material/.

CHAPTER 5

ArchDaily. 2010. "Marina Bay Sands / Safdie Architects". *ArchDaily* website, 26 July. https://www.archdaily.com/70186/marina-bay-sands-safdie-architects.

ArchDaily. 2016. "Oasia Hotel Downtown / WOHA". *ArchDaily* website, 7 December. https://www.archdaily.com/800878/oasia-hotel-downtown-woha.

Balian, H. 2015. "The Man Who Built Cambodia: Vann Molyvann's 1964 National Stadium". *Uncube Magazine* website, 3 March. https://www.uncubemagazine.com/blog/15359429.

Banham, R. 1966. *The New Brutalism.* London: Architectural Press.

Bhabha, H. K. 1995. *Nation and Narration.* New York: Routledge.

Binder, G. 2008. *Taipei 101.* Melbourne: Images Publishing Group.

Brookes, S. 2007. "Cambodian Modern: The Architectural Legacy of Vann Molyvann". *Most of the Shebang* blog, 31 December. http://www.stephenbrookes.com/new-writing/2007/12/31/cambodian-modern-the-architectural-legacy-of-vann-molyvann.html.

Canclini, N. G. 1995. *Hybrid Cultures: Strategies for Entering and Leaving Modernity.* Minneapolis: University of Minnesota Press.

Chalcraft, E. 2012. "Stacking Green by Vo Trong Nghia". *Dezeen* website, 9 July. https://www.dezeen.com/2012/07/09/stacking-green-by-vo-trong-nghia/.

Cheng, H.-C. and C.-M. Shih. 2008. "Reinterpreting Traditional Chinese Architecture in the Office Buildings and Skyscraper Architecture of C. Y. Lee". *Journal of Architectural and Planning Research*, vol. 25, no. 3, pp. 181–202.

Design Chronicle. 2014. "PARKROYAL on Pickering by WOHA". *Design Chronicle* website, 3 July. https://design-chronicle.com/parkroyal-on-pickering-by-woha/.

Dhiracitta, A. 2020. "Istiqlal Mosque by Friedrich Silaban – Shifting Perspectives on Colonial Architecture". *Rethinking the Future* website. https://www.re-thinkingthefuture.com/rtf-design-inspiration/a1417-istiqlal-mosque-by-friedrich-silaban-shifting-perspectives-on-colonial-architecture/.

Douglass-Jaimes, D. 2015. "AD Classics: Menara Mesiniaga / T. R. Hamzah & Yeang Sdn. Bhd.". *ArchDaily* website, 28 September. https://www.archdaily.com/774098/ad-classics-menara-mesiniaga-t-r-hamzah-and-yeang-sdn-bhd.

Edwards, N. and P. Keys. 1996. *Singapore: A Guide to Buildings, Streets, Places.* Singapore: Times Books International.

Fraser, F. 2015. "Navigating the Maze of Faith: 100 Walls Church by CAZA in Cebu City, Philippines". *The Architecture Review* website, 2 December. https://www.architectural-review.com/awards/ar-emerging-architecture/navigating-the-maze-of-faith-100-walls-church-by-caza-in-cebu-city-philippines.

Girard, G. 2021. *Leandro V. Locsin, Architect.* Basel: Birkhäuser.

Goodwin, K. 2016. "Cherry Orchard Cemetery by Fieldoffice Architects: 'A Subtle Conversation Between Man and Nature'". *The Architectural Review* website, 1 November. https://www.architectural-review.com/buildings/cherry-orchard-cemetery-by-fieldoffice-architects-a-subtle-conversation-between-man-and-nature.

Hahijary, B. 2016. "JKTarchitecture: Wisma 46 (BNI)". *iD Indonesia Design* website, 15 March. https://indonesiadesign.com/story/jktarchitecture-wisma-46-bni.

Hall, W. and L. Koren, eds. 2021. *Concrete.* London: Phaidon.

Harding, P. 2010. "Taiwan's Grand Hotel Welcome for Chinese Visitors". *BBC News* website, 23 January. http://news.bbc.co.uk/2/hi/programmes/from_our_own_correspondent/8475215.stm.

Hegel, G. W. F. 1965. "The Preface to the Phenomenology of Mind". In *Hegel: Texts and Commentary*, translated and edited by W. Kaufmann. New York: Doubleday, pp. 1–5.

Hess, A. 2004. *Googie Redux: Ultramodern Roadside Architecture.* New York: Chronicle Books.

Kroll, A. 2011. "AD Classics: Petronas Towers / Cesar Pelli". *ArchDaily* website, 24 January. https://www.archdaily.com/105895/ad-classics-petronas-towers-cesar-pelli.

Lee, M. 2011. "Pinnacle@Duxton". *Singapore Infopedia* website. https://eresources.nlb.gov.sg/infopedia/articles/SIP_1779_2011-02-18.html.

Lee, P. K. K. 1997. *Structures in the New Millennium.* London: Routledge.

Lico, G. 2010. *Arkitekturang Filipino: A History of Architecture and Urbanism in the Philippines.* Quezon City: University of the Philippines Press.

Malaysia Architecture. 2012. "Salinger House by CSL Associates". *Malaysia Architecture* blog, 11 February. http://msiaarch.blogspot.com/2012/02/salinger-residence.html.

Oka, M.; B. Bansai and E. Fox. 2016. *Architectural Guide, Yangon.* Yangon: DOM Publishers.

Pholsena, V. 2006. *Post-War Laos: The Politics of Culture, History and Identity.* Ithaca, NY: Cornell University Press.

Powell, R. 2004. *Singapore Architecture.* Singapore: Periplus Editions.

Purba, K. 2010. "Istiqlal: The Work of a Christian Architect". *The Jakarta Post*, 10 November.

Rasdi, M. T. and N. Hussain. 2016. "National Identity and the Architecture of Malayan Architect Co-Partnership". *Heritage Buildings of Malaysia* blog, May. http://myheritagebuildings.blogspot.com/.

Rowe, P. G. 2011. *Emergent Architectural Territories in East Asian Cities.* Basel: Birkhäuser.

Rowe, P. G. 2017. "Building Forwards and Backwards in Time: Architectural Modernism in East and Southeast Asia". In *The Modernist World*, edited by S. Ross and A. C. Lindgren. New York: Routledge, pp. 25–32.

Rowe, P. G. and L. M. Hee, 2019. *A City in Blue and Green: The Singapore Story.* Singapore: Springer Open.

San, J. 2013. "On the Waterfront of Singapore". *Domus* website, 29 March. https://www.domusweb.it/en/news/2013/03/29/on-the-waterfront-of-singapore.html.

Saunders, G. E. 2002. *A History of Brunei.* London: Routledge.

Schenck, M. and A. Garel. 2020. *Southern Vietnamese Modernist Architecture.* Helena, MT: Architecture Vietnam Books.

Schröpfer, T. ed. 2020. *Dense + Green Cities.* Basel: Birkhäuser.

Sopandi, S. and R. Hartanto. 2015. "A Cinematic Sandwich: Andra Matin House, Jakarta". *Uncube Magazine* website, 17 November.

Suthlapa, W. 2017. "Modern Tropical House in Ho Chi Minh City". *Living Asean* website, 11 July. https://livingasean.com/house/modern-tropical-house/.

Tham, I. 2010. "Architects' Pinnacle of Achievement". *The Straits Times,* 27 June, p. 12.

Tjahjono, G. and J. Miksic. 2003. *Architecture: Indonesian Heritage.* Singapore: Archipelago Press.

United Nations, 2018. *Population Dynamics.* New York: Department of Economic and Social Affairs.

Vorajee, I. 2019, "Federation Shares Stadium Progress". *Khmer Times,* 14 March. https://www.khmertimeskh.com/586361/federation-shares-stadium-progress/.

Welch, A. 2019. "Maha-Nakhon Bangkok: Thailand Tower". *E-Architect* website, 1 May. https://www.e-architect.com/thailand/mahanakhon-tower-bangkok.

Wong, Y. C. and S. T. Lee. 2005. *Singapore 1:1 – City.* Singapore: Urban Redevelopment Authority.

Yeang, K. 1996. *The Skyscraper Bioclimatically Considered.* New York: Wiley.

CHAPTER 6

Bulson, E. 2006. *The Cambridge Introduction to James Joyce.* London: Cambridge University Press.

Canclini, N. G. 1995. *Hybrid Cultures: Strategies for Entering and Leaving Modernity.* Minneapolis: University of Minnesota Press.

Eliot, T. S. 1919. "Tradition and the Individual Talent". *The Egoist*, vol. 6, no. 4, September, pp. 54–55 and no. 5, December, pp. 72–73.

Frampton, K. 1983. "Towards a Critical Regionalism: Six Points for an Architecture of Resistance". In *The Anti-Aesthetic: Essays on Post-Modern Culture*, edited by H. Foster. Port Townsend, WA: Bay Press, pp. 16–30.

Ginsburg, N.; B. Koppel and T. G. McGee, eds. 1991. *The Extended Metropolis: Settlement in Transition in Asia.* Honolulu: University of Hawaii Press.

Gupta, A. ed. 2008. *The Physical Geography of Southeast Asia.* New York: Oxford University Press.

Jambeck, J. R.; R. Geyer; C. Wilcox et al. 2015. "Plastic Waste Inputs from Land to the Oceans". *Science*, vol. 347 (6223), pp. 768–771.

Lim, G.; H. Ng and D. Zara. 2021. "Implementing a Green Recovery in Southeast Asia". Manila: Asian Development Bank. *ADB Briefs,* no. 173, March, pp. 1–7. https://www.adb.org/publications/green-recovery-southeast-asia.

Lim, W. S. W. and T. H. Beng. 1998. *The New Asian Architecture: Vernacular Traditions and Contemporary Style.* Singapore: Periplus Editions.

Numbeo. 2021. "Cost of Living". *Numbeo* website. https://www.numbeo.com/cost-of-living/.

Simmonds, R. and G. Hack, eds. 2000. *Global City Regions: Their Emerging Forms.* New York: Spon Press.

Trilling, L. 1972. *Sincerity and Authenticity.* Cambridge, MA: Harvard University Press.

United Nations. 2018. *Population Dynamics.* New York: Department of Economic and Social Affairs.

Biographical Notes of Regional Architects

Albert Aalbers (1897–1961) of the Netherlands and Indonesia was an architect who created elegant Streamline Moderne buildings in the Dutch East Indies, primarily during the 1930s. He studied at the Rotterdam Academy of Visual Arts and Techniques during a time when Dutch architecture was strongly influenced by Expressionism. He began working in Bandung as a freelance architect before opening the firm Aalbers en De Waal in 1935. He returned to the Netherlands in 1946 with the same firm.

Carlos Arguelles (1917–2008) of the Philippines was a prominent third-generation architect and a leading proponent of the International Style in the 1960s. He studied architecture at the University of Santo Tomas in Manila and at MIT in the United States. He also taught at Santo Tomas and was Dean of the College of Architecture from 1953 to 1959. Closely associated with the architectural development of Quezon City, he designed the modernist Philamlife Headquarters of 1962 and the Manila Hilton Hotel of 1968. He received the Gold Medal of the Philippine Institute of Architects in 1988.

Carlos Arnaiz (1975–) of the USA and the Philippines is the founder and principal of Carlos Arnaiz Architects, or CAZA, since 2011, and co-founder of the Studio for Urban Analysis (SURBA) in 2013, both located in Brooklyn, New York, but with branch offices in Manila, Lima and Bogotá. Born in the Philippines, Carlos studied architecture at the Graduate School of Design at Harvard University and teaches in the Graduate School of Architecture and Urban Design at Pratt Institute in New York City. Prior to founding CAZA and SURBA, he worked for several well-known firms. His work has been well published and includes a couple of projects presented in this volume. He has also been the recipient of a number of recent accolades.

Rachaporn Choochuey of Thailand is an architect and the co-founder in 2008 and design director of all(zone) architects, a collaborative practice based in Bangkok. She studied at Bangkok's Chulalongkorn University and at Columbia University in the United States, finally taking a PhD at the University of Tokyo in Japan. She is an active faculty member and teaches at Chulalongkorn University. Renowned for the poetic adaptive re-use and regeneration of older under-used structures, she has led projects like the MAIIAM Contemporary Art Museum, described here, and pursued contemporary vernacular projects such as the Open-Air Market and the large Duriflex warehouse, both in Bangkok. She is also the author of numerous articles about contemporary architecture.

Koh Seow Chuan (1939–) of Singapore is an architect and a founder of the Design Partnership in 1967, which was subsequently renamed DP Architects in 1975. He studied at the School of Architecture, Melbourne University, in Australia and worked with Malayan Architects Co-Partnership (MAC) before forming a partnership with William Siew Wai Lim and Tay Keng Soon. Beyond his career as an architect, he is a philatelist and philanthropist.

Denton Corker Marshall (DCM) of Australia is a large and well-regarded multinational architecture, urban design and planning firm founded by **John Denton** (1945–), **Barrie Marshall** and **Bill Corker**, all of whom graduated from the School of Architecture at Melbourne University and soon after established their partnership in Melbourne in 1972. Over time the firm has expanded considerably, now with offices in Sydney, London, Manchester and Jakarta and work done in something like 37 countries. They are the authors of a significant number of landmark buildings, including several in Southeast Asia, among them the recent Australian Embassy in Jakarta. Their subsidiary office in Jakarta, Duta Cermat Mandiri, has been particularly active in the Southeast Asian projects. Indeed, the work of DCM is the subject of several monographic publications edited by the likes of Haig Beck and Jackie Cooper and published primarily by Birkhäuser. In addition to many other accolades over the years, they received the Gold Medal of the Royal Australian Institute of Architects.

Jean Desbois (1891–1971) of France and Cambodia was the architect of Phnom Penh from 1931 to 1937 and the main designer of the city's Central Market, which is presented here. He studied at the École Régionale d'Architecture de Rennes in France. After Phnom Penh, he went to Hue in Annam, the French Protectorate encompassing central Vietnam in 1938, and returned to France in 1949.

Budiman Hoolan Hendropurnomo (1954–) of Indonesia studied at the Melbourne School of Design and joined Denton Corker Marshall's main office in the same city in 1981. Returning to Jakarta in 1983 to lead DCM's projects in Indonesia, he became director of DCM's newly founded Jakarta office in 1987, with the name Duta Cermat Mandiri. Under his leadership, numerous major projects were undertaken, among them a couple presented here, alongside the Kompas Multimedia Towers in Jakarta and the Maya Sanur Resort & Spa and the Apurva Kempinski Hotel, both in Bali. He is also the recipient of many Indonesian Institute of Architects awards, principally for sustainable design.

Tan Kok Hiang (1960–) of Singapore is a founding director of Forum Architects with his partner **Ho Sweet Woon** in 1994. He studied at the National University of Singapore, where he also now teaches. Forum Architects has been the recipients of numerous awards and their work has been widely published, including the Boon Tat Shophouse and the Assyafaah Mosque presented here.

Huang Sheng-Yuan (1963–) of Taiwan is an architect and principal of Fieldoffice Architects in Yilan, Taiwan. He studied at Tunghai University in Taichung and at Yale University. Before returning to Taiwan, he taught and worked in the United States. He teaches at Chun Yuan Christian University's Department of Architecture and at National Ilan University. He is also advisor to the Architecture and Arts Committee of the Taiwan Council of Cultural Affairs. Initiating projects in the Yilan area, his work seeks to integrate buildings into existing landscapes.

M. Ridwan Kamil (1971–) of Indonesia is an architect who founded Urbane Indonesia, a practice in Bandung, in 2004, partnering with **Achmad Tardiyana**, **Reza Nurtjahja** and **Irvan Darwis**. He studied at the Bandung Institute of Technology and at the University of California, Berkeley, in the United States. Politically active, he is the Governor of West Java and was previously Mayor of Bandung for five years. The firm, Urbane Indonesia, is international in scope and is the recipient of numerous awards.

Thomas Karsten (1854–1945) of Indonesia was an engineer who made major contributions to the architecture and town planning of the Dutch East Indies, most significantly concerning integration of colonial urban environments with indigenous elements. He studied at the Polytechnische School te Delft, the precursor to Delft University of Technology, the Netherlands. Escaping World War I, he moved to the Dutch East Indies and became an influential consultant on planning for major cities in the colony. He taught at the School of Engineering in Bandung and perished in a Japanese prison camp in 1945. Influential in public housing, among other causes, Karsten is the subject of a recent major monograph.

Christopher C. M. Lee of the United Kingdom and Singapore is an architect, and co-founder and principal of Serie Architects. He teaches at the Architectural Association School in London and at Harvard University's Graduate School of Design in the United States. He studied at the Architectural Association School and at the Berlage Institute as well as Delft University of Technology in the Netherlands. His practice is centered in London, Mumbai and Beijing.

Chu-Yuan Lee (1938–) of Taiwan is an architect and principal of C. Y. Lee and Partners in Taipei, founded with C. P. Wang in 1978. He studied at the National Cheng Kung University in Tainan and at the School of Architecture of Princeton University in the United States. A proponent of oriental culture in design, he directed the Taipei 101 project, presented in this volume.

Carl Lim of Singapore is an architect who studied at the National University of Singapore and founded Czarl Architects in 2009 as a local firm dealing with master-planning, interiors and displays, in addition to architecture. Among his projects is the Wat Ananda Metyarama Thai Buddhist Temple, prominent in Singapore's landscape and described here.

Jimmy C. S. Lim (1944–) of Malaysia is an architect who was a senior member of Project Architects in Kuala Lumpur from 1972 to 1977, before establishing his own practice, CSL Associates, in 1978. He studied at the University of New South Wales in Australia, working in a number of local practices in Sydney before returning to Malaysia. He was a founding member of the Heritage Trust of Malaysia and has also been active in local residents' organizations in Kuala Lumpur resisting uncontrolled development and destruction of the natural environment. He is renowned for his sustainable and vernacular-oriented work in residential and low-rise commercial architecture.

William Siew Wai Lim (1932–) of Singapore is an architect, urban theorist and activist. He studied at the Architecture Association School in London before moving on to the Department of City and Regional Planning at Harvard University in the United States. He began his professional career in Singapore at James Ferrie and Partners in 1957 but left to form the Malayan Architects Co-Partnership (MAC) in 1960, before joining the Design Partnership (DP Architects) in 1967 and establishing his own firm in 1981. Among numerous projects, he was a major contributor to the modernist People's Park Complex and the Golden Mile Complex before turning away to a more post-modern and vernacularly inspired architecture. He continues to write and lecture on a broad range of topics and is President of the Architecture Association of Asia and a founding member of the Singapore Heritage Society.

Antony Liu (1967–) of Indonesia studied at Tarumanagara University in Jakarta and began working with Pakar Cipta

Graha in Jakarta before setting up his own practice with **Ferry Ridwan** (1970–), also from Tarumanagara University, as Antony Liu + Ferry Ridwan / Studio TonTon in 2007. Since working together, they have designed a number of residences, resort hotels, churches and schools, as well as their own office presented here.

Leandro V. Locsin (1928–1994) of the Philippines was an architect strongly associated with the Marcos regime. After studying at the University of Santo Tomas in Manila, he began his practice in the 1950s, most notably with the Church of the Holy Sacrifice at the University of the Philippines, Diliman Campus, of 1955. Locsin was renowned for his brutalist architecture and buildings of 'floating volumes' such as at the Cultural Center of the Philippines of 1966 and its National Theater of 1969, presented in this volume. Most of his work was in the Philippines although he also designed the Philippine Pavilion for the World Expo '70 in Osaka, Japan. He was awarded the Order of National Artists of the Philippines in 1990 and his œuvre has been the subject of several monographs.

Nguyen Hai Long of Vietnam is an architect who founded Tropical Space with **Tran Thi Ngu Ngon**, based in Ho Chi Minh City. Long and Ngon both studied at the Ho Chi Minh City University of Architecture. They are strongly influenced in their work by the tropical climate and simple sculptural shapes. Their architecture also strongly reflects the people and culture of the place where it is being designed.

Andra Matin (1962–) of Indonesia, studied architecture at Parahyangan Catholic University in Bandung. Subsequent to working with the largest architectural firm in Indonesia, he established Andramatin Architects in 1998 in southern Jakarta. The recipient of several awards in Indonesia, major projects include the AM Residence, the Tubaba Mosque, Katamama Hotel and the Blimbingsari Airport. His work has been published internationally in *Architecture Review, Wallpaper* and *Archinesia*. He was also one of the founders of AMI – Arsitek Muda Indonesia (Young Architects of Indonesia), a collective of young architects active during the 1990s.

Graham McDermid of New Zealand is an architect and principal of the firm Architects Plus, founded in 2003, with offices in Christchurch and Wellington and active membership in the New Zealand Institute of Architects (NZIA). This practice spans a considerable range of projects, including Te Wharewaka, described here.

Vann Molyvann (1926–2017) of Cambodia was an architect who worked closely with Prince Norodom Sihanouk between 1955 and 1970 during Sihanouk's development program encompassing new towns, architecture and infrastructure. He was the primary author of the so-called New Khmer Architecture. He studied at the École des Beaux-Arts in Paris, returning to Cambodia in 1956. Among as many as 100 or so projects, the National Sports Complex of 1962 in Phnom Penh described in this volume is well-known, not least for its references back to elements of Angkor during the Khmer Empire.

Vo Trong Nghia (1976–) of Vietnam studied architecture at the Nagoya Institute of Technology and the University of Tokyo, earning a Master's degree. He established Vo Trong Nghia (VTN) in 2006 in Ho Chi Minh City. He has since established a reputation for sustainable architectural design integrating inexpensive local materials and traditional skills with contemporary aesthetics and urban circumstances. Major projects include the 'Houses for Trees' in Ho Chi Minh City, represented in this volume, and the Farming Kindergarten in Dong Nai, Vietnam. His work has been published in *Dezeen* and *Archinesia*, among other journals.

Eko Prawoto (1958–) of Indonesia studied under Y. B. Mangunwijaya, earning a Bachelor's degree from Gadjah Mada University, Yogyakarta, and subsequently a Master's degree from the Berlage Institute in the Netherlands. As an artist/architect with his own studio, he also teaches at Duta Wacana Christian University in Yogyakarta. Prawoto's practice is located in a village in Yogyakarta; his design approach is rooted in both the local natural and community circumstances.

Markus Roselieb of Thailand is a self-taught architect who originally studied medicine in Vienna, Austria, before moving to Thailand. He founded Chiangmai Life Architects and Construction in 2008 in Chiang Mai, specializing in the use of earthen and bamboo building materials married to very contemporary technical thinking. A major project presented here is at the Panyaden International School, of which he is also a co-founder. It is an alternative educational venue in northern Thailand with a campus comprised of earthen and bamboo structures, many with large thatch roofs.

Wolff Schoemaker (1982–1949) of Indonesia was a locally born architect and the designer of several distinguished Art Deco buildings in Bandung, Indonesia. Educated as an engineer, he became Director of Public Works in Batavia, today Jakarta, in 1914. In partnership with his brother, he established the architectural firm of C. P. Schoemaker and Associates in Bandung in 1918. From 1922 he taught at the Technical College of Bandung, which brought him into contact with Sukarno, who would become the first President of the Republic of Indonesia. Schoemaker traveled to the Netherlands in 1939, where he took a post at Delft University of Technology until his retirement in 1941.

John Colin Scott (1924–1992) of British and Te Arawa ancestry was a New Zealand architect who studied at the School of Architecture at Auckland University. Moving back to his hometown in Hawke's Bay, he was the architect of several private houses often inspired by traditional New Zealand structures like the *whare* and woolsheds. His Chapel of Futuna, presented in this volume, was the masterpiece of his career, combining elements of the Maori meeting house with traditional features of the church. He then continued to create fusions between Maori and Pakeha cultures, receiving the Gold Medal of the New Zealand Institute of Architects for his work.

Stephen Zawmoe Shwe of Myanmar is an architect and co-founder of the firm SPINE Architect in 2003 with his partner **Amelie Chai**. He studied at the University of California, Berkeley, and at Columbia, and she at Harvard University and also at Columbia. Prior to moving to practice in Myanmar, they both worked in New York City. They are known to be pioneers of contemporary architecture in Myanmar, such as the Zaya Thakedi Monastery, discussed in this volume.

Ng Keng Siang (1908–1967) of Singapore was an architect prominent in the early and transitional stages of modern architecture in the city-state. He studied at the Bartlett School of Architecture in London and returned to Singapore when the influence of the modern movement was beginning to take root. One of the first Singaporean architects to become a member of the Royal Institute of British Architects, he also served as President of the Society of Malayan Architects. He was the architect of the Asia Insurance Building, one of Singapore's first high-rises, described in this volume.

Friedrich Silaban (1912–1984) of Indonesia was a self-taught architect of the early generation and rose to national prominence by way of the 1955 competition for the Istiqlal Mosque in Jakarta, which is presented here. Together with Achmad Noeman, he founded the Indonesian Institute of Architects (IAI) in 1959. He received numerous accolades for his work, both locally and internationally.

Realrich Sjarief (1982–) of Indonesia is an architect who founded RAW Architects in 2011 in Jakarta. He studied at the Bandung Institute of Technology and at the School of Architecture at the University of New South Wales in Sydney, Australia. Coming from a family of long-time builders, he was no stranger to construction and produces work recognized for its simplicity and unpretentiousness, especially with regard to the use of local materials and craftsmanship. The Alfa Omega School, presented here, is one such example.

Wong Mun Summ of Singapore is an architect and co-founder of the local firm WOHA with **Richard Hassell** in 1994. Over the years, they have developed a unique and pioneering approach to tropical architecture and urbanism, weaving landscape and community space through porous structures, like those shown in this volume. The subject of at least four substantial monographs, Hassell studied at the University of Western Australia in Perth and Summ at the National University of Singapore.

My An Pham Thi of Vietnam is an architect who founded MM++ Architects in Ho Chi Minh City in 2009 with **Michael Charruault**. She studied at the University of Hanoi and worked for more than ten years in different international firms. Under her guidance, MM++ has earned a reputation for affordable, well-adapted and sustainable architecture, like the Townhouse in District 7, presented here. The work has also been quite widely published.

Ngo Viet Thu (1927–2000) of Vietnam was an architect who won the competition to design the Dinh Doc Lap, or Independence Palace, in Ho Chi Minh City. He studied at the École des Beaux-Arts in Paris and won the Grand Prix de Rome there in 1955. In 1962, he was the first Asian Honorary Fellow of the American Institute of Architects. As an architect and planner, he worked on several large projects in Vietnam. He was also a noted painter and his son, **Ngo Viet Nam-Son**, one of eight children, is the CEO of NgoViet Architects and Planners, a distinguished international practice.

Varudh Varavarn of Thailand is an architect and founder of Vin Varavarn Architects in Bangkok. He studied at King Mongkut's Institute of Technology in Bangkok and at the Architectural Association School in London. He established his own practice in 2005 and works on projects at a variety of scales, with particular emphasis on sensitive and imaginative use of materials and traditional precedents, like the Bann Huay San Saw Post Disaster School in Chiang Rai, discussed here.

Dam Vu of Vietnam is an architect who with **Anni Le** founded the firm Kientruc O, based in Ho Chi Minh City. They both teach at Ho Chi Minh City University of Architecture. Their architecture is noted for its keen observation of local culture in its modernity, such as the VAS Office Building complex in Da Nang, presented here. Their work is also well published.

Ken Yeang (1948–) of Malaysia and the United Kingdom is an architect, ecologist and planner renowned for his ecological and sustainable approach to architecture and the pioneering green aesthetic, which he began developing in 1971. He studied at the Architectural Association School in London, as well as at Cambridge University, where he received his doctorate with a dissertation on environmental architecture and planning. Yeang is executive director of Hamzah & Yeang, headquartered in Kuala Lumpur, but also with offices in London and Beijing. He and his firm are recipients of numerous awards, including the Dutch Prince Claus Award and the Aga Khan Award for Architecture, internationally, and several Malaysian Institute of Architects annual design awards, locally.

Acknowledgments

This book started in response to a simple request from Stephen Ross and Allana C. Lindgren of the University of Victoria in Canada for a short article for their book *The Modernist World* about architectural modernism in East and Southeast Asia, titled "Building Forwards and Backwards in Time". Fuller pursuit of the idea came from long discussions with a Singaporean post-doc at Harvard, named Har Ye Kan, or Xiayi, as we preferred to call her. It also involved our esteemed colleague at Harvard, Rahul Mehrotra, as we split the territory of our teaching responsibilities and he did South Asia, and we did East Asia, or at least that is what we all pretended. Also, in the background could be heard Hugh O'Neill at Melbourne University, urging us on to be more internationally and socially involved, as well as classmates, like John Denton of DCM in later life. Then too there were chance encounters with the likes of Budiman Hendropurnomo, the head of Duta Cermat Mandiri in Jakarta, Sean Chiao of AECOM and Andy Locsin and Senator Edgardo Angara in Manila, the Philippines. There were also more sustained contacts with Teng Chye Khoo and Limin Hee at the Centre for Liveable Cities in Singapore, Christopher Lee of Serie Architects in Singapore, Peeradorn Kaewlai and Warinporn 'Pia' Yangyuenwong in Thailand, as well as Teo Ah Khing and Ken Yeang in Malaysia. In addition, there were even longer and firmer encounters with Carlos Arnaiz, through our partnership at SURBA in Brooklyn, New York, and beyond, concerning the Philippines among other parts of the region. While she was at Tufts, Trang Vuong generously organized an enthralling trip to Hanoi, where Tran Ngoc Chinh, the head of the Vietnam Urban Planning and Development Association, went out of his way to be both helpful and informative. Our thanks also to Danny Wicaksono, Andra Matin, Adi Purnomo and the late Ahmad Djuhara of Jakarta, and Eko Prawoto and Ikaputra of Yogyakarta, who generously shared their city and architecture with us, as well as Luke Tan of Singapore, who helped us access the city's rich architectural history. All added to this portrait of modern architecture in Southeast Asia, although the flaws are solely ours alongside the enthusiasm for Austronesian contributions from two New Zealanders. Finally, we must express appreciation to Andreas Müller and Michael Wachholz at Birkhäuser for their unstinting encouragement all along the way, and to Rein Steger for creating the graphic design of this book.

About the Authors

Peter G. Rowe is the Raymond Garbe Professor of Architecture and Urban Design at Harvard University's Graduate School of Design and also a Harvard University Distinguished Service Professor. He served for twelve years as Dean of the Faculty of Design at Harvard and prior to that as the Chairman of the Department of Urban Planning and Design, as well as Director of the Urban Design Program. He is also currently the Founding Chairman of SURBA – the Studio for Urban Analyses in Brooklyn, New York. Born in New Zealand, Rowe is the holder of several honorary professorships in East Asia and the author, co-author and editor of numerous books, many dealing with the constructed environments of East Asia. Rowe recently authored, also with Yun Fu, *Korean Modern: The Matter of Identity.* He is also the author of *Emergent Architectural Territories in East Asian Cities,* and co-author of *Urban Intensities: Contemporary Housing Types and Territories* and *China's Urban Communities: Concepts, Contexts and Well-Being.*

Yun Fu is an Instructor and Design Critic in the Department of Urban Planning and Design at Harvard University's Graduate School of Design. Originally from New Zealand, he graduated in Architectural Studies from the University of New South Wales, prior to earning Master in Architecture and Doctor of Design degrees at Harvard. A winner of the Rome Prize at the British School at Rome, Yun is the co-founder of Semester Studio, a design and research practice for buildings, objects and neighborhoods. He had previously collaborated with Foster+Partners in London and ZAO/standardarchitecture in Beijing, and co-authored, with Peter G. Rowe, *Korean Modern: The Matter of Identity.* He was also a contributor to *Urban Intensities: Contemporary Housing Types and Territories* and *China's Urban Communities: Concepts, Contexts, and Well-Being.*

Illustration Credits

Chapter 1
11, 12, 14 Drawn by author based on Gupta, 2005.
17 top Stibig, H.-J. et al. 2002.
17 bottom Drawn by author based on Rowe and Hee, 2019.
19 Drawn by author based on Blench, 2009.
23, 26, 30, 33 Drawn by author.
36 Dower, 1999, p. 20.
43 Drawn by author.

Chapter 2
52 top Waterson, 1990, p. 119.
52 bottom Dawson and Gillow, 1994.
54 top Alexander Turnbull Library, from Brown, 2009, p. 62.
54 bottom Fox, 1993a, p. 154.
56 top Dawson and Gillow, 1994.
56 bottom Waterson, 1990, p. 235.
58 Fox, 1993b, p. 69.
59 top Dawson and Gillow, 1994.
59 bottom Photo by A. B. Godber, 1930, from Philips, 1952, p. 125.
61 Waterson, 1990, figs. 9, 10, 13.
63 top Public Domain, US National Oceanic and Atmospheric Administration.
63 bottom Waterson, 1990.
64 Waterson, 1990, figs. 10 and 14.
67 Waterson, 1990, p. 21.
68 Courtesy of Architecture +.
71 Courtesy of Leandro V. Locsin Partners.
72 Photos by Spaceshift Studio. Courtesy of Vin Varavarn Architects.
75 Photos by Bernardo Salce. Courtesy of Architetti Senza Frontiere Italia.
77 Photos by Eric Dinardi. Courtesy of Realrich Architecture Workshop.
78 Photos by William Vassal, John Gollings, and P. A. Pantz. Courtesy of ©RPBW-Fondazione Renzo Piano.
80 Design by Foster+Partners. Courtesy of the Aga Khan Award for Architecture.
82 Courtesy of Studio TonTon.
83 Photos by Hiroyuki Oki. Courtesy of VTN Architects.
84 Photos by Pasi Aalto. Courtesy of TYIN tegnestue Architects.
86 Photos by Gavin Woodword. From Walden, 1987.
88 Photos by Ahkamul Hakim. Courtesy of Eko Prawoto Architecture Workshop.
90 Photos by Robert Herrmann ©. Courtesy of vn-a.
91 Photos by Fernando Javier Urquijo. Courtesy of © studioMilou.
92 Photos by Paulo dos Sousa. Courtesy of Shigeru Ban Architects.
94 Courtesy of DCM Jakarta.
96 Photos by Andrew Nelson. Design by Heatherwick Studio.
98–99 Photographs by Darren Soh. Copyright Craig Sheppard. Design by Wilkinson Eyre.
102 Photos by Lucas K. Doolan. Courtesy of Bio-architecture Formosana.
103 Courtesy of DCM Jakarta.

Chapter 3
108 top Photo by Philippe Bourseiller.
108 bottom Photo by Gunawan Kartapranata / CC BY-SA 3.0, 2009. https://commons.wikimedia.org/wiki/File:-Borobudur_Mandala.svg.
110 Photo by CEphoto, Uwe Aranas, 2015. https://commons.wikimedia.org/wiki/File:Borobudur-Temple-Park_Indonesia_Stupas-of-Borobudur-03.jpg.
111 top Baldiri, 2008. https://en.wikipedia.org/wiki/File:Angkor_Wat_M2.png.
111 bottom Michell, 1988, p. 177.
112 top Baldiri, 2009. https://en.wikipedia.org/wiki/Angkor_Thom#/media/File:Angkor_Thom_M2.png.
112 bottom Connors Bros. https://www.shutterstock.com/image-photo/bayon-temple-angkor-thom-cambodia-1361749.
115 Author's collection.
116 Wu, L., 1999.
119 top Gerd Eichmann, 2006. https://commons.wikimedia.org/wiki/File:-Yangon-Shwedagon-350-gje.jpg.
119 bottom Ashok666. https://en.wikipedia.org/wiki/File:India_Meenakshi_Temple.jpg.
120 top Mike Prince, 2015. https://commons.wikimedia.org/wiki/File:-Mukteshwar_Temple_(19807741798).jpg.
120 bottom Dineshkannambadi, 2007. https://en.wikipedia.org/wiki/Vesara#/media/File:Dodda_Basappa_Temple.JPG
122 Drawn by author.
123 Courtesy of Marks Barfield Architects.
127 top Crisco 1492, 2016. https://en.wikipedia.org/wiki File:Looking_down_from_the_top_of_Cetho_Temple,_2016-10-13.jpg.
127 bottom Uwe Aranas, 2015. https://en.wikipedia.org/wiki/File:Brantan_Bali_Pura-Ulun-Danu-Bratan-01.jpg.
128 Shazz, 2006. https://commons.wikimedia.org/wiki/File:Original_Dharma_Wheel.svg.
131–133 Gopika Gopan. https://www.re-thinkingthefuture.com/architectural-styles/a2589-10-distinctive-elements-of-islamic-architecture/.
135 Photos by Luke Tan. Design by Forum Architects.
136 Photos by Hiroyuki Oki. Courtesy of Tropical Space.
139–140 Courtesy of Kwanchanok Weschasart.
142–143 Courtesy of PT Urbane Indonesia.
145–146 Courtesy of SPINE Architects.
148–149 Courtesy of Site-Specific: Architecture & Research.
151 Courtesy of GMP.
152 Courtesy of Norihiko Dan.
155 Photos by Luke Tan. Design by Czarl Architects.
157 Photograph by Hiroyuki Oki. Courtesy of Kientruc O.
159–160 Photos by Hiroyuki Oki. Courtesy of VTN Architects.
162–163 Photos by Hiroyuki Oki. Courtesy of Ho Khue Architects and ALPES Green Design & Build.

Chapter 4
166 Van Meurs, 17th Century. https://www.reddit.com/r/Map_Porn/comments/c0kobm/map_of_batavia_dutch_east_indies_1679_by_van/.
168 Adolf van der Laan. https://en.wikipedia.org/wiki/1740_Batavia_massacre#/media/File:Tableau_de_la_Partie_de_Batavia,_ou_s'est_fait_proprement_le_terrible_Massacre_des_Chinois,_le_9_Octob.jpeg.
170 top Collection of the National Museum of Singapore, 1970s. https://www.roots.gov.sg/Collection-Landing/listing/1190197.
170 bottom Phan. https://www.landolia.com/singapour/kampong-glam/29189/.
171 top Myanmore, 2017. https://www.myanmore.com/2017/11/myanmars-historic-secretariat-building-to-be-restored/.
171 middle and bottom Collection of Mr and Mrs Lee Kip Lee, National Library of Singapore. https://sgarchi.wordpress.com/2020/06/17/compradoric-architecture/; and https://sgarchi.wordpress.com/2020/06/17/compradoric-architecture/.
173 top https://en.wikipedia.org/wiki/Saigon_Governor%27s_Palace#/media/File:Hermitte%E2%80%99s_Palace_of_the_Government_(1873).jpg.
173 bottom manhhai, 2014. https://www.flickr.com/photos/13476480@N07/43692466032.
174 top John Tewell. http://www.lougopal.com/manila/?p=355.
174 bottom Kaho, Chuzai Living, 2019. https://www.chuzailiving.com/manila-american-cemetery-memorial/.
178 top Photo by Gunawan Kartapranata / CC BY-SA 3.0, 2010. https://en.wikipedia.org/wiki/Merdeka_Palace#/media/File:Merdeka_Palace_Changing_Guard_1.jpg.
178 bottom Coté and O'Neill, 2017.
179, 180 Coté and O'Neill, 2017.
182 top manhai, 2017. https://www.flickr.com/photos/13476480@N07/sets/72157687489159005.
182 bottom Veronica Boix, 2014. https://www.azureazure.com/travel/

destinations/asia-exclusive-colonial-mansions/.
183 top Charu Goya, 2020. https://www.travelwithcg.com/staying-at-belmond-governors-residence-in-yangon/.
183 bottom Wowieology, 2012. https://commons.wikimedia.org/wiki/File:St._Agustine_Paoay_Church_02.jpg.
185 top Coenraad Liebrecht Temminck Groll, Rijksdienst voor het Cultureel Erfgoed, 1988. https://commons.wikimedia.org/wiki/File:Gedung_Merdeka,_voormalige_soci%C3%ABteit_Concordia_-_20651406_-_RCE.jpg).
185 middle P. J. van Baarda. https://de.m.wikipedia.org/wiki/Datei:-COLLECTIE_TROPENMUSEUM_Villa_Isola_aan_de_Lembangweg_bij_Bandoeng_TMnr_60026636.jpg.
185 bottom Rafael Cazorla, 2012. http://www.postalesinventadas.com/2011/03/hotel-savoy-bandung-indonesia-mon-cher.html.
188 top Unknown. https://100travelstories.com/blog/geylang-singapore/.
188 bottom Jpatokal, 2009. https://commons.wikimedia.org/wiki/File:-Terraced_houses_along_Koon_Seng_Road,_Singapore_-_20090206.jpg.
190 top Two hundred percent, 2017. https://en.wikipedia.org/wiki/Five-foot_way#/media/File:Five_foot_way,_Ampang,_Selangor.jpg.
190 bottom LeonardKong, 2012. https://en.wikipedia.org/wiki/Five-foot_way#/media/File:Five_Foot_Way_in_George_Town_,_Penang.jpg.
193 top Brinda Shah, 2013. https://xotours.vn/blog/vintage-skyscrapers-the-evolution-of-the-tube-house-in-vietnam/.
193 bottom Natty domz, 2015. https://commons.wikimedia.org/wiki/File:-Bahay_na_bato_houses_of_philippines.jpg.
195 Photos by Rory Gardiner. Courtesy of Serie Architects.
197 Photos by Frank Callaghan. Courtesy of CAZA.
200 Photos by Soopakorn Srisakul. Courtesy of All(Zone).
201 Photos by Hiroyuki Oki. Courtesy of VTN Architects.
202 Courtesy of Chiangmai Life Architects and Construction.
206 Tropenmuseum, Amsterdam, part of the National Museum of World Cultures. Wikipedia and Wikimedia Commons.
207 National Heritage Board, 2021. https://www.roots.gov.sg/stories-landing/stories/Hawker-Centres/Tiong-Bahru-Market-Food-Centre.
208 Milei.vencel, 2012. https://commons.wikimedia.org/wiki/File:Phnom_Penh,.JPG; and Gerd Eichmann, 2007. https://commons.wikimedia.org/wiki/File:Phnom_Penh-Phsar_Thom_Thmei-08-innen-2007-gje.jpg).
211 Philip Jablon, 2009. http://seatheater.blogspot.com/2009/07/siang-savan-theater-luang-prabang-laos.html.
213 top National Heritage Board, c. 1960. https://www.roots.gov.sg/Collection-Landing/listing/1045919.
213 middle Tyers, 2018, p. 43.
213 bottom Bjoertvedt, 2018. https://commons.wikimedia.org/wiki/File:Singapore_Downtown_-_Finlayson_Green_2_-_Ascott_Raffles_Place_(The_Asia_Insurance_Building_1955)_IMG_9954.jpg.
215–216 Aga Khan Trust for Culture, 2012, https://www.archnet.org/sites/16088.
218 Courtesy of C+A.
219 Courtesy of O2 Design Atelier.
221 Courtesy of MM++ Architects.
223 Photo by Luke Tan. Design by Forum Architects.

Chapter 5
227 Patrick Kasingsing, Brutalist Pilipinas, 2021. https://www.facebook.com/BrutalistPilipinas/photos/a.1730217303798229/1906497276170230/
228 Courtesy of Leandro V. Locsin Partners.
230–231 Photos by Akio Kawasumi. Courtesy of Leandro V. Locsin Partners.
232 musnahterinjak, 2011. https://commons.wikimedia.org/wiki/File:-Masjid_Istiqlal_-_Panoramio.jpg.
235 Abhinav Publications Archival Photos and Manuel Oka, uncube, 2015. https://www.uncubemagazine.com/blog/15888275.
236 Architectural Guide Yangon. https://www.yangongui.de/inya-lake-hotel/.
237 Manuel Oka, Yangon Architecture, 2015, https://yangonarchitecture.tumblr.com/post/108201081133/todays-university-of-medicine-1-was-built-in.
238 Manuel Oka, Architectural Guide Yangon. https://www.yangongui.de/thakin-kodaw-hmaing-mausoleum/.
240 Tariq Khalil, Indonesia Design, 2017. https://indonesiadesign.com/story/discover-indonesia-cool-yankee-architecture.
242 top Allen, ArchDaily, 2011. https://www.archdaily.com/148641/googie-architecture-futurism-through-modernism/rider.
242 bottom Unknown. https://www.booking.com/hotel/tw/grand-hotel-taipei.html.
244 top de:Benutzer:Chtrede, 2008. https://en.wikipedia.org/wiki/Istana_Nurul_Iman#/media/File:Istana-nurul-iman.jpg.
244 bottom Unknown, 2018. http://aseansection.blogspot.com/2015/05/asean-palaces-of-power.html.
245 Photos by Asakawa Satoshi, Aga Khan Award for Architecture. https://www.akdn.org/architecture/project/salinger-residence.
248 Rudolph. A. Furtado, 2013. https://en.wikipedia.org/wiki/Independence_Palace.
250 top ModArchitecture, 2013. https://www.flickr.com/photos/88017382@N00/44268412072.
250 bottom Bao Zoan, 2016. https://medium.com/@mattcowansaigon/once-home-to-misery-now-a-place-for-humanity-35fe182fb0ee.
251 Photos by Virgile Simon Bertrand, 2016. https://www.dezeen.com/2016/09/13/the-national-sports-complex-phnom-penh-1964-vann-moly-vann-virgile-simon-bertrand/.
253 top Darren Soh, 2018. https://www.homeanddecor.com.sg/design/news/the-architectural-significance-of-golden-mile-complex-pearl-bank-apartments-and-peoples-park-complex/.
253 bottom Lim Han, 2018. https://www.mariefranceasia.com/th/culture-th/singapore-events-th/news-and-activities-th/10-nostalgic-malls-singapore-312402.html#item=1).
254 top Jhlim, 2013. http://adsoft-footstep.blogspot.com/2013/02/old-singapore.html.
254 middle and bottom Chongkian, 2013. https://commons.wikimedia.org/wiki/File:Negeri_Sembilan_State_Mosque.JPG.
257 Drawn by author.
260 Photos by Iwan Baan. Courtesy of CAZA.
261 Courtesy of Fieldoffice Architects.
263 Aga Khan Award for Architecture. Courtesy of Andra Matin Architects.
265 Photos by Jeremy San and Fabian Ong. Courtesy of Ling Hao Architects.
266 Morodok Techo National Stadium, https://www.facebook.com/MTN.Stadium.
269 Courtesy of Ken Yeang.
270 Photos by Patrick Bingham-Hall. Courtesy of WOHA.
272 Photos by Patrick Bingham-Hall and K. Kopter. Courtesy of WOHA.
275 Photos by Hiroyuki Oki. Courtesy of VTN Architects.
276 Photos by Hiroyuki Oki. Design credit: Vo Trong Nghia architects, Sanuki+Nishizawa architects.
280 Courtesy of César Pelli.
281 Courtesy of C. Y. Lee & Partners.
283 Photos by Srirath Somsawat and Wilson Tungthunya. Courtesy of Ole Scheeren.
284 Photos by Chia Ming Chien and Timothy Hursley. Design by Moshe Safdie Architects.
287 Courtesy of Arc Studio Architecture + Urbanism.

Chapter 6
297 McGee, 1991.
301 www.cewep.eu.
302, 305 Drawn by Author.

Cliometric Data Analyses
P311–321 Drawn by Author.

Index

Also by Peter G. Rowe

**Korean Modern: The Matter of Identity
An Exploration into Modern Architecture
in an East Asian Country**

Hardcover. 336 pages, 150 color illustrations
Published in 2021. ISBN: 9783035622614
Electronic version, ISBN: 9783035622621

**China's Urban Communities:
Concepts, Contexts,
and Well-Being**

Hardcover. 200 pages, 100 b/w and 200 color illustrations
Published in 2016. ISBN: 9783035608335
Electronic edition, ISBN: 9783035607062

**Urban Intensities:
Contemporary Housing Types
and Territories**

Hardcover. 232 pages, 75 b/w and 90 color illustrations
Published in 2014. ISBN: 9783038214779
Electronic edition, ISBN: 9783038211013

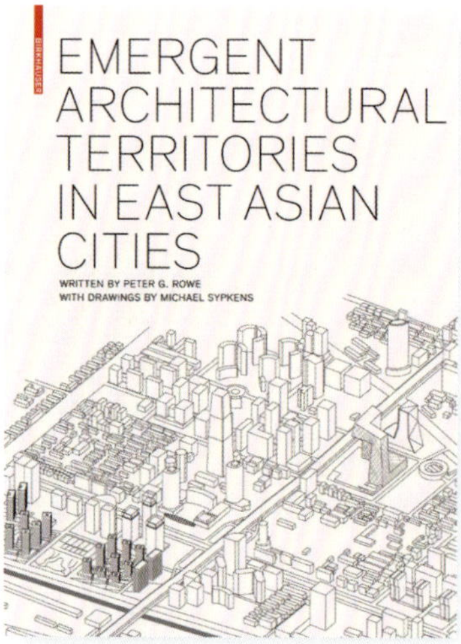

**Emergent Architectural
Territories in
East Asian Cities**

Hardcover. 208 pages, 120 b/w and 140 color illustrations
Published in 2011. ISBN: 9783764388157
Electronic edition, ISBN 9783034610599